To all at

TOM FREMANTLE'S restless caree[...]
teacher, journalist, dustman, ba[...]
nightclub and jackaroo on an Australian sheep station. He is
the author of *Johnny Ginger's Last Ride*.

Hope you enjoy it.

with best wishes,

Tan Ferral

MOONSHINE MULE

A 2,700-mile walk from Mexico to Manhattan

TOM FREMANTLE

ROBINSON

London

Constable & Robinson Ltd
3 The Lanchesters
162 Fulham Palace Road
London W6 9ER
www.constablerobinson.com

First published in the UK by Robinson,
an imprint of Constable & Robinson Ltd 2003

A copy of the British Library Cataloguing in Publication Data
is available from the British Library

ISBN 1–84119–725–4

Printed and bound in the EU

To Eliza, with love

Thank you for showing me worlds no atlas could ever touch

Contents

Acknowledgements

Without the bonhomie of hundreds of Americans this trip would very likely have broken me. As it was, whether in the boondocks or the big smokes you welcomed my mule and me, you encouraged us, cheered us on, supplied us shelter, food, drinks (sometimes far too many) and fully embraced the dream of reaching New York.

Special mentions must go to Loncito Cartwright, Justin McCord, Brandie, Kevin Wars, all the Welders, the Vaughns, Dorothy Ramsay, the Gurkas, Sid Duderstadt, Tracey Sage Weatherly, Rudy Martinez and all at the Alabama-Coushatta reservation, Chin Chong, all the Damloujis, Will and Miranda Clifton, Rodney and Emily Cook, the West family, Neil Varnell, Harry and Miss Bonny, Trenton Smith, Jim and Marilyn Lauder, the Watkins family, Ellie Braverman, all the Gastons, the Motleys, Steve and Ann Yauger, Page and Jane Henley, the Lineberrys, the Shirley family, Guy Troy, Jo and Sandy Rice, all the Bellingers, Margot McAllister, Roger, Kati and Sallyanne Hughes, Jay O'Hurley, Kathy Bilton, the Stoltzfus family, Sue and Loni Gadaleta, Lynne, Sergei and Mackenzie, Sid and Helen Frank, Holly, Tom, Ruby and Jackson Scalera, Heather and Xeno, all at Overpeck Stables,

Margarita Fugtroe, Hugh and Susan Fremantle and of course Browny, a princess among mules. To the many generous souls I've omitted, I'm sorry. You know who you are and I salute you.

To all at Swanbourne, especially Tom Finchett, David Edmondson, Peter Willie, Stuart Greenwood, Phil Timmins: thank you so much for your continual hard graft, without which it would have been impossible to elope with a mule. Thanks also to Ted Reeve, Ron Townsend, Walter Whitehall and Ray Tipping for valuable help through the years. Roger and Jean Jefcoate, Marion and Roger Lowe, Tony and Jenny Hilton have also been stars.

Alice and Julian Kennard, great friends and owners of Carmen the donkey; no finer beast could a trainee muleteer have wished for on a trial run. Eddie Fremantle, you were instrumental in securing Browny for which I'm most grateful. A huge thank you to Sylvia, Bruce and Al Corrie. Also to Riekje Van Drigalski, Tom and Mary Fry, Mark Saw, Bob Crow, Gina Rodriguez, Phil Kaisary, Sarah Laird, Geoff Goodman, Yoshiko Ridley, Ali Kwan, David Fox-Pitt, Virendra, Amar and Cath – fine friends all, Alice Westropp, Ben Kennard, Charlie Finchett and Hagar Tomer too.

Matt Todd, James Fry, Seb Piech and Nic Papa, many thanks for your sustained brio and for taking the time to march with me despite your busy schedules and wounded feet. Thank you to Sir Wilfred Thesiger for sage advice on mules and bush walking, Tom and Jim Sutherland for useful logistical tips, to Juliet Blayney for supplying mule medicines and to Charles Fremantle for valuable nuggets of family history. To Pat Chesterton, John Williams, Clive Harrington and all the team at St John Ambulance, Aylesbury, for dynamic help in raising enough funds for a new Community Care Vehicle and to Laura at Covenant House, New York. I am further beholden to my agent Barbara Levy and Carol

O'Brien at Constable & Robinson for championing the idea from the start.

Mum, Dad, Betsy, Iain, Fanny and Shaun: there for me as always. Amanda, you are a mother in a million to 'Oinks', not forgetting Jamie, her loyal and patient brother.

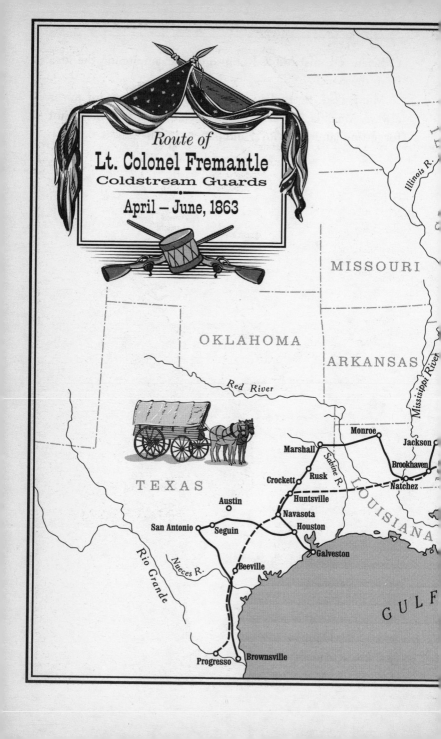

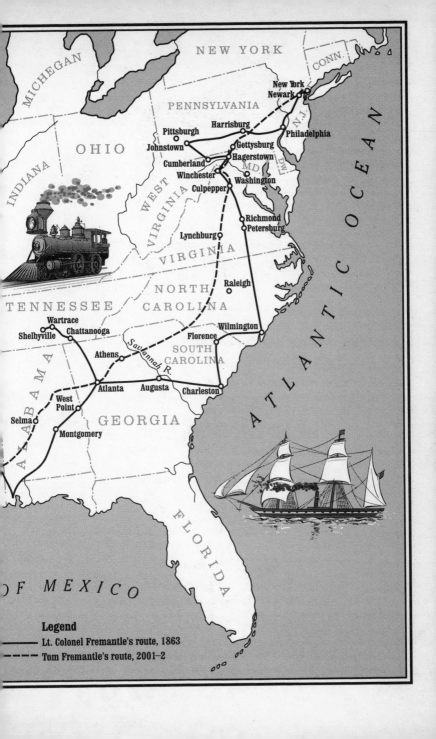

MICHIGAN

NEW YORK

CONN.

PENNSYLVANIA

New York
Newark

N.J.

OHIO

INDIANA

Pittsburgh
Johnstown

Harrisburg

Philadelphia

Gettysburg
Hagerstown

Cumberland
Winchester

MD

DW

Washington

Culpepper

WEST
VIRGINIA

Richmond
Petersburg

Lynchburg

VIRGINIA

Raleigh

TENNESSEE

NORTH
CAROLINA

ATLANTIC OCEAN

Wartrace

Shelbyville
Chattanooga

Wilmington

Athens

Savannah R.

Florence

SOUTH
CAROLINA

Atlanta
Augusta

West
Point

Charleston

Selma

GEORGIA

Montgomery

FLORIDA

OF MEXICO

Legend

——— Lt. Colonel Fremantle's route, 1863

- - - - Tom Fremantle's route, 2001–2

Prologue

'But where there is danger there grows also what saves.'

Friedrich Hölderlin

Once the chestnut buds and smashed beetles had been wiped from my windscreen the sign was easier to read: CLACKET LANE SERVICES.

I chanted it out loud to myself a couple of times and suppressed a smile. It was a far from romantic name, even for a garage on the M25. I wound down my jalopy's window to get a better look. Now it was unmistakable: CLACKET LANE SERVICES.

It is one of those names (like Basingstoke or East Grinstead) that even if whispered in a thrillingly seductive accent by Juliette Binoche – 'Clukeet Layne Servizes, *mon cher ami*' – or bellowed at full bore by Placido Domingo – 'Cla-a-a-ket La-a-ane Servizio-o-os' – would still hit a flat note. A name synonymous with the clatter of slot machines and the pong of burgers; petrol fumes hovering over it like a malign wraith.

Normally I wouldn't have paid any attention to a motorway pitstop but today was special. I was on my way to see the explorer Sir Wilfred Thesiger and it struck me that Clacket Lane was a wildly incongruous landmark with which to associate such a man – a veteran nomad who famously *hates* cars. Indeed, Sir Wilfred has spent the bulk of his ninety-three years as far from the roar and thrum of the internal combustion engine as his rangy legs would allow him.

I was now only ten minutes' drive from Thesiger's retirement home and, until Clacket Lane sprung into view, I had been lost in a daydream of sand dunes and camels, of tribesmen with kite-shaped shields and skies of unworldly blue. I had been trying to put myself in Thesiger's well-trod boots and picture Addis Ababa at the time of Haile Selassie, the Hindu Kush long before any hippies and, best of all, Arabia's starkly exquisite Empty Quarter, or *Rubh al Khali*, a name so splendid it could have been plucked straight from one of Scheherazade's magical tales.

But as I steered off the M25 I was jolted back to modernity and these heady images puffed away like genies into the summer breeze while I threaded my way north through some humdrum suburbs. The traffic eventually thinned out and several fields unfolded, one with a pony grazing in it. FRIENDS OF THE ELDERLY beckoned a sign. I drove on down a serpentine lane that swooped past a golf course before exposing a white, somewhat imperious building. The surrounding lawn, fringed with conifers, was so manicured it might have been shaved. I was glad the whoosh of motorway traffic was now out of earshot.

The world's greatest living explorer was easy to spot. While the other residents sat snoozing or playing patience on the porch, Thesiger, an alert, crag-faced man stood in the entrance hall propped against an intricately carved Zulu stave. He exuded a quiet dignity. Having only ever seen photos of Sir Wilfred, usually sporting Arabic robes, I was surprised to find him today in a rather spiffy three-piece suit and tie.

I suddenly felt a bit nervous, but as I approached he smiled warmly, his bright, curious eyes meeting mine head on. We shook hands and went to sit in the sun.

I had come to see Sir Wilfred about mules. Well, all sorts of other things – walking, nomadic inspiration, the fact I loved his books – but mules seemed a good place to start. In three days' time I was flying to Mexico City. I then hoped to hitchhike as far as the Tex-Mex border before striking out on a 2,500-mile walk through America ending up in New York. My only companion would be a pack-mule, who would keep me company and carry my swag.

'Mules are tough, very tough,' said the old wanderer softly. 'You have made the right choice of beast. Stubborn at times for sure, but intelligent and not fussy about what they eat and drink. In Abyssinia they were always respected much more than horses.'

As he spoke a powdery old lady in a blue shawl sat down next to us and flipped open a sketchpad. She looked out across the lawn and started to doodle.

'Once I used mules on a hunting expedition in the Arussi,' Thesiger continued, rolling his eyes in an effort to remember. 'They all got ill, probably due to bad grazing. To cure them the local muleteers killed a sheep, skinned it, ate it, and made collars out of its guts that they later hung around the mules' necks. An unusual cure; some of the mules got better, some didn't.'

'I'm not sure slaying a sheep would be the done thing in America,' I said.

'No, probably not,' replied Thesiger, combing back a long strand of silver hair from his forehead. 'I'm afraid I only know about Abyssinian mules. Camels, too.'

Abyssinia (now Ethiopia) is a place close to Sir Wilfred's heart. In 1909 Thesiger's father, having been appointed as England's minister to Addis Ababa, travelled over the wild

Chercher Mountains along with his young bride and a train of mules and horses. Young Wilfred was born in a mud *tukul* (hut) the following year, the oldest of four brothers.

'There is still a notice outside the *tukul* saying I was born there,' Thesiger told me. He said this shyly but not without pride; it was a forgivable flicker of vanity. Surely every explorer likes to leave a mark, a footprint in the sand.

The die of Sir Wilfred's remarkable life was cast as a young boy when he accompanied his father hunting for wildfowl, oryx and lions. He was smitten with the bush even then. It was not surprising that after graduating from Eton and Oxford, Thesiger gravitated back to Abyssinia to brave it among the proud, often barbarous tribes of the Danakil Valley. He served with distinction in Africa during the Second World War, then made his mark with the Saudi Bedouin in a series of punishing treks across the wastes of the Empty Quarter, about which he wrote the classic book, *Arabian Sands*.

Throughout all his travels, which in later life included seven years in the marshes of southern Iraq, several derring-do forays into Afghanistan and over two decades with the Samburu tribe in Kenya, Thesiger estimates he has walked over 100,000 miles. More than anything I wanted to know what compelled a man to wander this far, what created this tribal yearning. Was it obsessive? What could he teach me?

'Walking is by far the best way to travel,' he stressed. 'The most natural, the least intrusive. Something everyone can relate to. Walking with a mule is even better. I rarely rode mules – they were best as pack-animals. Like you, I preferred to walk.'

But making any sort of comparison between his highly disciplined quests and my own happy-go-lucky jaunt was, frankly, absurd. Thesiger was a pioneer, a mapper of the sands, an honourable gypsy who had 'gone native' down to the last detail. His idea of walking was barefoot, across the desert, a dagger at his side and a gun slung over his shoulder. In contrast my little tramp through America was nothing more than light entertainment. It was like comparing the voyages of Vasco da Gama to an afternoon's punting in Cambridge.

Thesiger suddenly rose to his feet. 'I need to buy some biscuits,' he announced. He gripped my forearm, rose up and off we launched through the cavernous house. Sir Wilfred was clearly still a champion walker, chicaning his way around the furniture and then climbing a long staircase on creaky but determined legs. I noticed his polished brogues were very cracked, looking as if they had already trudged through several lifetimes. Now and then, other residents greeted us. Sir Wilfred nodded politely but paid them little heed. I sensed there were few kindred spirits for him here.

We soldiered on down dark corridors. At one point Thesiger faltered, stopped and looked around, clearly a little lost. 'Is it this way?' he muttered to himself. 'Yes, yes, I'm sure of it.' He re-established his grip on the stave confident he was back on track. 'It's far more confusing in this place than in the desert,' he harrumphed.

Having secured a packet of chocolate digestives from the biscuit trolley, we paced back to the entrance hall. I had to be off soon but I wanted Sir Wilfred to sign my copy of his autobiography, *The Life of My Choice*. I rushed outside to the nearby car park and drove closer to the retirement home's stately frontage. My truck, a battered Isuzu Trooper, shuddered violently as I hit the brake making a noise like startled poultry.

Standing near by, Sir Wilfred, who believes the invention of the internal combustion engine to be the single biggest disaster in history, stared at the vehicle with thinly veiled chagrin. Leaning on my elbow for support, he suggested we retreat to his room for the book signing. We slogged up the main staircase once more and veered off down another corridor.

As to be expected Thesiger's bedroom is simple and uncluttered. All the decorations have been carefully chosen; the surviving treasures of a restless life. Two elaborate swords, one silver, one gold, hang in the far corner, presents from Arab sheikhs. A framed photo of Emperor Haile Selassie's 1930 coronation party shows twenty-year-old Thesiger standing proudly amid rows of bemedalled dignitaries. But the people most represented are his parents, their black and white portraits throwbacks to the halcyon days of the Empire. A haunting picture of a desert scene lit by a crescent moon also catches my eye.

'That was drawn by my father,' said Thesiger, sensing my curiosity. 'We were very close. He died when I was eight. I was at boarding school in England at the time. I hated school at that age. The other boys didn't believe my stories of Africa, the campfires, the hyenas, the lion shoots, all that. In bed I would dream of Abyssinia. The glow of the mountains, the colours of the sand.'

I commented that his mother looked very beautiful. 'Yes, she was,' he said with affection. He had clearly been devoted to her but women had never really taken centre stage in his life. He was a resolute bachelor, married only to the wilderness. Life as a nomad, though, had evidently had its price to pay. Other than his parents there were no photos of family, of children, of friends. He receives very occasional visits from old admirers, the odd writer and his one surviving brother, but essentially he is alone, albeit with a trove of inimitable memories.

'What's this wood?' asked Thesiger, handing me a thin stick leant against his desk.

'No idea,' I replied, running a finger along the smooth surface. 'Mulga, perhaps?'

'No, no, it's the shin bone of a giraffe,' he said with delight. 'It might come in handy on your walk.'

He took it back from me, brandishing it fondly. Spread open on his desk I noticed his latest book of photographs, due for publication in a few weeks. It was titled *A Vanished World* and had one of his trademark shots on the cover, a dramatic black and white portrait of a Kurdish tribesman. Many of his other books were stacked on a wooden shelf by his window. I also spotted a couple of novels by John Buchan. It dawned on me that Thesiger was very like a Buchan hero, a grown man with the courage to pursue a boy's dream. Thesiger put down the giraffe bone on the desk and picked up *A Vanished World*. He flicked through some of the pages. 'Danakil country!' he said, pointing at one of the photos. 'This poor warrior, here, was killed the day after I took this picture.' His comments did not surprise me. I remembered from his book *The Danakil Diary* that several of the tribes were notorious for killing and castrating rival warriors.

'Those tassels that hang from the warrior's dagger show how many men he has castrated,' added Thesiger.

'Would they have killed you?' I asked. 'As a foreigner?'

'Of course,' he replied merrily. 'All the Western-led expeditions before my trip to the Danakil had been attacked. Explorers, hunters or soldiers – almost completely wiped out. That was the challenge, the lure. For the young warriors killing was a way of proving themselves, almost like sport. Like football! It wasn't a gentle place.'

'Sounds barbaric to me.'

'Barbaric!' he fumed quietly. 'It's not barbaric.' He picked up the giraffe shin and pointed it at the window in the direction of my truck. 'That car of yours is more barbaric.' He waved the bone like a wand, an impassioned old wizard trying to zap my Isuzu and any other engine-powered car, bus or aeroplane into extinction, anything that interfered with his equilibrium of simplicity.

'But surely you have flown in an aeroplane before?'

'Of course, it's quicker,' he replied sharply. 'But if there were no planes I would still have walked, whether to Africa, Iraq, wherever. It would have simply taken longer.'

After a while we became absorbed in his book again. It was then that my mobile phone rang. Brrrrrrrr. I drew it from my pocket as quickly as the Sundance Kid and deactivated the trills of modernity. I hoped Thesiger hadn't heard. A mobile phone would be the final betrayal, but as usual, the old man hadn't missed a beat.

'Will you take one of *those* with you on your walk?' he asked dryly, humour in his eyes.

'Yes,' I replied, adding more enthusiastically, 'but only for emergency calls.'

'I can see why you want one,' he replied, scratching his crooked, Cyrano-like nose, a casualty of four years' boxing at Oxford. 'But a phone spoils the danger, don't you think? If you know you can be saved or have supplies dropped off, what's the point? In the Danakil you were truly on your own.' He paused, as if thinking out a chess move. 'The problem today is that Western youths are bored silly. In the Danakil you were never, *ever* bored. Never took anything for granted.'

I realised how alien my travels must have sounded to Thesiger. He had offered advice on walking, mules and nomadic life but that was where the parallels ended. I was going to walk through America, a land where the car is king, a culture of consumerism and convenience. I could think of few places he would feel less at home, with the possible exception of this dowdy London suburb where we sat.

Thesiger has never made any secret of his indifference to

Western society. Although he enjoyed aspects of Eton and Oxford, his time in England never stirred his senses. Cricket was 'appalling' and even the countryside he found 'intensely boring'. His heart was elsewhere. It was hardly surprising. This was somebody who, aged six, had witnessed the victorious army of Ras Tafari (later Emperor Haile Selassie) returning from the hand-to-hand battle of Sagale. Young Wilfred was overwhelmed by this spectacle of energy, thundering drums and glistening spears. He later wrote:

> That day made a profound impression on me, implanting a craving for barbaric splendour, for savagery and colour . . . I grew to feeling an increasing resentment towards Western innovations . . . and a distaste for the dull monotony of our modern world.

Thesiger has attracted some flak through the years. Some say his concern for the desert communities is paternal and unrealistic. Why should Westerners enjoy the fruits of capitalism but insist it is better for tribal communities to stay primitive? Thesiger, however, is no hypocrite and certainly no capitalist. He saw Africa before motorised transport, Arabia before the oil boom and Iraq before Saddam Hussein. He had every intention of living out his life as a nomad. Only failing eyesight and the death of a friend led him back to England in the mid-1990s from his home in Kenya.

Like Sir Edmund Hillary who has been horrified by the escalating pollution on Mount Everest since he reached the summit in 1953, Thesiger regretfully realises some of his maps of the Empty Quarter helped open up the area for oil companies. It pains him how oil money has all but destroyed the simple nobility of the Rashid, the Bedouin who joined him on some of his hardest walks. 'I never felt so at peace or so inadequate as among the Rashid,' Thesiger tells me. 'It's just not the same now. My motto has always been "the harder the strife, the purer the life". It's too soft for them today; they have cars, money. They've lost their sense of dignity'.

It was time for me to go. I had already overstayed by two hours. Characteristically, Thesiger insisted on walking me back down the stairs to my vehicle.

'Good luck on your walk,' he said, shaking my hand at the entrance hall. 'One thing I forgot to mention about mules – don't ever let them get away from you. They're terribly hard to catch.' He paused, still holding my hand. 'Come and see me when you return. Bring the mule along too.'

'I'd like that. Good luck with the Vanishing World book.'

'*Vanished* World,' Thesiger corrected me.

'Yes, of course.'

As I headed off towards Clacket Lane, I felt strangely elated. I knew that meeting this old man, so gloriously out of step with his times, had been a rare privilege. The sight of him waving his giraffe shin would long simmer in my memory. Not only had he fired my imagination, but more importantly, he had opened my eyes to an old, savage, more spacious world. A world where human dignity is really all that counts.

If I could capture just a little of Sir Wilfred's spirit, it would serve me well on my American journey. Besides, I only had to walk 2,500 odd miles, a mere 2.5 per cent of Thesiger's grand total. Yes, that made it seem a lot better. The fact they had no castration ceremonies in Texas was a plus point too. For the first time in months a sense of confidence and excitement swelled up inside me. I was all set. Tip top. Ready to stride off towards New York fleet-footed as a desert Bedouin.

All I needed now was my mule.

PART ONE

'I am here because of a certain man. I came to retrace his steps. Perhaps to see if there were not some alternate course. What was here to be found was not a thing. Things separate from their stories have no meaning. They are only shapes. Of a certain size and color. A certain weight. When their meaning has become lost to us they no longer have even a name. The story on the other hand can never be lost from its place in the world for it is that place. And that is what was to be found here. The *corrido*. The tale. And like all *corridos* it ultimately told one story only, for there is only one to tell.'

Cormac McCarthy,
The Crossing

CHAPTER 1

Colonel Arthur and the Mule Skinner

'We do not take a trip; a trip takes us,' so the saying goes. Since I was about to walk the equivalent distance of London to Timbuktu I tended to agree. Still, it seemed harsh to pin my upcoming odyssey purely on the 'trip', and I could hardly blame the mule either. In truth a host of potent influences had lured me towards America long before my meeting with Sir Wilfred.

In 1997 I had ridden a bicycle between England and Australia following in the wake of my swashbuckling ancestor, Captain Charles Fremantle. I had pedalled past the Coliseum and the Wailing Wall, over the Himalayas, through the jungles of Indo-China and into the Western Australian bush. I ended up at the port of Fremantle, just south of Perth, which had been named after him over one hundred and seventy years ago.

That was it, I told myself on arrival back in England; stop running, cultivate some roots. As Cat Stevens advised in his song 'Father and Son': 'Find a girl, settle down, if you want you can marry . . .' The fact that Cat Stevens has since changed his name to Yusuf Islam, grown an explosive beard and now only yodels the praises of the Prophet Mohammed did not waver me from my newly found domesticity.

Sure enough, I managed over three years anchored in Oxford, flitting between jobs. Then, once again, the tide tugged at my gypsy heart and the Sirens started cooing. But this time the Sirens were neither Cat Stevens nor the honey-voiced temptresses that charmed Odysseus: far from it. In fact there was only one Siren and he was another ancestor of mine, the imperiously named Lieutenant-Colonel Arthur James Lyon Fremantle of the Coldstream Guards.

I knew of Colonel Arthur (as I shall now refer to him) from the Fremantle family tree. Perched on his distant branch, my great great cousin always sounded rather limp and mossy, nothing like my ripe, full-budded seafaring forebears. What could Arthur offer compared to dashing, Australia-bound Captain Charles or plucky Admiral Thomas, one of Nelson's Band of Brothers? Arthur didn't even possess a dastardly streak like distant cousin, Richard Wynne, a jovial roué who boasted an equatorial paunch and side whiskers like Peruvian guinea pigs.

With all this sparkling competition Arthur was left in the shadows. It was not until I read about him in a historical novel by Michael Shaara called *The Killer Angels* that I realised his true potential. A friend of mine, Gina, chanced upon Shaara's Pulitzer Prize-winning book while trawling through a library in New Orleans. By a stroke of luck she spotted a chapter entitled 'Fremantle'. On hearing of Gina's exciting discovery I sensed my ancestor was well worth investigating further.

It came to light that Colonel Arthur had travelled through America in 1863 at the height of the country's violent Civil War. During his rip-roaring, three-month adventure, the 28-year-old soldier experienced all the rough and tumble of frontier life. He ate polecat, drank moonshine, played poker, dodged bullets, flirted with saucy belles and was arrested as a spy before finally witnessing the heroic but devastating Battle of Gettysburg. He then sailed back to England from New York and penned a bestselling diary about his travels. Wow, I thought, this makes even Captain Charles look like a pussycat.

In *The Killer Angels*, the author memorably describes Colonel Arthur as:

> a scrawny man, toothy, with a pipelike neck and a monstrous Adam's apple. [Fremantle] looked like a popeyed bird who had just swallowed something large and sticky and triangular. He was wearing a tall gray hat and a remarkable coat with very wide shoulders, like wings . . . He was the kind of breezy, cheery man who brings humor with his presence . . . he had not changed his clothes in some days and he looked delightfully disreputable . . .

This charming vignette of the Colonel certainly made him sound like a man who stood out from the crowd (as had his high-spirited father, 'Jolly Jack' Fremantle, also a soldier, who served as Wellington's ADC at the Battle of Waterloo). Indeed, ancestor Arthur instantly piqued my curiosity, but it was not until I tracked down a copy of his original 1863 diary that I became hooked.

The diary, *Three Months in the Southern States*, was at my parents' home in a locked cabinet, rubbing spines with a Maeve Binchy (my mother's) and a vast Sherlock Holmes omnibus (my father's). I pulled it out and blew off a patina of dust and mummified woodlice. On the sleeve jacket was a Confederate battle flag — blood red with a blue cross in the middle spangled with stars. It was in a very tatty state, as if it had been savaged by a Yankee bayonet.

I flipped open the first page and unfolded a map of the Colonel's route, stretching from the old port of Bagdad in north Mexico right up to New York. A dotted line zigzagged from one richly historic name to the next. San Antonio, Natchez, Chattanooga, Charleston, Richmond, Gettysburg. In the background were faded illustrations of cavalry swords and steam trains. An elegant ship, sails buffeted by the wind, blazed towards the Gulf of Mexico. The map smacked so much of *Gone with the Wind* I was surprised not to see a silhouette of Scarlet O'Hara and Rhett Butler smooching above Atlanta.

'Yes!' I thought ecstatically, my heart slapping into my rib cage like a visceral high five. 'Oh, yes.'

After devouring the first pages of Colonel Arthur's diary I knew there would be no turning back. However tightly I tied myself to the mast, it was just no good. Unlike Odysseus, I had no crew to restrain me, only my own easily lapsed sense of discipline. It was already too late. I was gone, long gone, back to a hopelessly romantic world; a world of courage, savagery, honour and prejudice; a world in which America had wrestled to define itself; a world as vanished as Xanadu but one in which I urgently desired to plant fresh footprints.

Now I needed to decide how to travel. My first instinct over those initial weeks was to hitchhike. After all, this is what Colonel Arthur had done in the summer of 1863. The young officer cadged lifts with drunken mule-train drivers, drifted across the Mississippi on a skiff, hopped on steam trains and, whenever possible, rode a horse. Hitchhiking today might prove a bit bland in comparison, I decided. It still boasted a devil-may-care quality but physically it was a cop-out. Besides, witnessing America from an air-conditioned vehicle or even the back of a pick-up truck would lose all Civil War resonance.

Then in a mood of wild optimism I decided to travel with a wagon and horses. My cousin Hugh, a New Yorker, dissuaded me from this idea. He sent me an article in the *New York Times* exposing how the fiercely traditional Amish people, who still use horse-drawn buggies, were being swept off the roads by large trucks. I realised if it was treacherous for wagons in these rural enclaves of Pennsylvania, then urban areas would clearly spell suicide. Besides, it would cost a fortune.

Having derailed the wagon plan there was only one thing for it – horseback. This idea excited me considerably but it had some severe drawbacks. Although my ancestor had been a whiz in the saddle, I had no idea how to ride at all. My horsemanship had last been tested as a seven-year-old at an apple-bobbing race in a local gymkhana.

The idea was to canter over to a bucket of water with an apple bobbing in it, dismount, grasp the apple between my teeth, remount and gallop back. I rode on my sister's feisty Welsh mountain pony, Lucky (a highly inappropriate name), and was disqualified after my mount ate the apple, drank the water, kicked the bucket into the crowd and then charged off with impressive alacrity, in the opposite direction to the other jockeys.

Too many viewings of *High Noon* as a child had clouded my judgement. Trotting into the sunset with Grace Kelly was only possible in a Hollywood Western, and only then if you were as cool as Gary Cooper. My sense of cool owed more to Tommy Cooper.

So riding wasn't such a good idea: but unless I was pre-pared to strike a Faustian pact with the internal combustion engine, it was the only option left. Then, just as I was about to buy my first pair of jodhpurs, destiny intervened. While perusing my ancestor's diary for the umpteenth time my gaze fell upon one particular illustration: a donkey. What was a picture of a jackass, a very large one at that, doing in an 1863 war journal? Surely donkeys had little use on the battlefield? Colonel Arthur certainly never mentioned them. Then it hit me. This wasn't a donkey or ass of any pedigree. What I was looking at was clearly a mule.

'A mule', I thought wistfully. 'That could work.'

*   *   *

'So I hear you are walking across America!' shouted Stefano down the line.

It was my final night before flying out to Mexico and the phone was hot with the playful insults of friends. The elation of my recent meeting with Sir Wilfred had long since evaporated and I was now in a funk, overwhelmed by last-minute anxieties. Spread on the kitchen table was a mass of books, magazines and photocopied information about America, the Civil War and mule husbandry. The last thing I needed was a phone call from Stefano.

'Since when have you been the mule whisperer?' he chided in his thick Italian accent. In the background I could hear a baby crying and the sounds of his family eating dinner.

'I'm meeting the beast for the first time in about a week,' I replied patiently.

'So you're walking all the way?'

'I'm walking in a continuous line from the Mexico border up to New York. The mule will carry my kit. I'm not riding it.'

'Do you know anything about mules?' asked Stefano, somewhat suspiciously.

'Only Abyssinian ones,' I admitted. 'I've worked lots with sheep though. Once I even milked a cow. I'll be fine.'

There was a long lull in the conversation. A door slammed shut and the background noise became instantly muted.

'You know something, Tom, you really are a character.'

'Thank you.'

'No, mate, I don't mean it as a compliment,' insisted Stefano. 'Some people use the word character to describe somebody strong-willed, adventurous or free-spirited. But when I call you a character I mean it in the sense you are a complete tosser.'

'Well, thank you, Stefano.'

'My pleasure. Listen, my friend, one more thing. I want you to remember these four words, "*in culo alla balena*".'

'What the hell does that mean?'

'In Italy we say it as a sign of good luck. It translates as something like "up the arse of a whale".'

'No wonder Italy always lose at football.'

'Hey, muleman, better up the arse of a whale than at the side of a jackass.'

But Stefano was probably right. I was a complete tosser and a selfish one to boot. I was leaving behind family, friends and responsibility to set out in the footsteps of an outlandish-looking ancestor accompanied by a creature known best for its grouchiness and deftly aimed kicks. Oh well, it was too late to turn back now.

To be fair, although most of my pre-journey homework had revolved around route planning, I had set aside a little time for mules. One book that now lay in front of me on the kitchen table was *The Modern Mule* by Paul and Betsy Hutchins. I had secured this having emailed a tiny outfit called Hee Haw Publications somewhere deep in the Texas backwoods. I loved the Hutchins' book – it made mules out to be highly distinct-ive beasts. Already from reading the opening chapter (plus

some back copies of *Brayer* magazine) I had learnt the following arresting facts:

> Mules are completely sterile; they are able to mate with great
> zest and imagination but will never reproduce. They boast
> nature's ultimate form of contraception. A mule is only
> created by the union of a male donkey and a female horse.
> Alternatively, a cross between a female donkey and a male
> horse is called a hinny, another sterile hybrid.

> Do not call a mule a jackass, an ass or a *burro* – all these
> words apply only to donkeys, tabloid journalists and anyone
> who plays golf.

> Mules are much more sure-footed than horses and are still
> used to ferry tourists (unless they are exceptionally plump)
> up and down the Grand Canyon. In several wars, especially
> the American Civil War and the First and Second World Wars,
> they have proved invaluable as pack-animals.

> Ranchers often keep mules in fields with horses or livestock
> as, being champion kickers, they can scare off coyotes, foxes
> or wild dogs.

This, however, is where the compliments dried up. *The
Modern Mule* and *Brayer* magazine were written for mule lovers
by mule lovers. To my dismay, I quickly discovered that in
most other literature mules are dismissed as villains. Take
these chilling observations written in 1872 by the traveller
Francis Galton:

> Mules require men who know their habits; they are powerful
> beasts, and can only be mastered with skill and address. A
> savage will not assist in packing them, for he fears their heels:
> the Swiss say mules have . . . odd secret ways, strange fancies
> and lurking vice. When they stray, they go immense dis-
> tances; and it is almost beyond the power of a man to catch
> them.

These comments perhaps say more about the Swiss than mules, but even so, not a source of great encouragement. Even in the classics mules and their masters come in for a drubbing. In Cervantes' novel *Don Quixote*, a group of heartless yokels who beat up the hero and his portly sidekick, Sancho Panza, are depicted as muleteers. The Bible isn't very generous either. The only story on offer is a negative one, in which King David's dashing son Absalom is garrotted on the bough of an oak tree while riding a mule under it.

Donkeys are far better represented. The aforementioned Sancho rides through the Spanish sierra on Little Dapple, a plucky ass. G.K. Chesterton's wonderful poem 'The Donkey' champions a holy animal that despite 'ears like errant wings' once had palms at its feet. A.A. Milne's creation Eeyore is forever forlorn while Bottom in Shakespeare's *A Midsummer Night's Dream* is a hopeless lummox. Yet both these donkeys, however flawed, at least boast literary endurance.

Of course horses have always been fêted. To the ancient nomads of Mongolia horses attained a mythical status, believed to be able to sweat blood and carry their riders headlong into immortality. Whether set in stone by the Persians at Persepolis or carved into the chalk of the Wiltshire Downs, whether charging Russian cannons at Balaklava or breasting the finishing line at Aintree, horses have long been beloved creatures. Pegasus, Rozinante, Red Rum, Black Beauty – household names all of them. Napoleon's stallion, Marengo, perhaps the most famous of military horses, still has his skeleton on display at the Army Museum in Chelsea almost 190 years after Waterloo.

But name one mule, just *one* mule. The only one I can think of is Muffin the Mule, from the 1950s children's TV show with a catchy theme song. The hapless Muffin is portrayed as a helium-voiced goof with wild ears and hyperactive hooves. *We want Muffin, Muffin the Mule, We want Muffin, Playing the Fool.*

No, we don't, I thought whenever the repeats appeared on screen, we want 'The Clangers' or 'Dr Who'.

Mules are the whipping boys of the entire equine world. If ever a creature was in dire need of a cavalry of spin doctors, the mule is it: a Millennium Dome of a beast. And what about all the cruel expressions – 'kick like a mule', 'stubborn as a mule'? Is there nothing positive for the poor creatures to bray about, except perhaps in 1930s Abyssinia?

On my kitchen table that evening there was one book that I hoped would redress the balance: Dervla Murphy's *Eight Feet in the Andes*, about a mother and her nine-year-old daughter walking through Peru with a mountain mule. I was confident that Murphy, a hardy and courageous soul, would applaud her beast of burden. I also had a copy of Robert Louis Stevenson's *Travels with a Donkey* and John Steinbeck's *Travels with Charley* in which the curmudgeonly author tours America in a camper van accompanied by his French poodle. I was optimistic that these tales of animal bonding would inspire me at the onset of my travels.

It was getting late. I pushed away all the books and paraphernalia from the table and unfolded a large map of Texas, the first place I would hike through. Texas really was enormous – the size of France someone had told me. I kicked off my leather walking boots and used them to pin down the Lone Star State, with one boot on Dallas and the other on El Paso. I earmarked the little town of Beeville, near Twin Oaks Ranch where my mule was being kept. It was about two hundred miles north of the Tex-Mex border.

I had one more phone call to make tonight, to Loncito Cartwright, the rancher who had agreed to supply my beast of burden. I had tracked him down through my cousin, Eddie, who worked for the Animal Health Trust in Newmarket. I had heard that Loncito was a 'good ol' boy', whatever that meant.

I glugged apprehensively on a glass of red wine and dialled the Twin Oaks number.

'Heeaylow.'

'Loncito, this is Tom, the Englishman.'

'Yeahhh.' There was certainly a drawl to his voice, but not a lazy one. This was a man who apparently rose well before dawn every morning to check his goats and cattle. 'Well, Tom, we've got you a mule.'

'Terrific, Loncito,' I said, punching the air with relief. 'You realise I might need a lesson or two on how to pack it.'

'Yeahhh, I've got a friend of mine to help you out. His name's Justin McCord. Great guy, real old cowboy.' Loncito stopped to clear his throat, then added casually. 'It depends on whether he's out of prison, though.'

'Prison!'

'Yeahhh, Justin likes to drink.'

'Surely they can't lock you up for that?'

'Naaaa, but he likes to fight too,' added Loncito with a phlegmy chuckle. 'Great guy though, and he likes mules. He'll be with you for the first week and show you what to do. He'll ride in a horse-drawn wagon while you walk. It will be like the old days, like when your ancestor was here.'

'Great,' I said feebly, aware that Justin, however good with mules, also sounded something of a handful. I framed a mental picture of Lee Marvin with a hangover.

'Should be an interesting time to visit,' continued Loncito. 'The stretch you are walking through is real Texas brush country, bone dry, rattlesnakes, one hundred degree afternoons, maybe even the odd twister.'

'Twister!'

'Yeahhh, don't worry though, it's late in the season,' Loncito quickly reassured me. 'That mule of yours won't mind. She's seventeen years old and tough as hell.' There was a pause as I digested the words, 'seventeen years old'. Surely even Pegasus had arthritis at that age.

'Seventeen years old, Loncito. Isn't that a bit past it for a mule?'

'Naaaa. She's a little hoary but not exactly past it. Mules can live to well over thirty. The fact she's mature will mean she's less skittish.' I was stunned into silence. 'See you in a few days then. Don't worry, we'll get you going. Justin will turn you into a regular mule skinner.'

'Mule skinner?'

'Yeahhh, someone who skins mules.' Loncito began to laugh at the end of the line. 'Just a bit of Texan humour,' he concluded before the line went dead.

Thesiger had told me, 'The harder the strife, the purer the life.' I got the feeling I was soon about to find out.

CHAPTER 2

Mexico

Flying over Mexico City my heart began pounding so hard I could see it beneath my T-shirt. At first I thought it was the sight of the mountains that stirred me, but soon realised it was nothing to do with them.

In contrast to the dramatic, snow-capped summits fringing capitals like Kathmandu or Edinburgh, Mexico City's lush peaks appear as mere blips. Here, above the ancient capital of the Aztecs, something else thrills the eye: a swirling hive of over twenty million people, the largest urban population on earth. From afar this immense panorama turns nature on its head, makes mountains into molehills, shrinking everything to the sort of skewed dimensions Gulliver witnessed at Lilliput.

On arrival I flagged down an airport taxi, a green Volkswagen Beetle, which decanted me near Sarah's home. Sarah is

an old friend who had been teaching English in Mexico City
for the last year. Her rented room lay in the heart of the Zona
Rosa, a confusing tangle of ancient and modern. Internet
cafes rub shoulders with Catholic shrines and hawkers tout
their sizzling tacos outside nightclubs with flashy names like
Osiris and Casa BoomBoom. Wandering through the streets
with my backpack, the whole area seemed in a state of upbeat
flux.

I dumped off my kit with Sarah's elderly landlady, who had
applied so much make-up she looked ready to lie in a coffin.
She was sweeping up leaves from her courtyard, a white
chihuahua yapping at her feet. After introducing myself I hur-
ried out to the neighbourhood bar where I had arranged to
meet Sarah. I found her sitting on a wicker chair on a
deserted pavement. VIVA MEXICO blazed a sign above her
head.

'*Saludos*, Thomas,' she greeted me in her thick Scottish
accent. She was deeply tanned, sporting sandals and a pair of
zanily designed bellbottoms. We embraced before squeezing
lime quarters into our Coronas and toasting absent friends.
Salud! Salud! The chime of the bottles stunned the torpid
evening air. We were overlooking El Angel, a statue with
golden wings and a serene visage, who cast her twilight
shadows down amid the palms and the street lights.

Sarah told me she loved being in Mexico. She spoke fluent
Spanish, enjoyed her teaching job and was dating a local man
who was training to be a doctor.

'So what is it Mexico has that Britain hasn't?' I asked.

'It's the men, Tom,' replied Sarah, tossing back her mane of
dark hair. 'Mexican men have this reputation for being
macho, but they're very gentle. In England a handsome man
is called a hunk — as if he's a hunk of rock or bread. In Mexico
a handsome man is called a mango. Far more sensual.'

'So is, er, someone like George Clooney a mango?'

'No way,' protested Sarah. 'Far too overripe, he's even older than you. But my boyfriend, oooh, yeah, now he's a mango.'

'And I thought you'd come here for more profound reasons.'

'No, no, mainly the men,' she admitted. 'And maybe, you know, the sunshine, the passion, the danger.' She laughed, swinging her necklace in her hands, its multicoloured baubles clacking together. Two young boys ran past dribbling a coconut shell along the road.

'So what about you? What was this ancestor of yours doing out in Mexico City?'

Actually, Colonel Arthur hadn't arrived anywhere near Mexico City, I explained to Sarah. The young Coldstream officer had been working as a military secretary in Gibraltar and, having requested four months' leave, desperately wanted a sniff of the action in America. He had caught a steamer to Cuba and from here jumped on a frigate that ferried him just south of the Texan border. To maintain his status as a neutral Brit, Colonel Arthur had to enter Texas via the port of Bagdad in Mexico. This was to slip under the Washington-controlled shipping blockade that was in force at the time.

'Arthur sounds quite dashing,' observed Sarah. 'Bit of a mango.'

'Not really. According to one writer he had pop eyes and poor hygiene. His only similarity to a mango was he had an Adam's apple the size of one.' I paused for a swig of beer. 'I'm glad he doesn't qualify as a mango, though. Makes him sound like a total wuss.' Sarah smirked at my huffiness.

'So if this mango-throated hunk didn't come here, why have you?'

'Mexico City is the best place for me to get to Bagdad,' I replied. 'I was going to hitch there but I've decided to go by bus. It takes over twenty hours.' I sighed at the thought of it. 'Then I'll track down the spot where the Rio Grande flows into the Gulf of Mexico – that's where Arthur anchored on April Fools' Day, 1863.'

'Why doesn't that surprise me?'

But Mexico City wasn't completely irrelevant to my journey, I stressed to Sarah. It could be argued it was here that the long fuse sparking off the American Civil War first ignited. In the autumn of 1847 the resplendently dressed General Winfield Scott, at the head of his triumphant US troops, accepted the surrender of Mexico's capital. The bloody two-year Mexican War was over. It was a victory that enlarged American territory by nearly a quarter – including South Texas, Arizona and California – but reduced that of Mexico by half.

Many influential Americans had been opposed to this land-grabbing conflict, seeing it purely as a way of muscling in on a weaker neighbour. The ongoing bickering about it led to some fierce political rifts, adding fire to the already explosive issues of slavery and state rights. The friction between America's North and South was escalating. On the plus side, the Mexican War had been an impressive tactical success and proved a valuable training ground for many coltish US officers. However, several of these young, gifted men would in fourteen years' time no longer be brothers-in-arms, but mortal enemies, facing up against each other in the most tragic event in America's history.

'Seriously though, good luck, eh,' said Sarah, snapping me out my reverie. She raised her bottle. 'Here's to Colonel Arthur. *Salud!*' We stood clumsily and our Coronas collided once more. Sarah's affectionate toast made me realise how close I was to kick off. In England it had all seemed so faraway but here I was, actually in Mexico City, the wind soughing through the palm trees, a golden angel casting dark shadows. For the first time a pang of fear shot through me.

*   *   *

Two days later I was tearing along Bagdad's dismal beachfront in a Fiat Uno having cadged a lift with a fisherman called Pedro. We were on our way to the mouth of the Rio Grande to see where Colonel Arthur had first set foot. Pedro was exuberantly friendly but not the best of drivers. One blind eye (the result of a car smash) and a bad twitch in his remaining one did not help matters. His myopia was further hindered by an array of geegaws dancing above his dashboard – a Virgin of Guadaloupe talisman, an air freshener shaped like a pine tree and a photo of Jennifer Lopez.

The sun had yet to break through the morning cloud but the heat was already spectacular. In the wing mirror I could see my face, sweaty as cheddar on the turn. We passed a voluptuous concrete mermaid, some green paint flaking off her tail. She looked awful, a piece of fairground equipment left out too long over winter. The barbed wire perimeter fence didn't enhance the area, nor did the beach parasols that stretched along the sand like a rash of mutant toadstools.

Pedro suddenly veered the Fiat across the beach, down towards the incoming tide where the sand was firmer. He thrashed the little car mercilessly, swerving to miss driftwood and the occasional carcass of a dead shark. The only other vehicle out this early was a polished four-wheel drive, fishing rods jiggling on its roof rack, as it cruised over the grubby shingle. After slaloming for several miles we ground to a halt.

'*Aquí*,' said Pedro, slamming the Fiat's door shut and pointing at a meandering stretch of water. '*Aquí es el Rio Grande.*'

I have to say the legendary Rio Grande looked little more than a flooded stream. A white lighthouse, stunted and derelict, sprouted out from the dunes beyond the beach. We were the only visitors other than a pot-bellied man in a sombrero dispiritedly casting a fishing line. Gulls mewed overhead. On the Texas side a border patrol vehicle was parked near to where the quiet river segued into the Gulf of Mexico.

When Colonel Arthur disembarked from his frigate *Immortalité* on 2 April 1863, he described Bagdad as 'a few miserable shanties, which have sprung into existence since the war . . . endless bales of cotton are to be seen.' There were no bales of cotton now. Seventy ships had also been anchored off the Gulf of Mexico when the Colonel arrived, many of them foreign vessels taking advantage of the favourable wartime market. Not a single ship was on the horizon today, the sea almost as tranquil and desolate as the sand. I snapped a few photos and headed for the car. It felt satisfying to stand in Arthur's footsteps but not in the least inspiring: perhaps that would come later.

On our way back up the beach the little Fiat became snared in the shingle. Fortunately, after much hearty shoving and tactical placing of driftwood under the wheels the straining vehicle shot free. When we pulled up near the green mermaid again, I insisted on buying Pedro breakfast to thank him for the lift. We pinpointed a wooden shack selling snacks, then hunkered down on the sand and dipped our *churros* – fried sugar twists – into cups of black, gritty coffee. Many of the other fishermen were in the shade of the beach parasols fixing their nets. A campaign poster for the upcoming local election flapped in the breeze.

My Spanish was too poor to have much of a conversation with Pedro, but this felt right. Restricted to the only tense I knew, I was happy to live in an unbroken, animated present, where anything could happen next. Pedro picked his teeth and winked at me with his ruined visage. He had a rictus smile, seemingly content just to be alive on this sunny day, watching the waves, the egrets pecking at the seaweed.

I rummaged in my pocket for my car keys, but noted with satisfaction that they weren't there. Nor was my mobile phone, my house keys, my diary – the usual gadgetry for survival. All I found were a few pesos and a dishevelled packet of Extra Strong Mints. Pedro plucked out one of the feisty sweets and crunched it apprehensively. Within seconds he spat it out. '*Fuerte, muy fuerte*,' he shouted fanning his face with his hands. The incident made him laugh so hard his Cyclops eye began to weep.

The tension of the last few weeks fell away. Here I realised I could play by a whole new set of rules. No mask of civility, no veneer of control, no behavioural nuances needed to face the real world. I was somewhere else altogether now, along with Pedro and Colonel Arthur.

'Let it go,' a voice whispered to me. 'Go on, just let it fall away.'

CHAPTER 3

The Last Battle

From Bagdad Colonel Arthur rode thirty-odd miles in a horse-drawn buggy to Matamoros, further down the Mexican border. Once permission had been secured he crossed the Rio Grande into the Texan town of Brownsville. Here, after only three hours of setting foot in America, the wide-eyed young adventurer saw his first corpse. A group of Texan cavalry officers had recently lynched a *renegado* called Montgomery. Montgomery, 'a man of very bad character', had been hurling abuse at the officers from the Mexican side of the river. He had been on neutral soil but that did not deter the no-nonsense Texans from taking the law into their own hands. As my ancestor observed in his diary:

> He [Montgomery] had been slightly buried . . . the rope still round his neck, but part of it still dangling from a small

mesquite tree. Dogs or wolves had probably scraped the
earth from the body, and there was no flesh on the bones.

For the next two weeks Colonel Arthur shuttled between
Brownsville and Bagdad soaking up the intoxicating frontier
spirit. He met General Bee who commanded the troops at
Brownsville and partied with the convivial, cocktail-swilling
Don Pablo, the Vice-Consul at Matamoros. He witnessed
fandango dancing at a society ball, Southern troops drilling
(which greatly impressed him) and pompously wrote off
Mexican girls as 'a plain-headed, badly painted lot and ridicu-
lously dressed'.

He soon realised that Brownsville was 'the rowdiest town
of Texas', which in turn 'was the most lawless state' in the
South where any sensible man carried a six-shooter. After ten
days of dining, gambling and boozing the Colonel wrote:
'I have now become . . . reconciled to the necessity of shaking
hands and drinking brandy with everyone'. My ancestor
clearly had a blast. During his visit the South was desperately
fishing for foreign aid, especially from Britain, so the
plummy-voiced guardsman's presence was a great bonus for
the generous, eager-to-please Texans.

It hadn't always been this way. At the outbreak of the Civil
War in 1861 my ancestor's sympathies had been: 'rather in
favour of the North, on account of the dislike which an
Englishman naturally feels at the idea of slavery.' However,
while serving in Gibraltar, Colonel Arthur became increasingly impressed by incoming reports of the gallant determination of the Southerners and irritated by 'the foolish bullying
conduct of the Northerners'. After only two weeks in Texas
one gets the impression my ancestor is already falling heavily
under the 'moonlight and magnolias' spell of the South.

Like Colonel Arthur I planned to start my travels in earn-
est from Brownsville, but Loncito advised me it would be way

too busy. Instead we had settled for the town of Progresso, about forty miles further inland, which would be more mule-friendly. This is where I would meet Justin (if he wasn't behind bars) the following afternoon – 1 September. I had plumped for September, rather than April, to avoid the mercury-busting heat that plagued Arthur during his travels. First though, I needed to do a couple of things in Brownsville.

*   *   *

After our adventure at the Gulf of Mexico Pedro and I headed straight for Matamoros, still the official frontier town into Texas as it had been in 1863. From the Fiat I noticed dozens of *maquiladoras*, or assembly plants, stretching into the scrubland. Many of them were American-owned sweatshops, Pedro told me, taking advantage of the cheap Mexican labour. We made it to the border crossing at lunchtime. I shook Pedro's hand, flashed my passport at Customs and crossed over the bridge into America. Below me stretched the Rio Grande, the water here much worse than at Bagdad, a scummy cocoa colour.

What struck me most on walking into Brownsville was that everybody still spoke Spanish. The shops and restaurants had distinctly Spanish names – *Café de Rey*, *Mercado de Luz*. Much of the downtown architecture was colonial, the streets wide and stately. Flocks of jackdaw-like birds chattered in the papaya trees. From one cafe cowboy ballads bled into the sticky air while the next minute a truck would pass by blasting salsa. This was not America, nor was it Mexico. It existed in a twilight world between the two, and I rather liked it.

I checked into the Economy Hotel, staffed by a pretty but melancholy Mexican woman. '*Vaya con dios*,' she said softly as she handed me my key. I trudged up the stairs with my backpack, pouring sweat, and crashed into my little room. After a cold shower I headed straight for the Brownsville Historical Museum to see if I could track down any evidence of my ancestor's visit.

I was rewarded almost immediately. Amidst the Second World War medals, the 1960s fire hydrants and a collection of rusty bedpans, was some Civil War memorabilia. Its centre-piece was a faded newspaper article that had appeared in the *Brownsville Herald*: 'British Officer Wrote Diary Here,' was the headline, followed by the more catchy subtitle: 'Life Was Gay But It Was Dangerous.' Strange how words my ancestor once used to define the gung-ho frontier spirit would now sound more at home coming from Boy George's biographer.

The article on show quoted Colonel Arthur's diary ver-batim during his two weeks at the Tex-Mex border. The text was accompanied with a Civil War sketch of Brownsville that depicted several mule-drawn buggies hurtling down the high street. I can't tell you how exciting it is to find a museum exhibit devoted to an ancestor in a remote frontier town in Texas. As for the inclusion of mules, it made me want to burst into spontaneous applause.

This incident meant much more to me than standing at the mouth of the Rio Grande, so much so I wanted to grab the other museum visitors and show off the article to them. Sadly, there were no other visitors. In fact, according to the curator's signing-in book, I was the first person to visit this trove of local history for a while.

*   *   *

Buoyed by my recent discovery I made a beeline to the offices of the *Brownsville Herald*, which had been running through the presses for over a hundred years. It was here I met Kevin Garcia, a precociously intelligent cub reporter. He had impatient gestures and a moustache as downy as baby hair. He knew very little about Colonel Arthur but was keen to run an article on the mule trip. When I explained I had no mule yet, he suggested we drive out to Palmito Ranch battlefield instead.

'The last battle of the Civil War,' Kevin explained. 'Very few people go there but it's well worth it. Really strange and haunting. You've got to see it.'

It was early evening now and the sun was dying, lending a purplish tint to the sky. On the way out of town we sped past Brownsville's elegant university. The campus had once been the site of Fort Brown, Kevin told me, which had been destroyed by a hurricane shortly after the Civil War. There was still a mass of traffic, both human and motorised, travelling to and fro over the Rio Grande. I noticed a poster of Vicente Fox, the newly appointed Mexican President. I had seen dozens of posters of him across the river but was surprised to find him here in Texas too.

'Fox and George Bush are getting on well,' said Kevin, making the sign of the cross as we passed a Catholic church. 'Mexican-American relations are at their best for years, Bush is even reassessing Mexican immigrant numbers. I'm happy about this, with a name like mine its obvious I love both countries. Kevin – Tex. Garcia – Mex.'

We were now well north of Brownsville, driving through flat brush country. Kevin's decrepit Chrysler was very comfortable, its passenger seat like a beanbag. Police vehicles passed by with alarming regularity; in fact I hadn't seen as much border patrol activity since cycling through Israel's West Bank five years ago. After about half an hour Kevin pulled over into a field of wild grass and prickly pear cacti. A brass plaque attested that the Battle of Palmito Ranch had taken place here on 13 May 1865, a full month after the Civil War had officially ended.

'Why was fighting still going on in Texas after it had stopped elsewhere?' I asked.

'We're talking over a hundred and thirty years ago, Tom,' said Kevin, who was shaping up to be an inspired tour guide. 'No text messages then. News travelled to Texas only by horse. Down here they heard nothing of the surrender so the war just continued.'

'Palmito Ranch was a tiny battle,' he added, stepping over a cactus with red buds, 'but the last Civil War soldier was killed in action here. Private John Jefferson Williams,' Kevin spelt out the name with a certain reverence. 'You know, I'd like to write a novel about that guy. He was a Northerner, a blacksmith from Indiana. Only eighteen years old but already with a wife and son. Shot right through the temple with a minié ball.'

As I wandered along listening to Kevin's commentary something struck me. Seeing the Civil War's last battle so early in my journey was a topsy-turvy way of going about things but oddly pertinent. I agreed with Kevin's instinct to write about Private John Jefferson Williams dying here amid the cacti, so young, so far from home. Williams was the final casualty in a war that claimed the lives of hundreds and thousands of soldiers. The human being whose death acted as a full stop to all the grisly arithmetic.

'Think about it, Tom, over six hundred and twenty thousand men were killed in the Civil War,' stated Kevin as if corroborating my thoughts. 'This exceeds the number of American soldiers killed in all the other wars our country has fought put together, including both the World Wars and Vietnam. It was more like a war between the old Greek gods.'

Over six hundred and twenty thousand men: I mulled over it, a statistic so bleak it was almost meaningless. But it did serve as a valuable reminder why historians remain obsessed

with the four years running from 12 April 1861, when the
opening salvoes were fired at Fort Sumter, up until 9 April
1865, when Robert E. Lee's troops finally surrendered at
Appomattox. One Civil War survivor put it beautifully when
he said Americans had 'crowded into a few years the emotions
of a lifetime'.

Kevin was right, I decided, the Civil War really did boast
Iliad-like qualities – the Trojans and Greeks of the 1860s. The
agrarian, traditional Southerners (alias the Confederates or
Rebels) in grey uniforms taking on the industrial, progressive
Northerners (alias the Union, Federals or Yankees) in blue.
The battle lines were frequently blurred, of course. Plantation owners fought side by side with farm boys; professors
and poets marched in line with stevedores and miners. It was
a war that also pitched friends against friends, brothers
against brothers and fathers against sons. A war with warriors
every bit as heroic and vainglorious as Hector or Achilles, and
as immortal.

Rallying the South were such men as Jefferson Davis,
Robert E. Lee, Stonewall Jackson, J.E.B. Stuart and Pierre
Gustave Toutant Beauregard, while championing the North
were Abraham Lincoln, Ulysses S. Grant, William Tecumseh
Sherman, Joshua Chamberlain and Winfield Scott Hancock,
to mention but a handful. Their names were a hodgepodge of
the biblical, classical, colonial, native-American and all-
American – an unforgettable cast of heroes and scoundrels,
or mixture of the two depending on your allegiance.

The initial reason for this clash of grey and blue was hugely
complex, yet in some ways disarmingly simple. In a nutshell
the South was fighting for the right to own slaves and to
secede from the Union (the Northern States) while the North
hoped to radically curtail slavery and retain *all* the states
under one Washington-controlled umbrella.

Perhaps the most succinct explanation for the war I had seen appeared on, of all things, 'The Simpsons' TV show. The episode in question concerned the fate of Homer's friend, Apu, the local convenience store manager. Apu is an Indian who is threatened with deportation. In order to pass a citizenship test and prove his patriotism he has to answer questions about American history. One of the questions fired at him is: 'What was the cause of the Civil War?' Apu replies with great sincerity about the divisions of wealth between North and South, the issue of state rights, the mounting political schisms. Clearly taken aback by such breadth of knowledge one of the examiners interrupts quietly: 'Hey, wait . . . wait . . . just say slavery.' Needless to say Apu passes the test.

Americans, despite many formidable qualities, are not known for their prowess in world history. In a recent high school survey 42 per cent of those seniors asked could not name a single country in Asia while a third thought the First World War started before 1900. Perhaps even more shockingly, in a separate survey 73 per cent of a sample group of US adults were stumped when asked what D-Day referred to. That said, the Civil War seems to be one area of history where many Americans know their onions, sometimes to an encyclopaedic degree.

This is hardly surprising when you consider over sixty thousand books have been written about the war – amazingly this works out at more than one book published every day since Private Williams was shot dead at Palmito Ranch. Films such as *Gone with the Wind*, *Glory* and *Ride with the Devil* have packed cinemas in the United States through the generations while Charles Frazier's fine Civil War novel *Cold Mountain* battled with Harry Potter for the literary top spot.

Then there's the mind-popping statistic about President Abraham Lincoln, perhaps the most enduring hero of the conflict, who is thought to have had more works written about him in English than anyone in history except Jesus Christ.

It was dawning on me that Colonel Arthur's diary was a distinct but very delicate brushstroke on a canvas of grand proportions.

'You know something,' Kevin called out to me, snapping back my attention. He was standing in the corner of the battlefield holding up a strand of barbed wire. 'This stuff was invented by two farmers from Illinois in the 1870s. Great for agriculture but look at all the horror it caused in the First World War. You realise, Tom, if barbed wire had been around only fifteen years earlier it would have probably *doubled* the Civil War casualties.'

As I walked over to him Kevin nodded his head and added sadly, 'Makes you think doesn't it? I'm not sure one country could have coped with that much heartache.'

CHAPTER 4

Pilgrim's Progresso

I'm not a superstitious man, but something about Progresso spooks me. Day of the Dead skulls swing from mesquite trees, incense sticks exhale sweet, sickly aromas while the wind chimes clang. Hey, I tell myself, I'm here because of a page falling open on a book, because of an ancestor of mine, nothing more. Pull yourself together and forget this lottery of fate mumbo jumbo, this dialogue with the heavens. You're here because of Colonel Arthur, the one with the pop eyes and weird dress sense, and don't you forget it.

Thankfully the mule turned up bang on time, which jolted me out of my ethereal jitters. I had been tense all the way over on the bus from Brownsville earlier in the morning, feeling more like a matador about to face his first *toro* than a long-distance walker soon to size up his beast of burden. Now departure was imminent I felt instantly better, soon we really would be walking into the sunset.

The scale of my reception party would have impressed Cleopatra. A convoy of trucks, horseboxes and trailers – one of them with a four-wheeled wooden wagon perched on top – ground to a halt in a whorl of red dust. Hell, I thought to myself, is all this on my behalf? Loncito jumped out from the leading vehicle. He was a heavy-set man with an easy smile and a pair of white Wellington boots that looked several sizes too big. He was accompanied by Kevin Wars, a friendly, soberly dressed rodeo rider who had supplied the mule.

Out of the next vehicle came Justin, his blue eyes and stubbly, angular face shaded by a baseball cap emblazoned with the name of a chainsaw manufacturer. Trailing behind was Brandie, Justin's lissom, blonde girlfriend (an ex-table dancer from Austin, I had been told), her angel-faced young daughter, Ariel, and a taciturn Mexican man, Fino, who wore a belt with a skull-shaped buckle. They certainly made a colourful posse.

It touched me greatly that this road show was completely for my benefit: this adventurer who didn't know his ass from his elbow, in every sense of the expression. All these good people had been prepared to drive almost two hundred miles to rendezvous with somebody they had never met and help him walk through their country. It was an act of generosity from a bygone age when time was not treated as a currency but as a moveable feast, something to be gauged only by a glance at the sun and stars. Indeed one of the first things I noticed was that only one of my support team wore a watch.

'Haa, you must be the Englishman,' bellowed Loncito. We all shook hands and exchanged a few pleasantries. Everyone seemed to be speaking in incredibly loud voices. 'Come and see your little mule, my friend.'

I peeked through the horsebox slats and inhaled the musky equine stink. In one compartment was a large, roan-coloured horse, which would pull Justin's wooden wagon. Behind her was a plump brown mule. She looked up at me, her eyes dark and inscrutable. She then snorted vigorously and lowered her head. Oh, well, not love at first sight, but I'm sure we could work on it. It would be like one of those old movies; she could play the haughty Katherine Hepburn role and I could be a patiently affectionate Spencer Tracey who finally wins her trust. We'd have to take our time. Nobody said she was going to be a pushover.

We were still on the Texan side of the border but I was keen to begin my journey on Mexican soil. Fino agreed to watch over the vehicles and horsebox while the rest of us walked over to the south side of the Rio Grande. This frontier is very different from Matamoros and Brownsville. There, I had been the only non-swarthy face. Here, almost all the throng shuttling over the bridge were pallid tourists. This in turn lured the beggars. Swimming below us skinny, nut-brown Mexican children hoisted up bamboo poles with buckets attached to them for the crowds to deposit their nickels and dimes.

Progresso is geared up almost exclusively for daytrippers, its stalls jammed with predictable Mexican fare: sombreros, jalapeno peppers, cacti fronds, straw puppets and phials of lurid-looking potions able to cure everything from obesity to impotence. Goat legs and shark fins swing from meat hooks. There are many dentists too, flashing signs such as BEST PRICE ROT CANAL, FILING FOR YOU, obviously popular with Texans wanting to slash their tooth bills. Further along are tangles of necklaces made from cowrie shells and masks of

Quetzalcoatl, the plumed serpent of fertility and life, ancient Mexico's most prevalent god.

We had a late lunch in a hot, crowded restaurant. Loncito called for quiet and said grace. 'My popa always tells me we ain't no better than pigs troughing on acorns without saying thanks to the Lord,' he observed. I plumped for *cabrito* or baby goat, which came in an immense portion roughly the size of a child's shoe. It was gamey and tough, but tasty. Justin and Loncito revved themselves up with several margaritas. I noticed they all used the adjective 'little' regularly in conversation. 'My little mule', 'that little bastard', 'with a little luck'. It was not patronising, they simply spoke as if everything in Texas was on a different, more spacious scale: louder too.

'Man, that Winston Churchill,' shouted Loncito. 'He was a fine Englishman wasn't he, Tom? Let's raise a little toast to him. Now Churchill had balls, real *cojones*. Still in office at seventy years old. Seventy years old! Yes, sir, that old man really blew the wind up my skirt.'

'Winston Churchill, yeeehaaa,' howled Justin, as if spurring on a stubborn mare.

I began to realise these Texans spoke a whole new language, an earthy, free verse poetry. It tickled me that someone like Loncito, this bulky rancher, used the expression 'blow the wind up my skirt' without a hint of irony. The fact Justin still yodelled 'yeeeehaaaaaa' all added to the sensation of entering an exciting new world. A place where men fight and swear, but insist on grace being said before meals, talk of their families with unabashed sentiment and drive two hundred miles to help out strangers. I was already falling for my fresh environment. The soft drawls and hard opinions of those on the table seemed to run against the haste and distraction of the new century. There was something almost tribal about these people. I sensed Thesiger would have approved.

After lunch we walked back over the bridge into Texas. At one point Justin stopped to give a blind Mexican child playing an accordion a few coins.

'Poor little guy,' he said. Maybe he wasn't going to be so tough after all.

By the time we returned Fino had led my mule and Maria, Justin's horse, out of the box. They stood side by side, heads sagged, tails whisking at passing bugs.

'Right, let's get this show on the road,' said Justin, jumping up on his wagon, which was top heavy with equipment – ropes, harnesses, mule tack, ice boxes, a gas cooker, a bag of rice, rashers of beef jerky and a bottle of whiskey. From under the wagon seat Justin pulled out a sawn-off 16-bore. He grinned, cocked it and looked down the barrels. I was very opposed to travelling with a weapon – I wanted to base the trip on trust – but decided Justin, who had just flicked his shotgun shut with the casual competence of Wyatt Earp, was not a man to challenge to a duel, either with words or bullets.

Justin harnessed up the mule, expertly balancing the two saddlebags either side of her steeply concave back. Despite the 100 lb burden – including all my camping gear, medical kit, books, diaries, a bag of oats – the little beast didn't flinch. I held her tight while Justin linked up Maria to the wagon with the help of Loncito and Kevin.

'By the way, what's the mule's name?' I asked, stroking my new friend. I was hoping for something with a nice Latino ring to it. Maybe Carmen, Gabriella or even Evita. Just as long as she wasn't called Muffin, I didn't mind. Traveller might be good, too, after General Robert E. Lee's horse.

'She's called Browny,' said Kevin, adding rather needlessly, 'she's brown, you see.'

'Would she answer to anything else?' I wasn't sure if I could face walking 2,500 miles with Browny the brown mule. Tintin may have had a dog called Snowy, but I doubt Thesiger would have had a camel called Goldy.

'You can try another name,' replied Justin, 'but she'll not listen. Anyway, you'll soon be calling her many names other than Browny, once she starts giving you the run around.'

'Browny it is then,' I conceded. Looking at the portly beast she didn't seem capable of giving anyone the run around. She looked barely capable of walking for the rest of the afternoon, let alone to New York. The one sign of life were her long brown ears, which spun about like hirsute antennae. I stroked one of them tentatively.

'Don't pet her ears, Tom,' snapped Justin, looking around while tightening one of Maria's straps. 'They are her most sensitive part. In fact don't pet her anywhere. She's your work mule not your pony.'

Now that Browny was harnessed up and Maria had been attached to the wagon shafts we were all set. It was already late in the afternoon and we needed to crack on to find a place to camp. I quickly took a couple of photos of the team. Justin gave Brandie and Ariel a group hug and slapped Fino on the back. I said my goodbyes and walked Browny a hundred yards ahead of the wagon before stopping to look back.

'Whatever you do Tom, never, *never* look back at that mule,' called Kevin after me. 'Don't look her in the eyes, she'll stop every time. Just keep going. Look back to check where Justin is, but don't look at that mule.'

It was clearly going to be a steep learning curve. Sensitive ears, ultra perceptive eyes – mules were proving surprisingly high-tech.

So this was it. I really was off, walking through a land my ancestor accurately described as 'flat . . . sandy and very dusty'. I continued to lead with Browny trailing slightly behind. She was proving unexpectedly biddable. Behind us I could hear the wheels of Justin's wagon rattling along the bitumen and Maria's loud clip clopping. Compared to Browny's delicate, well-padded strides, Maria sounded as if she had saucepans attached to her hooves. Already the sun was falling away, a distant lozenge of light in the greasy sky. We passed a field of sugar cane swishing in the breeze, its smooth, green waves, tall as men, rolling northwards.

Timber trucks and livestock trailers occasionally thundered by. We were still on a major road, although it did have a wide shoulder for Justin to steer the wagon. One by one the team drove past us, Loncito and Kevin whooping like a couple of Amazonian parrots, Brandie and Ariel waving and blowing kisses, Fino simply tooting his horn, a single plaintive 'Nerrrr'. We hoped to see them in roughly ten days, by which time we should have covered the two hundred miles to Twin Oaks Ranch. Here, Justin would leave me and I would continue on my own having become wise to the ways of mules. Well, that was the plan.

After an hour the sky had begun to darken and walking was becoming increasingly dangerous. One driver shouted at us in furious Spanish to get off the road. Justin suggested we pull over to camp on a swathe of grass fringing a nearby gas station. Once we had secured permission from the owner I tied Browny to a picket fence while Justin dealt with Maria and the wagon. I fetched water for the animals and doled out handfuls of oats. Before feeding, Browny slumped onto her side and began thrashing around with her legs in the air as if trying to rub away a bee sting.

'Don't worry about her,' said Justin, sensing my concern. 'Mules love to roll, the crazier the better. She'll do that every night of the trip until you get to New York. I'd be more worried if she didn't roll. That would mean something was wrong.'

Justin and I sprayed ourselves with mosquito repellent, and sorted out our sleeping arrangements, him in the back of the wagon and me in a North Face Tadpole, a tiny free-standing tent. We then unfurled a groundsheet, ate a couple of tacos and congratulated each other on our first five miles. Having finished their oats Maria and Browny began to graze, ripping away at the patchy grass. A formation of Canada geese flew over, roughly twenty of them, low enough to hear the gentle whoosh of wings. Lying back, a dram of Justin's whiskey coursing through my blood, I felt sublimely happy.

In the distance a band of gold light glimmered beyond the Rio Grande. As it fell below the horizon it seemed to shudder briefly, like a soul leaving a body, before plunging into darkness.

*   *   *

The following day we rose at dawn. Brewing coffee, packing up the wagon, feeding and grooming the animals took us over an hour. I realised that a large portion of every day from now on would be spent loading and unloading my long-eared companion. But it was time well justified. Walking with Browny enabled me to move with a simplicity Colonel Arthur would have understood. It meant I could crunch through the sagebrush alive to the spirit of the many soldiers, frontiersmen and chancers who had come before me. If I had to swallow a few mosquitoes, cultivate a few blisters, so be it, it was a small price to pay to be at one with this wild land, to feel its subtle pulses beneath my feet.

Before marching off I showed Justin a copy of my ancestor's diary. To my surprise he was fascinated by it, especially the excerpts concerning the Judge and Mr Sargent, the two rowdy characters who offered to transport Colonel Arthur by mule train from the Tex-Mex border up to San Antonio. The Judge was an MP and local magistrate who was travelling north and had volunteered himself as an assistant mule driver to foul-mouthed Mr Sargent, the principal skinner. According to Colonel Arthur, during his opening days on the mule wagon, they sounded a right pair.

> Mr Sargent is a very rough customer, a fat, middle-aged man, who never opens his mouth without an oath, strictly American in its character. He and the judge are always snarling at one another, and both are much addicted to liquor.

> We live principally on bacon and coffee . . . We have, however, got some claret, and plenty of brandy.

> During the midday halts, Mr Sargent is in the habit of cooling himself by removing his trousers (or pants), and having gorged himself, he lies down and issues his edicts to the Judge as to the treatment of mules.

As regards Mr Sarjent's treatment of his six 'God Damned' mules, my ancestor writes: 'He [Mr Sarjent] is always yelling. He rarely flogs his mules; but when one of them rouses his indignation by extraordinary laziness, he roars out, "Come here, Judge, with a big club, and give him hell."'

Clearly Mr Sargent was not a sensitive soul, although Colonel Arthur does note his redeeming qualities. He is especially impressed at one stage when the usually brutish Sargent applies a brandy-drenched poultice to a wounded mule 'which does it much good'. The ability to skin polecats and goats with equal ease and even recommend rattlesnake recipes is also in Sargent's favour and certainly helps vary the paltry diet of Colonel Arthur, the Judge and the other travellers as they trundle through south Texas's 'boundless prairies'.

'Right,' said Justin, snapping the diary shut, 'from now on I'm going to refer to you as the Colonel.'

'Then I'll have to call you the Judge,' I told him.

'Fair enough.' Justin stood up and wiped his forehead with his baseball cap. 'So what distance do you think we should cover today? Your ancestor managed anywhere from fifteen to forty miles. There's a little place called Lasara about twenty-five miles northeast. Can you manage that?'

'Remember Colonel Arthur was on a wagon like you, I've got to walk,' I replied petulantly, and noticed Justin smirking. I felt like a gauntlet was being thrown down, a macho initiation ceremony brewing. I decided to go for it and told him casually. 'Twenty-five miles, yeah, whatever. Piece of cake.'

It was to prove a huge mistake. By midday the temperature was nudging one hundred degrees. I was wearing a pair of sturdy but claustrophobic leather boots and soon my feet started, quite literally, to melt. It didn't hurt at first. I had done lots of walking in my time and prided myself on some harshly calloused soles. But like everything else in Texas, the heat is off the scale.

The morning had been fine. Browny marched alongside me and I felt alive to my surroundings, the cornflower blue sky, the maize fields, the hawks wheeling on the air currents. Many drivers would slow down to find out what we were up to or simply toot their horns and wave. Some shouted out: 'Wanna take me with you?' 'Go home, you crazy son of a bitch.' And perhaps most common of all: 'Man, I'd just love to do what you're doing but I got three young children/ ain't got no money/ scared of all the crazies out there/ got a belly the size of a sow at Christmas.'

This goodwill of strangers combined with the novelty of the landscape delighted me. I knew I was pursuing a dream as old as time, a primitive calling. The dream to escape, hit the road, wander. My journey was an immense privilege and I didn't want to let down those people who craved an adventure like mine but would never have the chance to undertake it. I had to be true to all those rainbow chasers, those sensible souls who despite strong urges chose not to run against the wind, whose sense of belonging held them back. Only the truly selfish could attempt a gig like this.

Then, of course, there were those who clearly considered my dream more of a nightmare. Those who drove past me with a glowing sense of *Schadenfreude*, knowing their lives were orderly, purposeful, constructive, while I was just a bum, a crank. They looked from their windows and instead of witnessing a dream in motion, saw a disaster waiting to happen. Of course, they might well be right. But I wanted to prove to them that I could make it through America, this superpower that supposedly boasted 'the best and worst of everything', wade through all the doom-mongering and hysterical statistics, without coming a cropper. I wanted to show, like Blanche Du Bois, that it is still possible to depend 'on the kindness of strangers'.

But more than anything on this opening day I had a strong urge to walk, to simply put one foot in front of the other for miles on end. Before departure I had read that the average American walks only 1.4 miles a week, that's barely 350 yards a day! What's more, this meagre yardage is most likely to be clocked up, not in a park or garden, but while loafing in the shopping mall or shuffling from the car to the office. Indeed for over 90 per cent of all trips outside their own front door — however small the distance — Americans use a car.

I found this immensely depressing. Walking is a joy, a biological urge. To neglect it, to walk 350 yards a day so that each step becomes an effort rather than an instinct, is surely the ultimate betrayal of nature.

Pilgrims through history have championed the spiritual and healing qualities of walking. To Middle Eastern Sufis walking or dancing was a way of being at one with God, while some of the more pious dervishes strove to become a 'dead man walking', with their soul in heaven while their body still roamed on earth. Kalahari bushmen believe that once the wind has blown away their final footprints that is the end of them, while Jesus Christ's last words to his disciples were simply: 'Walk on.'

Many men took this advice. Even before Christ, Alexander the Great made a demigod of himself by soldiering largely on foot through several continents. In more recent times sandal-clad Mahatma Gandhi pilgrimaged months on end through India championing independence from the Raj, while the gardens of Chartwell and Bleinheim Palace were the perfect stomping grounds for Winston Churchill to pace away his troubled 'black dog' moods.

But not everybody liked to use their legs. One horse-loving Shoshone chief proudly named himself Cameahwait, meaning 'One Who Never Walks'. Cantankerous Max Beer-bohm believed that footing it 'rotted the mind' and Thomas de Quincey in his book *Confessions of an English Opium Eater* goes as far as proclaiming that pedestrianism 'carries with it the most awful shadow . . . of the pariah'.

I have to say that fifteen miles into my first full walking day my sympathies were no longer with the more noble pilgrims but firmly on the side of Beerbohm and de Quincey.

Even by 4 p.m. the pulsing heat showed no sign of subsiding. The initial rapture of the morning had worn off, my once springy feet were now smarting with pain and I was walking with all the grace of a wounded penguin. I felt like the worst kind of pariah and although my mind was not actually rotting, it had long since stopped paying attention to the surrounding land, much of which had been ploughed up for next year's cotton. In contrast Browny plodded happily alongside of me, occasionally turning to bray at Maria, who Justin continually had to rein in to slow down to my miserable pace.

'How ya doing, Colonel?' shouted out Justin from his wagon. His voice, I was relieved to hear, was one of concern rather than smugness. 'You look a little sore.'

'Yeah, just a few blisters,' I replied. 'I'm going to stop for a while.'

Justin pulled up and fetched some water from a nearby stream for Maria and Browny. I slumped against a hackberry tree and nursed my decaying feet. My socks had stuck to my skin like masking tape. Once peeled off they revealed grossly wrinkled, very pale soles. My right foot was stained with a dull red smudge like that on a cricket bat after striking a new ball. The heel was especially raw and I decided to use one of my Extra Soft Second Skin blister patches. It amused me to imagine Thesiger standing over me appalled by such prissy antics.

After drinking a litre of water and dunking my head in the stream we continued north. Another ten interminable miles of meandering down looping country roads and we reached the village of Lasara. It was well after dark and the cicadas were in full chirrup. Little bats flittered in the moon shadows. My feet were such a mess I could happily have rolled into a ditch and slept, anything to take the weight off my ruined soles. We had been on the go for fifteen hours.

'Hey, cowboys,' shouted a voice in the darkness. Squinting ahead I could make out several human silhouettes standing by a porch framed with fairy lights. 'You two fellers need a place to camp?' asked one of them.

'Alleluyah,' I whispered. I have a feeling the same thing might have crossed Browny's mind.

*   *   *

Robert and Maria Garza proved the finest of hosts. The whole of their family – from elderly uncles to toddler nieces – had assembled for a Sunday evening powwow at their white stone farmstead. Hickory smoke from the barbecue permeated the air as we unloaded Browny and Maria on the back lawn. Storm lanterns and candles bathed us in a flickering, insect-rich glow.

Soon a swirl of thickly accented men, women and children surrounded us, handing out pork chops and bottles of beer. When I tried to explain the bona fide intentions of my journey I was cut off in mid-sentence.

'Hey, buddy, we can see what you're doing, you don't have to justify yourself to us,' said Robert, an athletic-looking man with a crew cut. He was holding hands with Maria, his petite, heavily perfumed wife. 'You are clearly on some sort of mission. We're cool with that.'

'Can I pet your donkey?' asked a young girl in a pink dress, her dark hair bunched into a pair of unruly pigtails. She stuck out a carrot towards Browny who snatched it and chewed ferociously, sending strings of drool in all directions. The girl laughed and ran away.

I struggled over to one of the garden benches, pulled off my boots and rubbed my burning feet. It was then I noticed my calves. I had been wearing shorts all day and had foolishly only smeared on sun cream in the morning. My calf muscles had been chargrilled to a luminous pink. I punctured several nascent blisters with my nail scissors, rubbed my feet with talc, bandaged them and slipped into a pair of flip-flops. The inferno blazing on my soles gradually cooled and I limped over to join the rest of the party who were now clustered around a large picnic table.

'Hey Colonel, you're walking like a Civil War veteran already,' teased Justin, who was clutching a tumbler of whis-key. 'We did twenty-five miles today and you look dead beat. What would Stonewall Jackson make of you? His troops could march that far with their eyes closed and carry all their kit.'

Justin's comparison with Stonewall Jackson was a bit unkind. Jackson was one of the South's star Civil War generals, a deeply religious eccentric and famous hypochondriac who, believing he had one leg shorter than the other, often walked around with one arm in the air to aid his blood circulation. He also had a curious penchant for sucking lemons as well as a gift for falling into Rip Van Winkel-type slumbers, even with shells exploding around him. However, Jackson was often a revelation on the battlefield, a master of the flanking manoeuvre plus an inspirational marcher.

During his famous campaign in the Shenandoah Valley in the spring of 1862, Jackson marched his exhausted army almost two hundred miles in two weeks. In that time his often barefoot, hungry troops won five battles and rounded up hundreds of Union prisoners. The following year Jackson was accidentally killed by friendly fire at the Battle of Chancellorsville, almost exactly a month after my ancestor arrived in America. Despite never meeting the legendary Stonewall, Colonel Arthur often refers to him in his diary, noting that the Rebel soldiers still spoke of him with utmost reverence.

'Stonewall's men had no nice new boots,' continued Justin, spinning the ice cubes around in his drink. 'They had no sun block, no blister pads. Towards the end of the war some soldiers were so hungry they had to chop up horse dung and eat the bits of grain inside it. Look at you, Colonel, wolfing down a pork chop, swigging on a Budweiser. You've got it soft.'

'Listen, Justin, it was my first full day, it was one hundred degrees and we covered twenty-five miles,' I blurted. 'Give me a break, OK.'

'Whatever you say, Stonewall, take it easy now.'

Justin and I stopped our verbal sparring and joined in with the family party. The Garzas were of Mexican descent but had been in Texas for a generation. Robert coached American football at a local college while Maria was an art teacher. The family were all dark-skinned and spoke English and Spanish with equal aplomb. They were fascinated by the trip and asked many questions, especially about the mule. 'How old is she?' 'What does she eat?' 'What will you do with her in New York?' I soon learnt that Browny was the star of the show and I was merely the sidekick. She was Butch. I was Sundance.

'How does it feel to be outdone by a donkey, Tom?' joked Robert, after the Browny inquisition had finished.

'Story of my life,' I replied pulling a mock gloomy face.

'Ah, come on,' countered Robert, waving his hands as if refereeing one of his football games. The beer had clearly gone to his head. 'You think you've got it bad, what about us Mexicans. We've had a terrible history, the human sacrifices of the Aztecs, the colonisation by the Spanish, the disease, all the pointless revolutions and corruption. One of our ex-presidents, Salinas, recently fled to Dublin with millions of pesos in his back pocket. What do you think of that?'

'Sounds like you don't miss the old country much.'

'Oh, certain things,' admitted Robert, his expression softening. 'But in America my children have choices. It's a good place to make a go of things. God has been kind to us.' He stopped and pointed to a cardboard skeleton suspended from the porch 'But as you can see I haven't completely forgotten my Mexican roots.'

'In America certain things are too sanitised,' he continued, scratching his shaved pate. 'Take death for instance. In Mexico during the Day of the Dead festival we all celebrate our ancestors, a bit like you with Colonel Arthur. But we drink too much, wear skull necklaces, hang skeletons in trees, sing, dance. We celebrate those bones of the past, talk about them, put flesh back on them. I like that. In modern America death is never spoken of, everyone's terrified of it. Everyone worships youth, wants to live forever.'

'Not me,' muttered Justin to no one in particular.

'In Mexico we love our old people,' enthused Robert. 'The older the person gets the more respect they earn. But America has some strange priorities. The old are seen as a burden, an embarrassment. I suppose that's why I like Texas, it's the Lone Star state. We play by our own rules, hold on to family values, the old fashioned ways . . .'

'Stop lecturing, Robert,' interrupted an elderly man with luxuriant sideburns sitting opposite. He looked tired, his pupils caged in nets of red wire. 'Shut up and sing us all one of your stories. You sing better than you talk.'

Robert laughed, flicking his wrist dismissively. 'No, no, I don't want to bore Tom and Justin with that.'

'Go on,' I insisted. 'I'd love to hear you sing.' All his family felt the same way.

'Please Uncle Robert.'

'Come on, Dad you've got a great voice.'

'Bob, baby, do it for me,' whispered Maria. A cheer erupted and Robert leapt on top of one of the benches. After taking several deep breaths he began warming up his voice, playing to the crowd, the lantern light dancing on his face.

'This is a song about a girl and a boy in a little Mexican town,' narrated Robert, suddenly serious. 'The two young lovers each carve their names on to a cactus plant and swear undying love to one other. Then the boy goes to war and they get separated. The boy only returns to the town in his old age. He finds the cactus. The girl's name is still visible, but his has been rubbed away. He is so distraught he collapses and dies. The song is not really about the two lovers, it's about the cruelty of history.'

And then Robert was off, his booming voice soaring through the heavy, hickory-scented night. I understood only snatches of the lyrics but I could tell Robert was performing with all his heart, singing with a mixture of fury and tenderness about doomed graffiti on a cactus, about Mexico, about his life, about all of us. Within seconds the children's laughter had been silenced. I forgot my palsied feet, my blistered shins, I forgot where I was, lost myself in a story I'd never heard before and yet somehow had heard a thousand times. Robert sang on and on, finishing off in a high-pitched crescendo, tears rolling down his cheeks and those of several members of his family.

Nobody clapped or cheered, and this seemed just right. All was quiet bar the backing chorus of the night. The only movement was the fireflies, fizzing off in wild trajectories like stars being born.

CHAPTER 5

Fists and Feathers

Over the ensuing days my relationship with Justin deteriorated, so much so we almost came to blows. It was less of a character clash and more a case of fortune spitting on us in one long, sour and relentless spurt.

We were now walking through our most remote stretch of Texas with over seventy miles of scrubland between the little town of Raymondsville, which we had just passed, and Kingsville, our next destination. My feet were looking like those of a medieval plague victim and my pace became increasingly sluggish. Justin sat on his wagon, an umbrella suspended to ward off the bullying sun, listening to Johnny Cash singing about bourbon and broken dreams.

One of the main problems was that Justin needed a drink and my wretched limping was delaying him from his next rendezvous with a bar. He also found it incomprehensible that I refused to jump on the wagon to speed things along.

'Who's going to know if you ride for a bit, Colonel?'

'I'll know, Judge,' I replied sententiously. 'I promised I'd walk in a continuous line. If I cheat now it will ruin everything. I realise I look pathetic but give me a day or two and my feet will be tough as camel pads.'

'Jeysus H. Christ,' barked Justin. 'I don't know who's more stubborn, you or your goddamn mule.'

The night after the Garzas' party we spent on the roadside by Highway 77, still some fifty miles from Kingsville. It depressed me slightly to think this was a distance a car could complete in less than an hour, while I, in my current state, would take up to three days.

The spot where we chose to camp was far from perfect. All along the highway the fringing farmland was fenced off, the gates locked. I envied Colonel Arthur who would have had the horizon to himself in 1863, unsullied by barbed wire and NO TRESPASS signs. For Justin and me our only option was to sleep on the verge amid the mesquite trees and *huisache*, a devilish weed with sharp thorns that plagues much of south Texas.

As we were unloading the wagon and feeding the animals a sheriff appeared. He was dressed all in black, his belt so polished it reflected the twilight sun like a prism. He was short and stocky, his shoulders rucked up with the defiance of a quarterback, a pistol on hip. His whole appearance suggested a man hungry to throw his weight around. I suspected we would be told to move on.

'Hey, you guys, mind if I take your picture for the local paper?' asked the man in black politely. His name was Will Tabasco, according to the nametag on his lapel. After we assented to the photo, Will drew out a small, silver camera from his top pocket. Justin struck a pose by the wagon while

I drooped an arm over Browny's mane. We were off to a surprisingly positive start with the law.

'I hope you fellers gotta gun,' said Will, fiddling with his zoom. 'Might get a little hairy here at night, you know. We often get Mexican immigrants in these parts. Wetbacks. That's what they're known as. It's because they have to swim across the Rio Grande. They tend to move in packs, like wolves, anything from six to twenty of them, heading north to find work. They're usually very poor and very hungry.'

Will zeroed in the camera for a close up of Browny. 'If they're decent they'll just take your food and money, but if you're real unlucky they'll hurt you and your animals.'

I glanced up at Justin. He looked a little shell-shocked. Maybe the 16-bore had been a good idea after all.

'You've gotta feel sorry for them really,' continued Will, leaning against a mesquite stump. He told us most 'wetbacks' simply wanted to earn a little money to send home to their families. They didn't realise how harsh the Texas desert was. Every year dozens of them lost their way and died of dehydration or rattlesnake bites. Will explained it was illegal for Americans to put up 'wetbacks' in their homes but this didn't stop some people.

'There's one old lady up the road,' Will gestured northwards. 'She's always helping wetbacks. Trouble is now she's been kind to one group, word has got back and they all go to her. When I went to see the old girl recently she looked me in the eye and said: "Arrest me if you have to, sheriff, but I will never turn away a starving man from my door."' Will laughed remembering the episode. 'Between you and me, I admire the hell out of her.'

He pocketed his camera and lit up a tiny, thin cigar. 'Well, God bless you, gentlemen, good luck out there,' he said, shaking our hands. 'Remember to watch out for rattlers.' Before heading back to the squad car he exhaled a plume of blue smoke. It coiled up from his mouth and then vanished, fast as winter breath.

Once Will had gone I began preparing some chicken dumplings while Justin grabbed hold of Maria's halter, lifted one of her front legs and dug out a stone lodged in her hoof.

'Hey, Judge,' I shouted over to him. 'How do you spot a rattlesnake?'

'You can't until you stand on one,' he replied helpfully. 'They're the same colour as the dirt.' He released Maria's leg and paced back towards the wagon. 'Just keep wearing those leather boots and long pants for protection, Colonel, you'll be fine.'

The Judge reached under the seat for his shotgun, cocked it and put two fat, red cartridges in the breach. 'I reckon rattlers are the least of our worries right now.'

* * *

After a restless night, alert to the slightest nocturnal hoot or rustle, we strode off north, a magenta-tinted daybreak beckoning us on. My feet were still in a pitiful state and progress was slow. I'd never known anything like the humidity here. My problem with the Texan sun, even in late summer, is that it doesn't know when to call it a day. It stokes itself up to a fierce temperature by mid-morning and sustains it until twilight, hitting a furnace-like intensity at around six in the evening.

Browny and Maria seemed remarkably oblivious to it; I suppose they were hardened locals. Justin, however, was starting to look miserable. Sitting for hours on end on a wagon watching an overripe Englishman limp his mule towards New York and all for a paltry wage – it was hardly surprising he was becoming a bit grouchy. He was clearly missing Brandie and Ariel and longing for a 'swig of the sauce' at his neighbourhood bar.

That evening was airless, preventing us from cooling down after another stifling day. We were both dirty, sweat-soaked and road sore. Justin had secured permission to sleep in a Dutch barn roughly thirty miles from Kingsville. On arrival we filled up Justin's jerry cans from a nearby hosepipe and sprayed down Maria and Browny, who whinnied gratefully before rolling in the dust.

I hobbled about setting up my tent and arranging mess tins for supper. Justin had begun to swear loudly at the slightest provocation – the mosquitoes, my slow pace, the fact we were eating chicken dumplings for the third night in a row. I decided to leave him in peace. I ate my meal on a straw bale at the back of the barn. After wolfing down pudding – a melted Snickers bar and a tin of fruit salad – I bundled into my tent to read Robert Louis Stevenson's *Travels with a Donkey*. The opal crescent of the moon shone through the canvas like a smile. I was asleep within seconds.

*   *   *

The following morning I woke at sunrise. 'You farkin' little sons of bitches!' were the first words that exploded from Justin. It was certainly an effective alarm call, making me spring to my feet and rub the sleep crust from my eyes.

'Ticks, hundreds of the little bastards, all over me,' Justin shouted, pointing to various parts of his body like an impassioned anatomy lecturer.

Justin wasn't lying, he did have ticks all over him, and so did I, minuscule black bugs burrowing into my face, forearms and calves, their little legs kicking about wildly as if stuck in jam. We both pinched and swatted at our bodies, swearing horribly. This frenzied spectacle continued for a while, radically slowing down our departure time and infuriating Justin to psychotic levels. To try and placate him I found an entry from Colonel Arthur's diary, proving my ancestor had to rough it too en route to San Antonio:

'I slept well last night in spite of the ticks and fleas, and we set off at 5.30 a.m.,' I read to Justin, quoting Arthur from 15 April 1863. 'After passing a dead rattlesnake eight feet long we reached water at 7 a.m. . . .'

'Forget the Colonel,' interrupted Justin. 'Come on, let's get out of here.'

But the ticks were just the start of our troubles. The next obstacle that confronted us was a bump gate. The bump gate is an ingenious Texan device that is opened by a vehicle driving gently into it. Once bumped into, the gate swings open and the vehicle shoots through it before it rotates shut, saving the driver the hassle of jumping out of his seat. Bump gates are tremendous if you have a tractor or truck. If you have a horse-drawn wagon and a nervous mule they are a royal pain in the arse.

Justin tied Maria to a fence post and sauntered over to hold the gate open for Browny and me. As I walked through I heard Maria neigh extravagantly. I looked back. There was a pistol crack of snapping leather and the next minute Maria had reared up, keranging one of her wagon shafts into the fence. As if in slow motion the shaft ruptured free from its metal clasp, kinking like a longbow at full stretch.

Justin let rip with a torrent of swear words that made his previous dawn chorus sound positively genteel. He charged over to Maria, took one look at his crunched wagon and threw his baseball cap down in disgust. His face turned puce, a dazzling combination of sun and blind fury igniting his features, the veins on his forehead pulsing like bad wiring.

'That farkin' little mule, I'd like to flog her,' shouted Justin, pushing back his receding fair hair. 'This whole farkin' situation. What a complete son of a bitch. Just look at my goddamn wagon.'

'It's not the mule's fault,' I said quietly.

'Farkin' little mule, you've got no control over her, she's always running up alongside my mare. You don't show her who's boss.'

To be fair to Justin this was true. My mule was devoted to Maria and always liked to be near her. Although I didn't like to admit it Browny was far more concerned about keeping Maria in eyeshot than me. I remembered reading about a mule's affection for horses in a publication called *Taylor's Eldorado*: 'The instincts of a mulish heart form an interesting study to the traveller,' advised the author, 'and sometimes the horse captivates the fancy of a whole drove of mules.'

'It wasn't the mule, Judge,' I insisted, 'something must have just spooked Maria.' Justin loved Maria, and she certainly was a magnificent and steady horse, so my comment was poorly timed. Criticising his faithful steed's nerve was likely to send the already simmering Judge right over the edge.

'Farkin' little mule,' Justin shouted again, thankfully not having taken in a word I said. 'What are we going to do now, eh?' He stopped to pluck another tick from his forearm. 'Jeysus Christ, what the hell am I doing here?'

I was suddenly seized by a raging anger. My soles were in agony. It was like this every time we stopped, the rush of blood draining from my feet. Getting going again would be even worse. I felt deeply frustrated: tired, hot and desperate.

'This wagon's had it,' Justin raged, kicking his heels and sending up a cloud of fine sand. 'I need a welder to mend the shaft.' And then he was off into another tirade. 'That farkin' little mule . . .'

'Justin, for God's sake!' I clenched my fist. I was now in that dangerous state where logic had deserted me.

I knew Justin, a self-described 'hard bastard' (and I had no reason to disagree with him) could swat me like one of the ticks burrowing into his skin. The Judge was a champion bar brawler, a master of fists who could fell me with a right hook, a mild slap, maybe even a well-aimed sneeze. But if I could throw just one punch it would be worth it. Whether I inflicted him with a full-on *coup de grâce* or the tiniest blemish I would fall to the dust happy.

'It's not the mule, Justin, okay!' I was shouting now. My legs were shaking and I could tell my voice sounded a little crazy. 'I'm no tough guy but I'm doing my best out here. Okay. So why don't you just pack it in, just . . .'

'Hey, Tom, cool it,' said Justin, looking at me strangely and softening his tone. 'This is not your fault. You may think I'm blaming you but I'm not, okay.' He raised his palms up in the air. 'I'm not blaming you, Tom. I'm not blaming the mule. Okay now, come on, whoa.' The violence swelling inside me deflated, the tension snapping fast as wire.

'Okay,' I said, backing away. 'Okay.' Once my blood decompressed an internal voice of logic inside me whispered: 'Phewwwy! Close call, Sundance, you would have been whopped out there.'

It also dawned on me that Justin had every right to be furious. This wagon was his pride and glory and was now broken up like a cheap toy. He was exhausted, filthy and a long way from home. I was the one who had put him here, the one whom he had volunteered to help. And here I was behaving like an outback prima donna.

But the confrontation was a turning point for us both. It was here fortune finally stopped spitting on us, controlled its gush of bad karma. Now it was time for serendipity to shine — for a guardian angel to intervene. He appeared in the guise of a rancher in a straw hat, driving slowly up to the bump gate in his Land Cruiser. 'You guys need a hand?' he asked. He sounded friendly even though his wilting moustache made him look as lugubrious as a spaniel.

'That's real kind of you, sir,' replied Justin doffing his baseball cap. 'But we need a welder, the wagon's pretty broken up.'

'A welder, no problem at all,' said the man, as if we were asking him for a cigarette or a directions to the post office. 'I've got one back at the ranch. Hand over the broken shaft and I'll fix you up.'

*   *   *

With the shaft straightened the wagon was back on track. So was the trip. The bloodless civil war between Justin and me had cleared the air and now things started to go our way. Over the next few days my soles finally developed the impregnable leathery rind I had been praying for and my pace quickened. This pleased Justin as did a fresh bottle of whiskey and a visit from the curvaceous Brandie on Saturday night.

Browny had her share of pampering too. A new set of mule shoes was bashed on in Kingsville, which the farrier said would last another six or so weeks (at this rate, I calculated grimly, she would be the Imelda Marcos of the equine world by the time we reached New York). Browny still remained devoted to Maria, but Justin assured me once the wagon was out of the picture and I was walking alone she would only have eyes (and ears) for me. I had yet to be convinced, but for now, despite the odd cantankerous moment, the old beast was coping well. We were building up a tentative rapport.

The landscape was improving too. The bleak sagebrush prairies and the shifting sand dunes near the Tex-Mex border had transformed into lush, undulating pasture. Instead of herds of hardy, outlandish-looking Indian Brahmans and Texan Longhorns, doe-eyed Jerseys and Holsteins now peered at us over the roadside fences. But perhaps the greatest joy was the rain. It came in sudden cool bursts, animating the drought-hardened locals in the way the first sun of spring delights Londoners.

To keep my kit dry I tied a canvas tarpaulin over Browny's packsaddle. During the heaviest showers, water ripping into the soft earth like gunfire, my mule reminded me of a storm-tossed skiff with her sails flapping loose.

*   *   *

As we made our way north Justin and I enjoyed noting comparisons between Colonel Arthur's journey and our own trip. My favourite contrast was that in 1863 Mr Sarjent treated his mules' cuts or sores with brandy, whereas Justin had prescribed me a tube of Desitin – a nappy rash cream – as a modern remedy. 'I ain't wasting good liquor on that old mule,' he insisted.

Justin was particularly amused by the fact my ancestor didn't remove his boots for ten days en route to San Antonio. Colonel Arthur certainly did have a *laissez-faire* attitude towards his feet. In contrast, as I was walking not riding, it was paramount I pulled off my boots at the end of every day or else risk a riot of sock fungi. I also vigorously talced and massaged my feet, buffing up my claw-like toenails as if they were pearls. The one 1863 hardship I could match was a ten-day stretch without a hot shower. Not quite in the mal-odorous Colonel's league but there was time yet. Fortunately, Browny didn't seem to mind.

The major landmark on this stretch of the journey, for both Colonel Arthur and me, was the immense King Ranch which stretched far and wide across the scrubland near Kingsville. My ancestor's mule train pulled up there on the night of 19 April 1863.

At 825,000 acres the King Ranch is now supposedly the largest of its kind in the world, covering an area bigger than

Luxembourg. It was set up by a dynamic river boat captain, Richard King, a decade before my ancestor arrived in America. King purchased the ranch's first cattle from an impoverished village in north Mexico. When he heard many of the villagers were starving, King, an altruistic man, offered to move them to Texas along with the cattle. Today there are still several cowboys on the ranch who are sixth-generation Mexicans. The King Ranch is also famous for its Santa Gertrudis cows, a quirky hybrid of Indian Brahman and British Shorthorn, famed for being the first beef cattle bred in America.

The trouble now, Justin told me as we plied through Kingsville, is that old traditional breeds, especially the Texan Longhorns, weren't much in demand. After the Civil War they were the best cattle around, able to be droved thousands of miles to far-flung markets all across the Wild West. There were no fences then, of course, Justin reminded me. Now barbed wire was everywhere and cattle were only moved about in trucks. Ranchers were plumping for 'fancy, heavy-set' European breeds instead.

'The Longhorn is like you, Colonel,' Justin teased. 'Scrawny and able to walk forever but no longer any real value. Just kept as a novelty. The new breeds are big and lazy. But they're easy to rear and taste good and that's what we want these days. It's all in the name of convenience.'

Although the King Ranch was way too plush for Justin and me to stay the night it excited me to think that the ancestors of today's ranch workers may have met my ancestor. It dawned on me he may have even feasted on one of the contemporary cows' forebears.

Sadly, though, Colonel Arthur never crossed paths with Richard King himself, who was away from the ranch on business at the time of the excitable guardsman's visit. Arthur was entertained instead by Mrs Bee, the wife of General Bee,

the officer he had partied with in Brownsville several weeks
before.

Colonel Arthur describes Mrs Bee as, 'a nice lively little
woman, a red hot Southerner, glorying in the fact she has no
Northern relations or friends.'

Mrs Bee was not the only Southern belle to impress
Colonel Arthur. Indeed, one of the great strengths of his diary
is recognising the spirit and stoicism of the many Southern
women, especially in the countryside, whom he encounters
on his gallivant. He writes particularly of the no-nonsense
grit of the ranchers' wives who are forced to hold the fort
while their men-folk are off fighting.

At one point Colonel Arthur writes:

> when this war is over the independence of the country [alias
> the South] will be due, in a great measure, to the women . . .
> [who] have invariably set an example to the men of patience,
> devotion and determination. Naturally proud, and with an
> innate contempt for the Yankees . . . they are prepared to
> undergo any hardships and misfortunes . . .

Colonel Arthur is especially moved after hearing the story of
a widow 'whose three sons had fallen in battle one after the
other, until she had only one left, a boy of sixteen.' When a
Confederate officer visits the grieving mother to offer his
condolences, she tells him bluntly: 'As soon as I can get a few
things together, General, you shall have Harry too.' Colonel
Arthur, clearly turning a blind eye to the mother's blatant
hardness, ends this particular diary entry with the words:
'How can you subdue such a nation as this!'

Although Colonel Arthur was wrong about the outcome of
the war, his views on Southern women were perceptive. It
should be remembered that by 1865, staggeringly almost one
of every three Confederate soldiers had died from disease or
wounds. Those men who did make it home were beaten,

dispirited and often maimed – Southern manhood was at its lowest ebb. It was to fall on the women to care for the wounded, the orphans and widows, and mostly they did so, capably and without fuss.

I too had been impressed with the few Southern women I had met so far, none more so than Beth, who I stayed with on my penultimate night before reaching Twin Oaks.

*   *   *

Justin already knew Beth so we had no trouble locating her sprawling farmstead via a maze of country lanes. Her garden had clearly been invigorated by the recent rain and was alive with bright, jungly vegetation. After the neutral colours of the desert, the blossoms on her ranch driveway seemed to boast an almost neon glow.

Browny and Maria were stabled in a barn at the back of the house. It had a steeply arched, overlapping roof, which enveloped the entrance like a hat. Our animals were provided with separate stalls and rolled about rapturously in the soft, crisp straw. When she stood up Browny had flecks of gold in her mane.

Beth is a human dynamo, somebody who makes an instant impact. Strong, dark and formidably fit, Beth is also missing a hand, which is substituted by a row of five realistic but static plastic digits. If Justin had not told me this, I'm not sure I would have noticed, as Beth never gives any indication of her disability. She drives, shoots and cooks with a fierce, fluid energy, constantly on the move, her fitness almost like a disease.

'Now that we've sorted out the mule,' she said, ushering me into her drawing room, 'let's go shooting. Yes! Fun, fun, fun.' Beth has a strong Texan drawl and pronounces fun as 'furn', and yes as 'yeyus', adding one or two syllables depending on the complexity of the word. She was about three steps ahead of the rest of the group which, other then me, included her pretty, soft-spoken daughter, Dabney, a lawyer from the nearby port of Corpus Christi and Dabney's fiancé, Will, a great friendly bear of a man who worked in advertising. Justin had already peeled away from us for another tryst with Brandie.

Beth put on a waxed jacket and handed me a can of Coke and a 12-bore. We were off to shoot clay pigeons in a gully at the bottom of the garden. The clays sprung out from two traps perched in the surrounding hackberry trees. Will, cartridge belts wrapped around him like a Zapatista revolutionary, handed out the ammunition. Dabney coordinated the traps with a hand-held remote control. The clays sprung out in a variety of ornithological guises.

'These are springing teal,' explained Beth, blasting the ascending brace of clays to powder. 'Got 'em,' she shouted in delight. 'That's a pair of fast quail, Tom,' she warned me, as two discs tore over my head with such zest I never had a chance to even raise the gun. The only thing I could hit was a single 'slow turkey', the ornithological equivalent of a barn door. It cracked reluctantly in half, unlike Beth's birds that dutifully disintegrated on impact as if in an arcade game. Will and Dabney proved equally adept at slaughtering their quarry, however erratic the flight paths. When we finished, ears ringing, the air was thick with sharp, acrid smoke.

'Right, Tom,' Beth stated, after we had picked up the spent cartridges. 'I want to show you something special.'

We walked half a mile or so through the pecans and hackberries, still brandishing guns, to look at the site of Beth's latest brainchild – a family chapel. Will and Dabney were to marry there next year. Potentially it was a beautiful spot to set aside as holy ground, a forest glade fringed by a commanding sweep of parkland. Silver doves swooped above us before crashing into the conifers to roost.

Beth started pacing up and down marking out the dimensions of the chapel, dry twigs snapping under her feet. Will's
two black Labrador puppies, Hemingway and Lulu, were let
off their leash and frolicked in her wake.

'You stand there, Will, and you over there, Tom.' Beth
pointed out where she wanted the foundation stones. 'You
there, Dabney, that's it. Get down, Hemingway. Down!
Right, let's see, I'd better be the fourth corner of the
chapel.'

We all stood in a square, holding up our guns like sylvan
sentinels. The puppies ragged with each other roughly where
the aisle would run.

'What do you think, Tom?' Beth asked, swiping at a mosquito. 'It's going to be made of white wood with stained glass
windows. Nice and simple. What do you think, huh?'

'Great idea,' was all I could think of to say. I found it
incredible that I had only just met Beth, and here I was
involved in making decisions about her daughter's wedding.
So much so I was even playing the role of a gun-toting
foundation stone. This was something I was struggling to get
my head around in Texas; that within minutes you weren't so
much treated as one of the family: you were family. A prodigal
son, a trusted confidant, whatever was required – even if it
was just for the evening.

The reasons for Beth wanting a family chapel ran deep, she
explained, as we continued with the measurements. Her
husband had been struck down with cancer several years ago.
Beth had nursed him at home before he died. She had clearly
loved him deeply and now injected all her energies into the
ranch and her remaining family. She revealed her husband had
been a 'mustard keen' traveller, and had spent over ten years
sailing around the world, before settling down and marrying
her in his early forties.

'It was awkward for him, being settled,' Beth admitted, slinging the gun over her shoulder as we headed back to the ranch. Will and Dabney walked behind, each held one of the pups in their spare hands.

'He often still had that urge to be at sea,' she explained, lost in quiet reverie. 'I love the sea too, but for my husband it was like his home. I was always more at home with the ranching. It's a way of life too. There's a lot of machismo bluster, but actually ranchers are compassionate, resourceful people, deeply rooted to the land. We have to help each other or we wouldn't survive.'

For some reason I framed a mental picture of Justin. Justin giving money to the blind Mexican boy with the accordion, whispering soft words of encouragement to Maria, helping me lift Browny's packsaddle, holding Brandie's hand. For all Justin's macho swagger, 'compassionate' and 'resourceful' were appropriate words for him. After all, he had taught me, his cack-handed cadet, to load a mule with the dexterity of a master skinner.

'Hey,' a wild thought struck me and I turned to Will and Dabney. 'You two could have Justin ride you to your honeymoon on a mule-drawn carriage.'

'Yes, yes,' agreed Beth. 'He could wear a white coat and a top hat and the mule could be covered in blossom!'

As we wandered back I spotted a tiny hummingbird by the roadside. I picked up the brightly plumaged corpse and bought it over to Beth who was chastising Hemingway for barking at her cows. The hummingbird was no bigger than my thumb and weighed less than a pound coin. One of the things that astonished me about this often desolate part of Texas was the amount of exotic bird life. Over the past days I had seen a mass of gulls, waders, hawks and scissor-tails flying over-head.

'It's a ruby throated hummingbird,' said Beth, peering into my palm. 'It's probably flown across the Gulf of Mexico. Over five hundred miles. You know this little hummingbird's wings beat up to fifty times a second.' Beth fluttered the fingers of her good hand to demonstrate. 'All that way, all that effort. Only to be hit by a car or truck. How *cruel*. How *sad*.'

I felt grateful that the clay pigeons this afternoon had only included game birds. I had no problem shooting at a 'springing teal' or a 'slow turkey', but downing a 'flushed hummingbird' would have been too much. Not that I'd have hit it.

'While out sailing at sea we saw all sorts of gulls,' continued Beth, squinting her eyes as if focusing a pair of imaginary binoculars. This talk of migration had clearly stirred memories of her ocean-roving husband. 'One of my favourite birds is the Arctic tern. An incredible little thing. In one year it can fly over twenty thousand miles. Twenty thousand miles! Think about it! That's nearly all around the world.'

I suddenly felt immensely inspired. Whenever I was tempted to jack in the mule walk from now on I would draw strength from Beth's description of the ruby throated hummingbird and the Arctic tern. My journey seemed rather meagre in comparison to these tiny, feathered gypsies with their indefatigable wings. It also seemed rather trivial compared to this gutsy Southern rancher single-handedly – quite literally – tending her land, building her church, living her dream . . .

After dinner, I retired to a guest room called the Dog House. It was neat and spartan with Texan landscapes all over the wall. I didn't fall asleep for hours, ideas and memories flapping around my mind like impish bats.

*   *   *

The next day Justin and I clocked up the last fifteen miles to Loncito's home at Twin Oaks Ranch. It was easy going, a balmy tailwind propelling us along. On arrival Justin insisted on buying me a drink at the local bar. Once out of the bright evening sun the bar's dark interior was cool as a cave. Quiet, lonely-eyed men cradled their bourbon while pool balls clacked in the background.

Justin and I sat on high stools at the bar, drinking Shiner Bock, a locally brewed beer, sharp and malt-rich. It went to my head in no time. Justin picked at his beer mat and joked with the barmaid. A notice board hung by the peanuts. It was filled with photos of khaki-clad men holding up recently shot deer by their antlers.

'Well, Colonel, I bet there were a couple of times you could have punched me since Mexico.'

'Oh yeah, once or twice, Judge,' I admitted. 'Actually, no, a hell of a lot more than that.' He laughed and told me it was for my own good. He said I would find myself in situations far worse later down the line, which I would have to deal with all alone. I knew he was right, and was grateful he had stretched me. So far I had only undergone the initiation – the next few weeks would be the real test.

'So, cheers, Colonel.' He raised his glass. 'I wasn't so sure about you at the beginning, all that limping about. But you made it. You can take a couple of days off now. So here's to New York, and that old mule!' We clashed drinks.

Justin and I stayed up late, buying each other Shiner Bocks. He told me about his three sons – 'good boys, real proud of 'em' – from a previous marriage. They lived out of state but he was regularly in touch and one of them was visiting him soon. He spoke of the annual wagon rides he took part in, how much he loved horses. He even mentioned some of his more epic fights, the fact he could be a fool if he drank too much. How Brandie was good for him, stood up to him, coped with his wild moods, had the finest midriff in Texas.

We paid up and made our way to Loncito's farm gate. Justin told me I could hop on the wagon now, as I would walk this same stretch of road when I headed north. He joked that it wouldn't jeopardise my code of honour. He was right, and I thought it would be fun to have at least one go holding the reins.

We tied Browny to the back axle of the wagon and lurched off up the dirt track. From where I was sitting all that could be seen of Browny was her nostrils and eyes, her ears flattened by the wind. She reminded me of a crocodile swimming on a lake, facially calm but legs pounding beneath. We careered down the track, Justin yeehaaing like he had back in Progresso. When he handed me the reins I yeehaaed too, beer-flushed and exhilarated by the speed, the dust kicking up behind us in a smoky contrail. Up ahead a row of mesquite trees stood on a levee, their shadows like ancient hieroglyphics. It was as if they were revealing a secret language to us, guiding us on through the blue and starless night. I could hardly believe the first leg was over. Just me and my mule now.

CHAPTER 6

One Day in September

On arrival at the ranch Justin and I learnt that Loncito's mother had just died. There could not have been a worse time for me to stay at Twin Oaks. I had never met Mrs Cartwright but by all accounts she was a much-loved matriarch, not only in the family but in the whole surrounding ranch community. Everyone was badly shaken.

Loncito remained the perfect host but I felt my presence was intrusive. For all his good-natured hospitality his grief was palpable and I didn't want to impose myself on his already demanding schedule. 'This is Texas, Tom,' he reminded me firmly, 'you have to stay.'

On the morning of September 11, still a little bleary from my night with Justin, I kept out of everyone's way and busied myself with routine chores. I fed and hosed down Browny (who was sharing a paddock with Spit and Rusty, two other

mules). I washed my clothes, aired my tent and scrubbed my
mule's saddlebags. Then I took Loncito's two pointers for a
long walk around a nearby lake.

As we pounded through the sagebrush, a pair of scissor-
tailed flycatchers flew by in a flash of white feathers and wild
screeches. The two pointers ran and stopped, their retroussé
noses twitching, then ran and stopped again: it was as if they
were remote controlled. At one point a goat sprang out from
a creek bed, looked at us, and sped away. As I watched its
silvery tush retreating I half expected to hear the tinkle of
bells.

I returned to the ranch in the early afternoon. Loncito, his
wife Crystal, and their three children were away for the day,
so I had the place to myself. All I could find to eat was some
chocolate ice cream. After a diet dominated by chicken
dumplings this was a decadent treat and I feasted as I wrote
up my diary. I was surrounded by Mexican landscapes,
painted by Loncito's mother. They hung from the farmstead's
dramatic white stone walls – made from locally quarried
caliche, each slab roughly the size of a microwave oven.

While scribbling notes in the sitting room I caught sight of
a record player behind my sofa bed. Loncito had a landslide
of vinyl LPs stacked up against it. I put a warped, crackly
album by The Kinks on the turntable. I always refuse to travel
with a Walkman. For this reason hearing great music, having
been starved of it on the road, always delights me. I danced
around for a while, air guitaring to 'Waterloo Sunset'. The
record was badly scratched and soon the stylus started to
jump, surfing across Ray Davies's final chorus.

I tried the radio instead. For some reason the radio's knobs
sported tassels on them, a bit like those on a Moulin Rouge
striptease artist. This analogy made me smile. 'You've been
spending too much time with that old mule, Colonel,' I could

imagine Justin warning me. The radio's reception was poor, crackling with static.

'This is the worst attack on American soil since Pearl Harbor . . . the two planes . . .'

The voice faded and then cut out, as did my frivolous mood. I twiddled the channel knob. The radio was struggling to pick up a signal, as if it was being driven through a succession of interlinking tunnels. Odd splashes of sound and then nothing.

'. . . The exact casualties are unknown at this stage but could be many thousand . . . the Twin Towers are no longer . . .'

The penny still had not completely dropped. Initially I thought I had tapped into some apocalyptic afternoon play, the type they sometimes have on Radio 4. But every station was broadcasting news – no music at all – which hinted that something more sinister was afoot. Soon it was clear, even with these paltry snatches of information, that something calamitous was unfolding. I dashed around looking for a television set, lifting drapes, poking around in cupboards, but there was none.

I returned to the radio, twiddling at it again in a state of incipient panic.

'Osama bin Laden and his terrorists are now . . . we are still unsure . . . military strikes . . . Afghanistan.'

I urged myself to be patient and controlled the knobs with painstaking exactness, as if trying to crack a safe. Finally the distorted broadcast became clear.

'This is a tragic day for New York, for America, for all of us,' said a commentator gravely. 'Whatever happens now, the world will never be the same again.'

The Kinks were put back in their sleeve and my diary snapped shut. I poured myself a cup of coffee, sat back and listened. After about twenty minutes I'd heard enough.

I walked out to the mule paddock and fed Browny an apple. The old beast provided some company, the reassurance of another living creature, but her world was untouched. In truth, my world was untouched too, out here in the Texas boondocks. My only link to New York was my cousin Hugh and his wife, Susan, who both lived far from the Twin Towers. Yet even from my mule paddock, over two thousand miles away, it was clear this day, September 11 2001 would have some sweeping consequences.

When travelling I pride myself on rarely feeling lonely. But right now I longed to be around fellow human beings. I sat down in the sand near to Browny and pulled out some family snapshots from my wallet. I flicked through them slowly like a priest with a rosary.

In New York City, amid the collapsed and smoking towers, the maelstrom of chaos and anger, I imagined millions of people secretly touching photos, twisting wedding rings and kissing crucifixes: all of them fumbling in the darkness for a talisman of love.

*   *   *

The next day I visited A.C. Jones High School in the local town of Beeville. I had agreed to give a talk about my travels to the students. Loncito drove me there after a fig roll and black coffee breakfast at a country store. The store's walls were covered with the usual photographs of khaki-clad men holding up slain white-tailed deer, black boars and plump, silver catfish, their barbels slumped in expressions of exquisite sadness. The hunters were beaming and wide-eyed, some sporting caps with earmuffs. It was as if a variety of Gary Larson cartoons had come to life.

In Beeville GOD BLESS AMERICA bunting had been draped across the façades of some houses and fast food joints. Near the high school entrance we drove past a Stars and

Stripes slumped at half-mast like a windsock. In the car park I noticed a pick-up truck with the slogan AN EYE FOR AN EYE, A TOOTH FOR A TOOTH stuck to its back window. Parked diagonally opposite was a red Chevrolet, its passenger door blazing DON'T MESS WITH TEXAS OSAMA – WE'LL KICK YOUR ASS.

At the school I was introduced to Heather Welder, a vivacious and bespectacled senior teacher. Heather bristled with energy, her hair bunched into an elegant brown swallow's nest. She led me through freshly mopped corridors to the first class. There were about twenty or so seventeen-year-olds chatting amongst themselves. Before Heather had a chance to say anything the opening strains of 'The Star Spangled Banner' crackled over a loudhailer.

All the class stood up, some staring ahead grimly, others looking at the floor. After the national anthem, 'God Bless America' was played. Several of the children joined in with the words or simply mouthed them. A pretty black girl with tousled dreadlocks began to cry. After the song was over Heather called for two minutes' silence.

'The reason for this is to pay homage to those who died yesterday,' said Heather calmly. 'I have had requests from many students for the silence. In all my years of teaching I'm not sure I've ever felt as proud.'

And it really was moving watching these teenagers, so silent and respectful, contemplating what this distant event in New York meant for all of them. After the two minutes, Heather ushered me to the front of the class and made an introduction. It felt like an impossible act to follow – two minutes of silent hopes and prayers, a moment of almost sacred poignancy, followed by a fool with a mule. Heather didn't say that of course. With true Texan chutzpah she made my walk sound on a par with Hannibal crossing the Pyrenees.

I talked a bit about the reasons behind my journey, about Colonel Arthur, the first days on the road with Justin. I had the usual forest of stretched hands pleading to ask about Browny. A few of the geographical questions were a bit off kilter: 'Hey, Mr Fremantle, what's it like living in New England?' But the most burning questions were about Afghanistan. Heather had revealed in her introduction that I had visited the country during my bicycle ride to Australia.

'Why did the Afghans do that to us?' said a boy in a Texas flag T-shirt – red, white and blue with a Lone Star in the corner. He was genuinely incredulous. 'Why do they hate us?'

'They don't hate us,' said the black girl who had been crying earlier. 'They hate our government. We are the super-power, the boss. They see us as manipulators and they don't like that.'

'Did the Afghans you met hate us?' asked Heather.

I had only briefly visited Afghanistan while on a trek to a village in the remote northeast corner of the country. It remains to this day the most extraordinary place I've ever set foot. 'It was a scene from the pages of Tolkien; alive with mystery, a landscape of infinite severity,' I had written in my diary at the time. Throughout my stay there, I was watched over by a tobacco-chewing seventeen-year-old guide armed with a Kalashnikov. The whole experience had been fuelled with fear and great excitement. Everyone I met from shepherds to village elders had treated me with nothing but kindness.

I tried to relay this to the teenagers in front of me, to emphasise that not all Afghans, or Muslims, could be put under the same umbrella of distrust. The Afghans I had met back in 1996, only weeks before the Taliban overwhelmed the country, had been polite and generous – all fiercely opposed to bin Laden's style of austerity. I told the students I sympathised with America wanting to retaliate against the terrorists, but surely not against Afghanistan as a whole.

'We should bomb them,' said a sour-looking boy, his fringe sticking up like spruce needles. 'And kick all the Arabs out of our country.'

Spiky fringe's brand of grumpy nihilism was rare, and met with opposition by his classmates. Texas had a poor reputation education-wise, languishing near the very bottom of the state leagues, with an especially insular approach to history: much of the past being remembered from a fiercely Lone Star perspective. But I was impressed by the attentive, open-minded attitude of the bulk of the teenagers in front of me. All of them were upset, wanting to strike back at the terrorists but still concerned about the prospect of a full-scale holy war. The greatest frustration for most was being unable to do their bit. Texans throughout their history have often been the first to volunteer for the fray and the state still has a wildly disproportionate amount of military bases compared to other parts of America.

'The worst thing is being so far from it all,' commented the clean-cut boy with the Texan flag T-shirt. 'I just want to lend a hand, show we can rise above this thing.'

*   *   *

I talked for most of the day: Heather leading me into class after class lined with timetables and bright posters. After lunch I ended up with one especially animated history group. The young, casually dressed teacher, Cory, pointed out to his students that both my ancestor and I had visited America at a pivotal time.

'Colonel Fremantle travelled through America when it was ripping itself apart in a terrible Civil War,' he stated in a calm, friendly drawl, holding up *Three Months in the Southern States*.

'Tom Fremantle here is walking through a very different America. For all of yesterday's horrors, what happened in New York really does seem to be uniting our country. Pulling us together more than we have been for a while.'

I gave a brief talk to the class about my mule trip, which was met with the usual round of quick-fire questions. When I finished the class returned to their syllabus – the subject of Reconstruction, the turbulent period after the Civil War when the South was reintegrated back into the Union. While the students tackled a short written test I quietly chatted to Cory. I especially wanted to pick his brains over an article in one of the morning newspapers in which September 11 had been compared to 'a modern-day Antietam'.

Cory explained that the battle at Antietam Creek on 17 September 1862, near the little town of Sharpsburg in west Maryland, was the bloodiest day of the Civil War. By the end of it nearly six thousand men lay dead or dying, while another seventeen thousand sustained wounds. On the morning of my visit to Beeville, the number of Twin Tower casualties in New York was still uncertain, thought to be around three thousand.

'Surely the big difference,' I said to Cory, 'is that on September 11 everyone was innocent. Antietam was horrible, but at least they were soldiers, knew they had to fight.'

'You're right,' agreed Cory, rubbing a pencil on his chin, 'but remember some of the soldiers at Antietam were teen-agers, same age as my class here. Many of them were coming under enemy fire for the first time – "seeing the elephant" as they called it then.'

'Yesterday shocked Americans regarding terrorism,' he added. 'But Antietam woke up the country to the true nature of the Civil War. In many ways the early 1860s was the most miserable time ever to have been a soldier.'

Cory emphasised to me that the old clumsy ways of fighting – like marching in slow lines towards the enemy – were still used at Antietam. These outdated infantry tactics collided tragically with new, sophisticated weaponry, such as mortars and minié balls, which could cut down men in swathes.

'The medicine on offer to deal with the Antietam casualties was another tragedy,' whispered Cory, watching over his silent class. 'Medical knowledge was still too primitive to deal with this sort of carnage. In the early 1860s pus was even viewed by doctors as a good thing. A sign of a wound healing! Of all the countless men who died in the Civil War – for every one killed in battle, two died from disease and dysentery.'

'The other thing about Antietam,' Cory waved his pencil at me to make his point. 'It was the first battle where official war photographs were taken. Soon after the fighting a man called Matthew Brady displayed his photos at an exhibition in New York. They were gruesome – lines of bloated or spread-eagled corpses – but they had a huge impact, opened the public's eyes to the vulnerability of the soldiers.'

'Like hearing about the Twin Towers collapse on the radio,' I interrupted. 'I haven't seen the television yet but it has clearly had a big impact.'

'Yes, the TV footage was certainly humbling,' nodded Cory. 'Nobody will forget those planes in a hurry. I suppose the photos of Antietam were like the TV of their time. They remind us we don't want this to happen again.'

When the students' test was over Cory made his apologies and resumed his teaching. I continued reading up on Antietam from a selection of Civil War books at the back of the class.

I learnt that the battle raged throughout most of that hot September day and that it was probably the hardest twenty-four hours fighting of the entire Civil War. Gunfire crackled and bayonets clashed in places such as The Cornfield, Bloody Lane (a trench so full of dead it was possible to walk along it without touching the ground), Burnside's Bridge, Dunker Church and other immortal landmarks. Casualties for blue and grey were roughly the same, although strategically it was a Union victory as the Rebels were forced to turn back from their march towards Washington.

After the battle a Northern soldier wrote with moving candour:

> The truth is, when bullets are whacking against tree trunks and solid shot are cracking skulls like egg-shells, the consuming passion in the breast of the average man is to get out of the way. Between the physical fear of going forward and the moral fear of turning back, there is a predicament of exceptional awkwardness.

He added that 'in amid the hiss of bullets and hurtle of grapeshot . . . the whole landscape for an instant turned slightly red.'

When I looked up from my books the class was starting to wind down, the students packing up their stuff.

'I'd like to end on an uplifting note,' stated Cory, still pacing the classroom. 'Some newspapers are drawing comparisons between yesterday's events and the battle of Antietam, the bloodiest single day on our country's soil. It's important to know the morning after Antietam, the two armies called a brief truce. Men in blue and grey, who had been fighting only hours before, lay down their arms and swapped tobacco with one another as they collected their wounded.' Cory paused to drink from a cup of coffee on his desk. 'War can bring out the best in people as well as the worst.'

*   *   *

Before walking north towards Louisiana with Browny I made a whistle-stop tour of San Antonio, the first major city

Colonel Arthur visited in America. Although I had vowed to walk in a continuous line to New York, I granted myself the privilege of making detours in cars or buses to some of the more far flung places on my ancestor's route. To walk the whole of his zigzagging itinerary would have taken years rather than months. My only rule was that I had to return to my mule before marching on.

Colonel Arthur's visit to San Antonio was even briefer than mine. My ancestor noted that 'trade was at a standstill' and many goods had soared to 'famine prices'. Coffee, for instance, was $7 a pound (still cheaper than a couple of frappuccinos at Starbucks, mind you). The Colonel stayed at the Menger Hotel, run by a German – one third of the city was German at the time – who was on the verge of shutting it down due to lack of business. My ancestor also took a peek at the elaborate Castilian-style missions (fortified churches) of San José and San Juan, which had been set up in the 1730s by the Franciscans for converting native Indians to Christianity.

San Antonio was a very different place for me. During Colonel Arthur's visit ten thousand people lived there, today the population has an extra two zeros tagged on and trade is booming. The Menger is still there, now the plushest hotel in town with doormen and fountains. In the city centre elegant skyscrapers full of casually dressed oil prospectors and property developers sprout up amid the classical Spanish architecture. The San Antonio river threads lazily through it all; palm trees lining its banks, their leaves like flaccid combs, occasionally plopping into the pale, shivering water.

It's a place that's full of pizzazz: a nice combination of Mexican colour and Texan energy. Even the beautiful Franciscan missions Colonel Arthur saw are still thriving either as tourist attractions or else as active churches.

The most famous mission is of course, the Alamo, where for thirteen days in the winter of 1836 roughly one hundred and eighty Texans held out against up to four thousand Mexicans. Although the Alamo's defenders were a rag-tag bunch (mostly Americans with a small contingent of chancers from England, Germany and Denmark), the three principal heroes were Davy Crockett, James Bowie (of knife fame) and Captain William B. Travis, best known for his letter pledging 'Death or Victory'. For almost all the defenders it ended up as death. The only two survivors were thought to be Bowie's and Travis's black slaves. For the Mexicans, under General Santa Anna, casualties were huge too, well over one thousand.

The valiant defence of the Alamo gave the legendary General, Sam Houston, time to whip up some reinforcements and rout Santa Anna's troops at the Battle of San Jacinto two weeks later. Houston's men charged through the Mexican lines with the battle cry 'Remember the Alamo'. Now no longer under Mexican rule, Texas became an independent republic (the only US state ever to achieve this) for nine years until 1845, when America took control again.

Today, I have to admit the Alamo is my least favourite of San Antonio's missions, and surely the least authentic. It has been spruced up, re-roofed (there was no roof during the battle) and covered in more flags than an Olympic pageant. There is also rather a needless replica of Davy Crockett's waistcoat. The Alamo's latest claim to fame, one of the guides told me, is the fact loopy rock star Ozzy Osbourne urinated against its front wall several years ago and was subsequently banned from Texas.

In my mind, the heroes of the Alamo have been soiled by 'Disneyfication' far more harshly than by Mr Osbourne. Crockett, Bowie and Travis and every slain man, whether American or Mexican, deserved their last stand to be left in peace, to be remembered as it was in 1836. A myth of this proportion is all the more poignant for words left unsaid, not spelt out with bright flags and bogus waistcoats. I have no problem with an Alamo museum and gift shop, but in a separate building, not on holy ground.

*   *   *

I spent my one night in San Antonio at the home of Loncito's sister, Claire, and her husband George. They had generously laid on 'a mule skinner's dinner' for me and invited a gaggle of friends over. Everyone stayed impressively upbeat despite the spectre of September 11 hovering over the conversation, but guests were clearly worried about the freefalling economy. Two oil-dealing brothers were tense having recently invested in a three-mile deep well south of the city. A power-dressed woman revealed that punters at her new bar had dried up since the attacks, and a rancher who sold goat meat to a largely Middle Eastern clientele was nervous about the implications on his trade.

The following morning the headlines did nothing to assuage people's fears. The *San Antonio Express* heralded: 'US Prepares For War.'

'With two teenage sons that is not what I want to hear,' said Claire over morning coffee. 'Everything seems so out of control.' As we chatted a portable TV in the kitchen flashed footage of militant groups in Pakistan burning the Stars and Stripes.

After breakfast I leafed through a copy of *Time* magazine and noticed an article, like the one I had spotted in Beeville, comparing September 11 to the battle of Antietam. It was by a reporter called Nancy Gibbs.

'This was the bloodiest day on American soil since our Civil War,' she wrote, 'a modern Antietam played out in real time, on fast forward, and not with soldiers but with secretaries, security guards, lawyers, bankers, janitors. It was strange that a day of war was a day we stood still . . .

'It was as though someone had taken a huge brush and painted a bull's eye around every place Americans gather, every icon we revere, every service we depend on, and vowed to take them out or shut them down, or force us to do it ourselves.'

I put the magazine down. I was lucky, I decided. Tomorrow I would hit the road with my mule, oblivious to all the sound and fury, the rumours of apocalypse.

*   *   *

Back at Twin Oaks Browny and I were waved off by Loncito and his 80-year-old father, Lon Senior. The elderly cowboy sported a wide-rimmed hat beneath which danced a pair of electric grey eyes. He was tanned the colour of the earth and looked, as did his son, utterly at one with the surrounding land. When I turned back for a final wave, Loncito's toddler son had joined them both. Three generations, a dynasty in motion, standing under the Twin Oak trees that they ruled over and which in turn ruled over them.

So much of America, I was to discover as the walk progressed, has been tamed. It still looks like countryside but has been manicured into something else altogether: nature on a leash, a eunuch wilderness diluted to the needs of man. In this part of Texas, for all its isolation, nature still runs wild, it burns you and snaps at your heels, kicks sand in your face then floods your boots, constantly catches you unawares. For this reason life is vulnerable and so lived to the full, a fine and precious thing.

Justin brought this home powerfully when he caught up with my mule and me a few days after we had set off from Twin Oaks. As he had predicted, without the wagon and the seductive clip clopping of Maria, Browny only had eyes for me. Justin pulled up in his rusty Ford truck with Brandie in the passenger seat. She jumped out first – big smile, flip-flops, exposed midriff. Justin had found me a new halter rope, some elastic bungies and a bottle of Summer Fruits Gatorade, the colour of blood. His initial scepticism towards the journey had been replaced by unbounded enthusiasm and I was touched.

Brandie, who worked as an X-ray technician in Beeville now her dancing days were over, had sweetly bought me some bandages from her clinic. As my soles had now formed a hard membrane I hoped I wouldn't need them, but it was good to be safe.

We stood by the roadside chatting while Browny grazed, tied up to a nearby signpost. Having been camping the last few nights, I asked about the latest news regarding the attacks on New York.

'Oh, we'll kick someone's ass soon,' said Justin, very matter of fact. 'It was terrible what happened, all those people dying. But I think the best way to deal with it is to carry on as before. Be strong. I've got horses to break, mules to trade. I can't sit stewing about it.

'The thing is,' he said, more pensively. 'Whatever happens, even if this whole world goes up in smoke, hell, Colonel, life is bound to go on, isn't it?' He picked up a handful of sand and examined it. He said nothing for a while then added, his words tumbling in a rush.

'That land we travelled through coming up from Mexico, Colonel. You remember? It looked dead most of the time, didn't it? Think about it. Dry, hot, cracked, hard.'

'I'm glad you noticed, Judge!'

'Well, let me tell you, my friend,' he stressed, flicking the reins of his imagination, 'that land is full of life, life that has created its own way of survival. It has plants that can stuff themselves with enough water to last months of drought, it even has insects that devise their own refrigeration systems. That sagebrush you walked through like it was on fire.

Remember! The only way that survives is because it has its own oily skin, same as a fisherman's coat.'

Justin was off now, his thoughts yeehaaing at full-tilt. 'The places where the land has not been messed with. Where folks aren't fat and soft and don't live in areas chock full of houses. Where folks look out for each other instead of in at themselves. Where nobody chooses to live except old buzzards like me. That's where life will hang on.

'Look at you,' he stated, pointing my way as if at a peculiar museum exhibit. 'I've never seen such a wimp. Hell, Colonel, you would probably even step out of a bathtub to take a piss but, hey, you adapted, you survived. Sheeyit, my friend. It will take a lot to wipe us humans out.'

'Especially you Texans,' I teased.

'Hell, yeah.' We all laughed, Justin throwing his handful of sand in the air, before he added more seriously: 'Oh hell, yeah.'

'Well, Judge,' I thought to myself, packing my new kit into Browny's saddlebags. 'You may drink too much, have a horrid temper and cook the worst chicken dumplings this side of Mexico, but deep down you're a wise, good-hearted old skinner. You truly are.'

CHAPTER 7

Lone Star of Confusion

In his book *The Lost Continent*, Bill Bryson sets off in search of Amalgam, a mythical place that champions all the best aspects of American small-town life. He never finds it. It's a shame Bryson didn't make it to the little community of Goliad because, despite its clunky name, it's a dream location. I reached there three days after the roadside farewell with Justin and Brandie and immediately fell in love.

Goliad is straight out of a film script and lives up to all the stereotypes. It is the sort of place where locals call each other 'Doc' and 'Miss Dorothy'. It has a diner where a wholesome waitress with a big smile – a Sandra Bullock dead-ringer – serves iced tea. You can imagine a wise and avuncular old-timer like Morgan Freeman as the preacher. Cher would be perfect as the pill-popping town gossip, full of waspish one liners, while Reese Witherspoon could play the peach-cheeked belle. A mysterious Hispanic drifter, Antonio Banderas, fresh off a Greyhound could add to the cultural ragout. Pepper it up with cruel-humoured redneck, Tommy Lee Jones, who gets his just deserts in a bourbon-induced hunting accident, and there you have it.

Doc, Miss Dorothy and the friendly diner where the waitress really did look like Sandra Bullock – or perhaps I'd been too long in the company of mules – were truly part of Goliad. The rest, of course, is fantastical nonsense. In truth I had no idea what lurked beneath Goliad's seemingly lovely surface, but my first impression was very fine.

Goliad's town square was dominated by live oaks, many of them over one hundred years old, their dark, sun-drenched leaves the colour of avocado rind. The oaks were all dripping with Spanish moss, pale lichen that looked like something spun by a team of magical spiders. Underneath the droopy foliage the townsfolk sat on benches, reading newspapers or eating sandwiches. Without exception they peered up to say, 'How y'all doing?' when Browny and I walked by. In the centre of the square was a stately courthouse and surrounding it was The Blue Quail Café, The Goliad Chemist and a host of other local businesses, all bustling with life.

Yes, I could live here, I told myself. But I often thought this about places I had only experienced for a morning, or a lunch break, my opinions still untrammelled by the confusions of time.

Goliad was proud of its past and boasted a mass of historical markers. Some pretty grisly stuff was recorded – mass hangings, hurricanes, that sort of thing. The town's biggest claim to fame is the nearby La Bahia fortress where hundreds of American soldiers were brutally executed by Mexican troops in March 1836, shortly after the Alamo, but before Santa Anna's comeuppance at San Jacinto. One of the more recent markers referred to an incident when a herd of Longhorn cattle lost control in a parade and stampeded across town, attempting to shish kebab any unfortunate bystanders.

Goliad was clearly fully in touch with its contemporary history too. The Stars and Stripes and 'God Bless the USA' signs hung in dozens of front yards suspended from flagpoles or basketball hoops. WOUNDED BUT NOT DEFEATED, warned one placard, draped across a restaurant window.

I spent a couple of hours scribbling postcards while Browny grazed near the town square. Church bells occasionally bonged. After a catnap in the shade of the live oaks I headed off again, a jaunty spring in my step. As my mule and I marched north out of town a wild-looking man accosted us. He had dark eyes with dilated, owl-like pupils, his neck striated by bright veins.

'What are you protesting about?' he shouted at me, waving his arms. 'You're one of those terrorists, aren't you? You've come to kill us all.' While September 11 had created an esprit de corps with many Americans, this man had clearly slipped the net. He was fuelled with a raging distrust.

'I'm not protesting about anything,' I assured him. 'I'm just on a cross-country walk.' The thought of little Goliad being next on bin Laden's hit list seemed hugely improbable. The man continued to eye me up warily. Instead of cans of Spam and books on mule husbandry, he clearly thought Browny's saddlebags were bulging with anthrax.

'You're a protestor!' he bellowed again. Browny was becoming jittery and I held her tight, stroking her neck. I now realised the poor fellow was either drunk or insane.

'You're a terrorist! What else would you be doing here otherwise?' he ranted on, his sour breath in my face. 'Get that donkey out of town.'

'She's not a donkey, she's a mule.'

'Bastard!' he snapped once more and then began backing off. His eyes were all over the place, as if following a roving butterfly. 'You protestors are all bastards.'

'I'm not a protestor, a terrorist or a bastard, nor is my mule. We're on a walk . . .'

'You're a terrorist bastard, I know it!'

There was clearly no arguing with this unswerving logic. I left the hysterical man to spout vitriol at any other illegitimate Al-Qaeda muleteers that happened to pass his way. I suppose even Goliad had to have its drunken conspiracy theorist – a perfect cameo for Gary Oldman perhaps.

*   *   *

I was loving every minute of small town Texas. Each of the communities Browny and I walked through had a pulsing heart, a strong sense of civic pride and often some bizarre local customs. By far the strangest custom I heard about was in the town of Cuero, two days' walk from Goliad. Cuero proudly dubs itself the 'Turkey Capital of America', and holds an annual fifty-yard race – the Gobbler Gallop – to prove it.

Since the early 1970s Cuero's swiftest turkey has been battling it out with another hot-footed gobbler from Worthington in Minnesota – a town that competes as the Turkey Capital of America. The two little communities take it in turns to host this prestigious poultry Olympics. Although a good-natured contest, it has had moments of high drama, as any local will tell you.

Two years ago Cuero's turkey dropped dead on the starting block, suffering from a combination of stress and heat exhaustion. A replacement sprinter was quickly recruited from a nearby farm. During one race a decade ago both birds charged off in the wrong direction. This year, due to the Gobbler Gallop being scheduled directly in the wake of September 11, Cuero's turkey, rather than being flown as usual, was driven several hundred miles to Minnesota. Despite the long journey Cuero's bird romped home, breasting the finishing line in a record-smashing 47.35 seconds.

'Nothing will stop the Gobbler Gallop,' one old lady told me in a Cuero grocery store. 'Rain, injuries, not even that bin Laden.'

But I soon learnt there was more to Cuero than just turkeys from a flamboyant local, Sid Duderstadt. Sid passed Browny and me on the outskirts of town that afternoon and invited to put us up. He told me there was a nearby paddock where the mule could graze.

Sid was a dishevelled, thrice-divorced businessman who remained relentlessly upbeat. He lived in a white-brick bachelor pad in a northern suburb where I popped inside for a drink of water before unloading Browny. LIFE'S TOO SHORT NOT TO LIVE IT AS A TEXAN! gloated a *fortissimo* magnet on his kitchen fridge. What was it with these Texans! I tried to imagine an equivalent back home but BUCKINGHAMSHIRE – THE ONLY ONE FOR ME! or MILTON KEYNES – WHERE ELSE? just didn't sound right.

I was particularly grateful to stay under Sid's roof as Matt, a friend of mine from Oxford, was arriving in Cuero that evening. If I had a set address it would make it easier for him to track me down rather than if I was camping rough. At Sid's office I checked my email and found out Matt was due in on a Greyhound within the hour. Sid drove off to pick him up. The pair of them had returned by the time I unpacked Browny and staked her out.

'Whoa, they were strict at Customs,' said Matt, dumping off his rucksack in Sid's cluttered porch. 'They even confiscated my nail scissors.'

Sid, sporting dark glasses, a Stetson and cowboy boots, popped us all a beer and told us to get ready – we were off to see an American football game. I was getting used to this kind of thing. I was worried Matt, a father of three who had taken a week off from his environmental consultancy work to join me, might be a little wary putting himself at the mercy of this happy-go-lucky stranger. I needn't have worried.

'I'll miss my family,' Matt told me, well into his second beer. 'But being on the road is a real treat. This week can be as unpredictable as you like.' He was not to be disappointed.

When we reached the football stadium it was packed. The game was only a high school play off but had a Super Bowl buzz: brass bands, digital flashboards, cheerleaders jiggling their pompoms. The Cuero team was, predictably, called the Gobblers and were up against their big rivals, the Sealy Tigers. We joined the ranks of Gobbler fans. Many were waving around black rattles, which supposedly made a noise like a gobbling turkey. The diehard fans wore green shirts, the Gobblers team colour, emblazoned with the slogan 'Go Mean Green'. To get in the mood Sid bought us all hot dogs and hat-sized cups of fizzy drink.

The atmosphere was rowdy but good-natured: a true family occasion where grandparents, toddlers and ardent groupies all mixed happily. There was none of the insidious violence of an English soccer stadium. After the brass band finished belting out 'America the Brave' and 'The Eye of the Tiger' the tannoy fell silent. A soft but authoritative voice took over:

'Tonight we should all remember those who lost their lives on September 11. We will not forget them. Never will we be cowed by cowardice nor terrorised by terrorism. We must be patient. God Bless America, everyone. Now let's play football.'

The next two hours were a mystery to me. Sid and Matt tried to explain the rules but I might as well have been watching a foreign film without subtitles. It seemed a very staccato affair, lots of beefcake players facing off against each other then briefly jostling for possession before the ref intervened. Once in a while a lightning sprint would be attempted but was always cut short when either the runner got squashed or the whistle blew. Still, I enjoyed the Mexican waves, the cheerleaders' dance routines and chanting 'Go Mean Green, Go Mean Green' at every opportunity. Not that our chanting did much good. I don't remember the score but it was clear the Gobblers had been savaged by the Tigers.

'Man,' said Sid, taking a drag on one of his clove cigarettes. 'That was a tragedy. You think Cuero takes its turkey race seriously, that's nothing compared to our High School football.'

Sid explained that if the Gobblers triumphed in the leagues it not only instilled the whole town with a sense of pride, it created all manner of fringe benefits. Victory would subtly enhance Cuero's profile, boost the local economy and even encourage outside investment. Every aspect of the game smacked of fierce commitment. Even the cheerleaders were hugely competitive. Recently there had been an incident in another small town in Texas where a jealous woman had hired a hit man to murder the mother of her teenage daughter's cheerleading rival.

'High School football can make the Super Bowl look tame,' Sid said, jumping into his pick up. 'Anyway, our game's over now, let's party.'

After a quick trip home, Sid drove Matt and me to his local rifle club for an evening soirée to celebrate the start of the dove shooting season; a sort of Texan version of the Glorious Twelfth. I sat in the back of Sid's pick-up as he sped along, the smoke from his clove cheroots adding an exotic tang to the night. Soon we were in woodland, cicadas chirruping, the headlights occasionally catching the white tail of a retreating deer. A congregation of tiny stars shone above.

We heard the din of the party long before the rifle club came into view. Then, in a remote glade amid the conifers, appeared what looked like a small, timber-framed warehouse. A throng of people, all in hats, stood outside.

I'd been to some strange theme parties in my youth but nothing to rival this one. The music ranged from 1980s disco chestnuts to wild bluegrass yodelling, but what was truly extraordinary was the dress code. Most of the groovers looked ready for battle – camouflage trousers, combat jackets, black army boots – and that was just the women. The men sported the same wardrobe, but accompanied by tattooed forearms, wide-rimmed hats and spaghetti Western moustaches. In contrast my pale orange Marks & Spencer T-shirt and nautical plimsolls were the ultimate in outré dandyism.

The hall was spartan, musty and surrounded by all manner of deer antlers. A stuffed fish – the size of a small shark – was mounted in a glass display case near the bar. This is a rifle club, I thought to myself boozily. Some joker actually shot this fish! There was a big poster of Charlton Heston, the darling of America's gun owners, brandishing a rifle. DEFEND OUR RIGHT TO SHOOT! he urged the revellers. Why did Charlton Heston need a gun, anyway? He coped perfectly well with a sword in *Ben Hur*, a lance in *El Cid* and as Moses, sporting a beard the size of a polar bear cub, he shouted at the rabble on Mount Sinai, 'Thou shalt not kill!' Oh, sorry, except clay pigeons, Texan doves and anything that tastes good on the barbie.

I had no problem with bona fide hunters having weapons – but it worried me that so many Texans secreted a handgun purely for self-defence. Over the last month I had spoken to locals who boasted of pistols in their hip pockets and handbags or else under their truck seats or pillows. One night early in the journey a couple had let me use their washroom where I discovered a Smith and Wesson revolver on the toilet cistern. When I jokingly asked if it was used for shooting alligators in the bath, I was told casually: 'You need a gun in this town, son.' In a state that had shown me, a stranger with a mule, such kindness it seemed extraordinary that Texans didn't seem to trust each other much. It's a contradiction I still struggle to understand.

Throughout the disco Matt and I drank far too much. I vaguely remember being dragged on the dance floor by a fifty-something lady so stupendously endowed that, when she bopped, her cleavage almost pogoed its way clean out of her combat top. Her peroxide hair glowed in the dark. She was blessed with a lovely smile but this was diluted by the fact she seemed to have applied her make-up with some sort of DIY power tool. Still, I was happy, full of beer and dancing the night away with surely the most spirited grandmother in town. Life could be a whole lot worse, I thought.

'Where are you from, honey?' she shouted at me over the closing chorus of 'Hi Ho Silver Lining'.

'England.'

'Geez, that's nice. Makes a change to dance with someone from out of town. Know what they say about local men, honey?'

'No idea.'

'They say knock all the bullshit out of a Texan and you could bury him in a matchbox. Wheyhey, how 'bout that?' She laughed uproariously. 'I'm from Virginia, honey. The most beautiful girls in the world live there . . .'

At this stage Sid tactfully intervened, peeled me away from my fragrant partner and chaperoned me back to his pick-up. I fell into the back seat. Matt sat in the front with a 'what the hell have I let myself in for' grin on his face. Sid fired up the truck.

'Welcome to Friday night in Cuero, gentlemen,' he stated gravely, making a poor stab at an English accent. He blew a smoke ring and I watched it waft up like a shimmering halo above the dashboard. Then we were off, tearing through the clove-scented forest.

*   *   *

The alarm went off at dawn the next day. I blinked tentatively, praying for a clear head. Bugger, I hadn't got away with it – it felt like someone had opened up my skull and poured in a ladle full of toxic porridge. Matt could clearly take his liquor much better than me and was scampering about Sid's house preparing for the day's walk. I popped several aspirin and pulled on my boots. After a coffee and some Cheerios I felt a little better.

I loaded up Browny, wincing every time I yanked one of her girth straps. Sid appeared just as we were heading off and generously presented us with a couple of wooden staves, made from white eucalyptus. Matt accepted his but I turned mine down, partly because it was taller than me and partly because any passing animal lover might get the wrong idea and think I used it to wallop Browny. Sid embraced us both (everybody in America hugs each other with wild abandon: men, women, bears) and handed over the address of a lady called Tracey, a friend of his from Yoakum, a small town some seventeen miles up the road.

Matt coped well with his first day's walking. The morning was cool, with the odd shower freshening the heavy air, but by lunchtime the heat was severe. We reached Yoakum early in the evening, a sleepy, attractive place full of old-fashioned stores with hand-painted signs. By this stage Matt was burning up. His face was blushed with sun and his feet increasingly tender. When we tracked down Tracey's house, an elegant mock colonial manse, he collapsed on her lawn under a sprinkler.

There was no sign of Tracey so I prowled around her street to see if any of her neighbours knew of her whereabouts. It soon became clear this was the thick of the Bible belt. In many of the gardens were sign posts with chilling biblical prophecies: HE THAT SACRIFICETH UNTO ANY GOD, SAVE UNTO THE LORD ONLY, HE SHALL BE UTTERLY DESTROYED, Exodus 22: 20 preached the house two doors down. WITH MEN IT IS IMPOSSIBLE, BUT NOT WITH GOD: FOR WITH GOD ALL THINGS ARE POSSIBLE, Mark 10: 27 was the more engaging message from the garden opposite.

Fortunately Tracey pulled up in her truck before I had to search further. She was an attractive, frizzy-haired lady who exuded a sassy confidence. In the small garden at the back of the house Matt held Browny while I hosed down her sweat-caked flanks. Katie and Marsha, Tracey's bubbly blonde teen-age daughters came out and helped unfurl a bale of hay. When all was done Tracey poured us all iced teas and ushered us into the kitchen.

'What's with all the religious sign posts in the other gardens?' I asked.

'All the towns around here have loads of churches,' replied Tracey, carving up a joint of cold lamb. 'Religion's big. There ain't a whole lot else going on. Some small towns have as many as six or seven churches. Often when the Baptists set up a church, some members disagree with its style of preaching, so a splinter group starts up, then another and another. It's hard to keep up sometimes.'

'Are you Baptist?'

'No, I'm Episcopalian,' she drawled, touching a crucifix that hung around her neck. 'I love the Lord but I'm not the best of Christians, I've been divorced four times.'

'Mom, where's Iran,' interrupted Katie. She was doing her homework on the kitchen table. 'We've got to do a report about the war against terror for history.' Katie was running a finger over a world atlas. Matt helped her out and stuck his finger on Tehran.

'So if we kill these guys,' Katie said to Matt, 'then we can use their country as a base.' It was an innocent comment by a bright young teenager but a little worrying that she considered her president able to obliterate whole nations with a flick of a finger. 'But these guys,' she pointed at Pakistan, 'they are helping us, aren't they? So we don't have to kill them.'

'Hopefully we won't have to kill that many people,' stressed Tracey, winking at Matt. 'Just bin Laden and his friends would be quite enough.'

Marsha's homework was equally fascinating if a little less demanding. She was reading a book called *Captain Underpants and the Wrath of the Wicked Wedgie Women*. After dinner Tracey ordered the two girls to bed, despite Marsha's repeated requests for Matt and me to read about the intriguing but clearly perilous Wedgie Women in an English accent. Matt smothered his feet in talc and plasters and crashed out on the sitting room floor. I felt for him, I'd been through all that blistery horror last month.

Tracey and I stayed up chatting in the candle-lit dining room. She admitted it was strange for her – this free-spirited divorcee – living in quiet, puritan Yoakum.

'I'm no picnic,' she confessed. 'I struggle in my relationships with men because I do things my way. Women round here tend to be quite subservient, but hell, not me. I won't compromise myself for anyone, except my kids.' She prodded gently at the dripping wax on one of the candles.

'Here, let me show you something, Tom.' Tracey shot up and walked over to a wooden trunk in the corner of the room. She opened it and pulled out a sepia photograph, which she threw down in front of me. It showed a beautiful woman in a 1920s dress. 'I reckon this is who I get my wild blood from.'

'Who is she?' I asked, studying the photo.

'Not she,' Tracey whispered mischievously. 'He! This picture is of a man named Lois Plume, my great uncle.'

'No way!' I analysed the picture more closely and sure enough the caption read. 'This is the famous Lois Plume, curiously dressed as a woman.'

'He's not bad, is he?' joked Tracey.

Apparently Lois was born in Yoakum but it wasn't really the place to launch a career as a crossdresser. So teenage Lois ran away to New York's Greenwich Village where he got work as a bit-part actor and learnt to dance the charleston. He didn't make his name until he moved to Hollywood and became a transvestite, long, long, before it became de rigeur. It was all shocking, groundbreaking stuff. He was even supposed to have been Rudolph Valentino's lover for a while. When she revealed this last fact, Tracey raised her eyes in a 'how about that?' look.

'The amazing thing is Lois returned to Yoakum in his early thirties,' she continued, snuffing out one of the candles with her fingers. 'Weird really, because nobody had any time for him here. Maybe he got fed up with the fame thing. He was only thirty-three when he died, some sort of mysterious disease.

'Lois is a bit of an embarrassment to the family,' mused Tracey with a detached smile, twisting on her crucifix again. 'Yoakum is a very traditional, god-fearing place. That's why Lois is hidden in a secret trunk, his Pandora's Box, or Lois's Box, as I call it. I only mention him to a few people, but I'm proud of great-uncle Lois, he displayed real balls. Well, not exactly displayed – hid them more like. But you know what I mean. He's a Texas cowboy in his own way, taking on the world with his lipstick and cocktail frocks. If anyone had the frontier spirit, he did!'

I laughed uncontrollably. I think the reason Tracey's yarn tickled me so much is that it was so unexpected. Texas up until now had been such a relentlessly macho environment and here, out of the blue, was this peculiar but heroic charleston-dancing gender bender, this cowboy in a cocktail frock. I told Tracey that Lois's tale was a marked contrast to the previous night where the women had worn combat pants and camouflage paint at the Rifle Club dance.

'They say Texas is not a place but a state of mind,' said Tracey, suddenly serious. 'Sometimes it's a crystal clear state of mind, other times very confused.'

* * *

Colonel Arthur also had some 'very confused' experiences during his travels south from San Antonio to Houston. Having flogged (clearly with Del Boy Trotter relish) his battered portmanteau and the clothes inside it for over \$320 – in England it was only worth £8 – he cadged a lift on a mule-drawn stagecoach. His carriage was crammed with nine people and many more on the roof. The Colonel's principal problem was tobacco. As he writes: 'In the afternoon tobacco-chewing became universal, and the spitting was sometimes a little wild.'

Colonel Arthur tolerates the chewers within his carriage who 'aimed at the windows with great accuracy, and didn't *splash* me.' However, he was careful not to lean his head outside to 'avoid a shower of juice from the mouths of the Southern chivalry on the roof.' To amuse himself he shot at jackrabbits through the window with his revolver.

All things considered the Colonel stays fairly sanguine and praises his fellow stagecoach passengers who in spite of 'their peculiar habits of hanging, shooting, etc., which seemed to be

natural to people living in a wild and thinly populated country
. . . They had a sort of bon-hommie [sic] . . . and extreme
good nature, which was very agreeable.'

Later on his journey, as he nears Houston, Arthur travels
by a combination of steam train (luxury after the stagecoach)
and cotton wagon. He eats 'miserable' food, shares a bed with
an 'enormously fat German' and, on arrival at the port of
Galveston, a brief rail road ride from Houston, dances an
American cotillion, which he dismisses as a 'very violent
exercise' – no doubt the 1863 equivalent of Sid's Rifle Club
disco.

Arthur enjoys the landscape though, and passes through
'some very pretty country, full of beautiful Indian corn' and
cotton fields crisscrossed by rickety ox-pulled wagons.

Although he stayed in the spiffiest accommodation when
he had the chance – such as the Menger Hotel in San Antonio,
or the homes of Rebel grandees – Colonel Arthur was more
than happy to slum it much of the time. Confederate officer
Gilbert Moxley Sorrell revealed that the Englishman was 'a
very small, slight man, wiry, and much enduring . . . I don't
believe he changed his clothing or boots while he was with
us,' adding that Colonel Arthur, 'roughed it with the hardest,
and took everything as it came.'

After the relative luxury of Tracey's sitting room carpet
Matt and I were back to roughing it too. Over the next few
days we camped in a park, a rodeo arena, the backyard of a
motel, and in the charming little town of Round Top (population 77 according to its sign) we bivouacked under a large
magnolia while Browny frolicked in a nearby meadow full of
sunflowers and blue-winged butterflies. In the morning a
local couple brought us out some plums and let us shower
under their bracingly cold garden hose.

Beyond Round Top, Matt and I covered a stretch of country
known by locals as 'the devil's backbone', its lush vertebrae

rolling like choppy surf towards the horizon. Hardly any of the land was cultivated unlike Colonel Arthur's day: it was mostly sweeps of pasture grazed by cattle, horses, donkeys and, far less frequently, mules. When we walked by the various beasts would charge up to the fence line and holler at Browny, who, tossing her mane dismissively, would strut by with a look of exquisite froideur.

The main hazards confronting us were the narrow bridges that arched over the many creeks and streams. Browny's pace stayed a steady 3 mph, a rhythm unchanged since the time of Hannibal, although at a push I could rev her up to 4 mph. This meant some of the longer bridges could take over a minute to cross, leaving no room for manoeuvre if two cars sped over from opposite directions. To avoid any potential accidents I would hussle Browny across (the beast showed no fear of heights at all), while Matt whooped encouragement from behind, waving his stave at any oncoming cars like a deranged shepherd. It worked a treat, and although it brought entire communities to a standstill, nobody ended up getting hurt.

This is more than can be said for the many road-kill armadillos, which got hurt with savage regularity. British hedgehogs are paradigms of street savvy compared to these scaled and suicidal creatures. Certain stretches of road were like an armadillo Culloden, their shattered, visceral remnants scarring the bitumen. Almost as bad as this animal debris (which also included raccoons, skunks and many birds) was the human-spawned litter thrown from car windows – at times the verge turned into a landfill of plastic bottles, tin cans, Styrofoam, nappies, crisp packets. There were plenty of anti-trash, fine-threatening DON'T MESS WITH TEXAS signs but they didn't seem to do much good.

The litter especially enraged Matt, an ardent greeny, but his disappointment at Texan ecological sloppiness was tempered by the generosity of the locals. On his final day we walked twenty-five miles, ending up in the pretty little town of Navasota. As usual we were winging it, with no idea where we would spend the night. It was getting dark and we were all flagging, including our over-burdened beast.

Just as we were toying with the idea of dossing down on the next available acre of turf we heard a voice: 'Can I help you?' A lithesome black girl sitting on a picket fence was semaphoring wildly for us to come over. Above her head was a red sign blinking RUTHIE'S PIT BARBECUE. She told us her name was Sharona and that her boyfriend, Charles, owned the restaurant.

Ruthie's looked nothing more than a well-upholstered shack. Matt and I were ushered around to the side entrance where we set up camp on a patchy swathe of grass studded with dogwood trees. Hickory smoke belched out from the kitchen vents. Within five minutes Charles and Sharona returned with coffee and two plates of steaming beef, for which they fiercely refused payment. The meat was some of the best I've ever tasted, delicately seasoned and sumptuous, falling off the bones as easily as petals from a rose.

'What ya doing out walking with your four-legged hussy?' asked Charles, gesturing towards Browny.

When I mentioned Colonel Arthur, Charles laughed with a deep, resonant boom. 'Man, I like this walk you're doing but why d'ya want to follow some old army guy,' he insisted, chewing on a rib. 'Most of us black folks just want to forget that war, look to the future. You should follow ya mule, not ya past. Respect ya ancestor fella, but don't follow him.'

It was interesting to hear a fresh interpretation of the journey and we all stayed on chatting until the mosquitoes became too much to bear. Matt and I escaped to the tent, where we toasted Browny for covering almost one hundred and fifty miles over the last week. I wrote up my diary while

Matt read a biography of Laurie Lee. Outside swarms of luminous bugs could be seen zipping around in the gloaming.

The following day Matt and I took a swim in the gently purling Brazos river near to where General Sam Houston signed the Texas Independence document in 1836, almost a decade before America took the maverick state under its wing. Apparently even now, up near the New Mexico border, Texas has a little posse of determined but barmy vigilantes still championing Lone Star independence.

After our wallow in the Brazos and a hearty breakfast of egg, cheese and potato burritos it was time for Matt to head home. He gave me a handshake and Browny a skinner's embrace before hopping on a Greyhound back to Houston. My mule and I were alone once more for the final Texan leg.

CHAPTER 8

Skewed Angels

Two days later I marched into Huntsville, having slept the previous night in a derelict caravan in the tiny, one-mule town of Shiro. Huntsville was the first major place — about thirty thousand people — I had confronted with Browny. I imagined a series of chronic flyovers and spaghetti junctions, their smooth, twisty arteries yet to be scuffed by hooves. As it turned out I need not have worried. Within minutes of reaching Huntsville's outskirts, a local businessman by the name of Lyn Boone pulled up and offered me a sofa bed in a log cabin. It was an ideal spot, he told me, about three miles south of town near some woods where Browny could graze.

When I arrived at the cabin, having bypassed much of Huntsville's fast food suburbia, I was met by Davy, an intense, sallow-faced Mexican. He told me he worked for Lyn's company, which specialised in locating and dynamiting potential oil fields. He said since September 11, the explosives industry had become much more vigilant and tightly controlled. For this reason he was busy with fresh paperwork and would be out most of the time. He told me I should just make myself at home. It was an act of good, old-timer decency by Lyn and Davy, who both knew next to nothing about me.

'I just like to help out a fellow human being,' Davy told me. 'Simple as that. Besides, you can hardly make a quick getaway with that mule.'

That night I crashed out on the cabin's plump cushioned sofa; the sort of homely item of furniture you could reach down the back of and pull out three biros, a half eaten mint, a pair of broken sunglasses and an old copy of *Explosives Weekly*. From my prostrate position I also noticed I was surrounded by angels: angels hanging from the roof, angels made of straw, of wood, wire, plastic, angels with pulsing neon wings or with skewed haloes like miniature basketball hoops. Davy clearly collected them and now here I lay, watched over by this host of heavenly kitsch.

I slumbered deeply on the sofa until the sun lanced through the window blinds the next morning.

There was much to be done during the next few days. First on the list was a visit to Sam Houston's colossal, white concrete Doppelgänger, called a Tribute to Courage – The World's Tallest Statue of an American Hero. Seeing the statue did not take much effort on my behalf, in fact just by cricking my neck it was visible through the window above my sofa bed. I suppose I'll have to get up and introduce myself properly, I decided blearily. I threw some fresh hay in Browny's paddock and walked over to the towering Texan, who in life was six foot six but in death towered a massive sixty-seven foot, supposedly visible from seven miles away.

If I worked for the Texas tourist board I would describe Houston's statue as a Brobdingnagian masterpiece. As I don't I can safely say that it is the most appalling example of 'I'm the Biggest' naff I've ever seen, even worse than those giant roadside pineapples or lobsters that occasionally sprout out from American highways. A much more respectful tribute to the great man was to be found at the Sam Houston Memorial Museum in Huntsville town centre. I hitched a ride there with Davy who dropped me off at the museum's romanesque main building, fronted by four fluted columns and an attractive domed roof.

Samuel Houston was one of life's trailblazers. He was born in Virginia in 1793, became a US Senator as a coltish thirty-year-old and a Governor of Tennessee only six years later. In 1832, after a brief, at times debauched spell living with the Cherokee Indians, he headed south to Texas and defeated the Mexicans at the Battle of San Jacinto before being named President of the Republic of Texas a few years later. Like so many great men, the Civil War all but destroyed Houston. Tragically, he was deposed as Texas's top dog at the war's outbreak after vigorously opposing secession from the Union. He died in his Huntsville home (also in the museum grounds) a broken man, in 1864.

By sheer chance Colonel Arthur met Sam Houston only ten weeks before the ailing Texan's death. The two men crossed paths in a railroad carriage bound for the port of Galveston. My ancestor describes Houston in less than flattering terms:

> Though evidently a remarkable and clever man, he is extremely egotistical and vain, and much disappointed at having to subside from his former grandeur. The town of Houston is named after him. In appearance he is a tall,

handsome old man, much given to chewing tobacco, and blowing his nose with his fingers.

Colonel Arthur later notes: 'Sam Houston lived for several years amongst the Cherokee Indians, who used to call him "the Raven" or the "Big Drunk". He married an Indian squaw when he was with them.'

According to information in the museum, Houston's marriage to the Cherokee squaw was brief, as was his marriage to his first wife Eliza, which only lasted three months. The love of his life was his third wife, Margaret, with whom he had eight children.

After overdosing on all the Houston memorabilia – including the inevitable leopard skin waistcoat given to him by the Cherokees – I made a beeline for the information kiosk. I wanted to quiz someone on Houston's relevance today.

'He's still huge,' said the curator, Richard, looking up from behind his well-polished desk. Richard had the ashen complexion of a man who spends too long in sunless rooms poring over books and drinking strong coffee.

'Only today,' he announced excitedly, 'I had a call from a student claiming that Sam Houston slept with many Cherokee squaws other than his wife, one who produced him illegitimate twins. Well, let me tell you, Houston left the Indians in November 1832,' Richard tapped his forehead knowingly, 'and these twins were supposedly born in April 1834. So, that's either the longest gestation period in history or complete bulldust. We get enquiries like this all the time, Texans are still obsessed with him.'

'Do they still admire him?'

'Houston – oh they love him. I get at least thirty calls a year from people claiming to be related to him. Some people even get their DNA checked to try and prove it. None of them ever manage to. I've disproved the lot of them.'

'That sounds a bit harsh.'

'Hey, I'm a historian,' countered Richard, 'not an astrologer. I tell them the truth, not what they want to hear. It's how Houston would have wanted it.'

'So you like Houston?'

'Oh yes, yes,' the curator enthused. 'He was a maverick, drank too much, womanised, could be proud and selfish. But he was also a complete hero, a brave soldier and an unshakable politician. Unlike so many in his position, he was prepared to champion the Indian people and he treated his slaves almost like family.'

'What about the Civil War?'

'Sam was immensely principled,' stressed Richard, blowing his nose with the sort of Houstonian lustre my ancestor described. 'His refusal to join the Confederacy at the start of the war was heartbreakingly courageous. He knew he would be vilified but stuck by his guns – it horrified him when one of his sons, Sam Jnr, fought for the Rebels and was badly wounded. It's a tragedy Houston died so unpopular in Texas having done so much for the state. But at least Texans now see him for the hero he is.'

Richard rubbed his paunch with both hands. 'Hell!' he exclaimed. 'If I could drink as much as he did in his life and still achieve so much, I'd want to be remembered.'

*   *   *

After thanking Richard for his time I walked back into the town centre. While troughing on a plate of fried eggs and corned beef hash I pondered over Colonel Arthur's description of Sam Houston. It interested me that my ancestor had been so dismissive about this extraordinary man. But a pattern was starting to emerge. It was clear that as his journey progressed Arthur was becoming almost ludicrously one-sided in his opinions. Every Confederate officer or sympathiser my ancestor met was showered with superlatives while anyone with even a sniff of Union about them was likely to be snubbed.

He also took rather a haughty attitude towards minority groups. As the historian Garry Gallagher noted: 'He [Fremantle] considered the Mexicans a brutal people, mocked their Catholic religion, and disparaged their dress style. Germans, Irish, Poles and other ethnic members of southern and northern society received similar criticism.'

To me, the fact that Colonel Arthur becomes such a Confederate stooge is one of his great weaknesses as a diarist — especially over slavery. Despite his easygoing manner and formidable stamina, Arthur can at times be a bit of a prig. He insists on recording *all* toasts to the Queen, he bristles slightly at the intimacy of hand shaking, and is happy to use the 'Ladies Car' in a train, until he discovers, to his chagrin, that 'one is liable to be ousted by a female.'

Of course Colonel Arthur is, to an extent, a prisoner to the politics of his day. I respect his patriotism and his admiration of Southern valour and can even overlook his minor prejudices, but it would be useful if he had, at times, seen the big picture. Of the few detailed eyewitness diaries about the Civil War, most are understandably written from a trenchantly Yankee or Rebel viewpoint. The Colonel, despite his Confederate sympathies, was an Englishman, a non-partisan spectator, who could have provided if not a neutral, at least a broad-minded perspective. Instead he produces a highly readable adventure but strongly laced with Southern propaganda.

Colonel Arthur is especially chummy with the Confederate 'aristocrats' who are proud of their English roots and whose 'manners and feelings resemble those of the Old Country.' At times he lapses into fawning prose, especially when he first meets noble, vice-free Robert E. Lee at Gettysburg, whom he describes as 'the handsomest man of his age I ever saw' and 'as near to perfection as a man can be'. Lee was undeniably a great General but this sort of adulation just makes Arthur sound like a star-struck teenager. It is not surprising a recent article in *Vanity Fair* describes *Three Months in the Southern States* as 'one of the most vivid, if least intelligent, Civil War diaries'.

With this in mind it is clear why rough and ready Samuel Houston got a bad rap from my ancestor. To Colonel Arthur not only was he an Indian-canoodling, tobacco-chewing boor with a semi house-trained approach to nasal etiquette, but, much worse, a sap to the Union. Colonel Arthur is happy to recognise Houston's greatness but cannot resist cutting the big Texan's ego down to size with a rather mean-spirited character assassination. It shows an uppity side to the usually good-humoured Colonel.

*   *   *

Other than Huntsville's obsession with Sam Houston – the town's university and cultural centre are both named after him – these days it has another controversial claim to fame: Death Row. Huntsville is America's capital punishment nerve centre, executing three times as many criminals as anywhere else in the country. Death Row itself, which currently houses over four hundred inmates, is located in farmland a few miles out of town, but there are still several high-security prisons within the civic envelope.

Wandering around it is easy to spot evidence of the prison compounds. There are walls topped with razor wire, prominent watchtowers and convicts in white pyjama suits working in the surrounding farms, picking crops, erecting fences, collecting trash. Perhaps the most unusual sight are the prison-bred horses; all branded with a convict-like number on their rumps. Indeed, rather than disguising its criminal populace Huntsville positively flaunts it. There is even a Texas Prison Museum near the town square.

The museum's most popular exhibit is an electric chair called Old Sparky. Over a forty-year period Old Sparky was responsible for 361 executions, up until the Supreme Court banned the death penalty in Texas in 1964. Capital punishment was reintroduced to the state eighteen years later but only if carried out by lethal injection. Set at the back of the museum Old Sparky really is a nasty-looking contraption, lit up in a dull, spooky glow like the Mastermind chair.

'Old Sparky sent a shock of 2,000 volts for 3–4 seconds,' read the charming information plaque. 'This was then reduced by 1,000 volts to stop the body catching fire.'

Much more interesting than this redundant blood-frazzler was an exhibit detailing the last meal request of a Death Row inmate called Morrow J.H., who clearly stayed both calm and unrepentant until the end.

'This is my last meal,' wrote Morrow, 'and damn it, I want it served hot on however many plates and bowls it takes . . . for mixing . . . it up together, and I want it served at 1 o'clock this afternoon.' For anyone interested he requested one small steak (tender, no bone, no fat, cooked rare medium) with French fries and large butter beans. For dessert he plumped for a piece of fluffy coconut pie.

The museum also displayed a rogues' gallery of other previous inmates. These included petty criminals such as the blues singer Leadbelly and the 1950s Las Vegas stripper Candy Barr. Then there are hard-core gangsters like Fred Carrasco who in 1974, after an eleven-day prison siege, attempted to escape with a Ned Kelly-style metal helmet on his head. The helmet didn't do Carrasco much good; he died in a hail of bullets along with a fellow inmate and two hostages.

My favourite item of felon memorabilia was a letter written by Clyde Barrow, of Bonnie and Clyde fame, from his Huntsville cell. The cheeky missive is addressed to Henry Ford and congratulates the famous inventor on his 'dandy' V8 Model. The notorious outlaw writes that he has frequently used it as a getaway car and 'the Ford has got every other car skinned.'

On my way out of the museum I resisted the urge to enlist on a Tourist's Prison Driving Tour — 'See what life inside is really like!' — or to buy an 'I Did Time In Huntsville' T-shirt. I freed myself and strolled back to the cabin past the fields of convict horses.

*   *   *

The following day got off to a bad start. I had planned to take a side trip to Houston. Colonel Arthur made a whistle-stop tour of the city and the nearby port of Galveston in early May 1863 and I was keen to follow in his wake. Now that Browny had Davy to throw her fresh hay in my absence I felt no guilt about deserting her for a couple of days.

When I arrived at Huntsville's dingy Greyhound office it was clear something was wrong. A throng of agitated people surrounded the information desk. A young auburn-haired woman was shouting that she had been waiting in town since yesterday. 'I've seen my brother in prison,' she railed at the Greyhound staff. 'And now I just gotta get home.' Davy had warned me that many of the bus passengers would be newly released cons or else Houston-based friends and relatives of prisoners.

I bought a can of Dr Pepper from a drink dispenser in the corner. The purring machine nursed several dents where previous customers had hit and kicked it. Rusty juices oozed from its wobbly base. An old man sat slumped against the machine's side talking to himself. He had watery blue eyes, withered cheeks and a wen on his forehead, a bit like a piece of dried up chewing gum. When I looked at him he smiled and then continued his conversation with himself.

On one of the plastic chairs in the waiting room was a copy of the local paper, the *Huntsville Item*. I picked it up and noticed the following article on the front page:

PASSENGER SLASHES DRIVER'S THROAT, KILLS 6 PEOPLE ON GREYHOUND BUS

A passenger on a Greyhound bus slashed the driver's throat with a blade, grabbed the wheel and crashed the vehicle (yesterday, 3 October) killing six of the 41 people aboard and prompting the company to temporarily shut down service across an already jittery nation.

The driver was in a stable condition following surgery for a 5″ cut to his neck. The 34 others aboard were also injured.

The FBI said the 29-year-old assailant was among the dead. 'We believe he was acting alone,' said R. Joe Clark, the FBI's agent in charge. 'I would say this was a disturbed individual . . . this is not an act of terrorism.'

This sad tale clearly explained the kerfuffle at the information desk. But all was not lost. I learnt that Greyhound buses were now up and running again, just with a few more delays than usual. I booked a Houston-bound ticket for the early afternoon and read Steinbeck in the waiting room. When the bus finally arrived it was jam-packed. I squeezed in at the back next to a burly, gimlet-eyed man clutching a hessian sack full of cans of cat food.

The bus glided down Highway 45, past Sam Houston's gigantic white statue. Soon the only view was that of towering pine trees interspersed occasionally by shopping malls. I dozed against the window. The bus seemed to stop repeatedly, at one stage for over half an hour. We did not reach Houston's fringes until the light was fading.

Houston was clearly a very different place from when Colonel Arthur had visited. He had described the outskirts as: 'very pretty, and studded with white wooden villas, which are raised on blocks like haystacks.' From the bus window it looked far from pretty, more like an expansive building site studded with flyovers and industrial zones. Now I was near the centre, skyscrapers burst up like unworldly silver stumps amid the dowdy precincts.

Mildly disorientated I snatched my rucksack from the Greyhound's vault. I suddenly realised I had done no home-work about Houston whatsoever. All I knew was that NASA was based near by and that Tom Hanks had once told some-body here that he had a problem.

I, too, had a problem. I had no idea where I was, where I would stay or whether I was in a good part of town or a bad one. I was wearing the most inappropriate outfit – bright, Hawaiian-style shorts, plimsolls and a touristy T-shirt I had been given by a good-hearted hillbilly that read 'SHIRO – TEXAS Blink and You Miss It'. My money belt stuck out from my side like a holster. This sort of pastoral innocence was fine in the boondocks: not in Houston. 'Hey bro, you need a taxi, hey little bro,' several hustlers converged on me.

It didn't take long to work out the Greyhound station was not the best part of town. So far I had never felt on my guard in America. In the countryside, I received the odd suspicious look, but never felt threatened. My mule was like a talisman, protecting me from all harm. Without her I suddenly felt vulnerable. I struck out on foot towards the city centre, beneath a series of shadowy overpasses. Clusters of homeless sat in groups drinking from bottles in brown paper bags. One or two of them shouted at me, I waved and speeded up. One old man pursued me for a while, swearing abuse. I broke into a run splashing through a series of filthy puddles.

It was almost dark now. The streets in this part of town were littered and deserted. There were signs for pawnbrokers and bail bonds and the odd derelict store. Graffiti was rife. I didn't want to stop. I would wait until I was in a crowded, more reassuring place before studying my guidebook. It dawned on me it would be the first time I had bothered to look at it all trip. Usually I had simply asked a friendly looking local for a place to camp: made it up as I went along. Here in Houston, it was a whole new set of rules. I finally stopped running and slowed down to a more relaxed yomp.

I reached a busier street. Office workers were clocking off and enjoying pre-prandial drinks in the cafes and wine bars. I had been on the move for what felt like miles. I stopped, adjusted my rucksack and walked on until I came to a palm-fringed complex with cinemas, restaurants and a Hard Rock Café. To my delight there was a herd of multicoloured cows outside it. As Milton Keynes – famous for its herd of concrete cows – is my hometown, I have always felt affection for bovine sculptures. This group was particularly wacky. One of the cows was wearing an astronaut's uniform with a space bubble over its face, another sported a cowboy hat and my favourite looked as if painted by Jackson Pollock having had an artistic epiphany in a Dulux factory.

Sweat-soaked, adrenaline-pulsing, I slumped against one of the heavily splotched heifers and ferreted out my guidebook. Yes! There was a YMCA only a short walk away. I wonder if there will be any pasture for Browny, I thought to myself, then laughed at my stupidity. Despite being surrounded by a herd of psychedelic cows I was still clearly missing my mule.

*   *   *

The following day, hot on Arthur's trail, I caught another bus to the port of Galveston. Sadly the train Colonel Arthur had hopped on when he met Sam Houston no longer existed.

At the time of the Civil War Galveston was not only Texas's biggest port; it was also the state's most prosperous city. Houston in contrast was nothing but a tiny backwater. As the fighting intensified on the coast, Galveston's population retreated inland, but once the war finished in 1865 it soon regained its former prosperity, comfortably outdoing torrid, swampy Houston.

In 1900 that all changed when a devastating hurricane whooshed through the port, ripping up buildings and killing at least six thousand people. Galveston never really recovered, and after a dubious period in the 1950s as a sin city, known for gambling and prostitution, it has now cleaned itself up to become a low-key seaside town. Conversely sultry Houston, benefiting greatly from a combination of nearby oil fields and air conditioning, is now one of the five biggest cities in the USA.

The centre of Galveston is based near the tip of a finger-shaped spit, which is where my bus pulled up. I wandered down The Strand, the wide, oleander-lined main drag, admiring the few antebellum buildings that survived both the Civil War and the big storm. All the forts Colonel Arthur visited in 1863 had been destroyed and the Hendley Market, which was used as a lookout during the war, now sells knicknacks – aromatic candles, whoopee cushions and Marilyn Monroe postcards. From Galveston's harbour my view was dominated by container vessels and fishing boats, whereas Arthur would have witnessed the impressive fleet of blockade ships lining the horizon with the odd wreck poking up from the nearby surf.

I enjoyed Galveston, but finding it hard to put myself in Colonel Arthur's boots decided to catch a Greyhound back to Houston the following morning. While waiting for my connection I saw on a TV screen at the bus station that America had started bombing Al-Qaeda targets in Afghanistan. Everyone was talking of the 'War against Terror'. Tony Blair briefly appeared on the screen next to President Bush. It was a repeat news clip of the President telling the masses: 'The US has no truer friend than Britain.'

Ever since Bush uttered these words shortly after September 11 several strangers, on hearing I was British, had shaken my hand and commended my country's stance. To my amazement some of the more effusive types even hugged Browny. Colonel Arthur had also won favour thanks to his nationality. During his travels my ancestor encountered many Southern Anglophiles keen to curry favour with him, still optimistic Britain might come on side. However, he was also abused by the odd Rebel fed up with Britain's constant prevarication.

Colonel Arthur dealt with his critics very effectively. 'Sometimes a man remarks that it is rather "mean" of England not to recognise the South,' he wrote, 'but I can always shut him up by saying that a nation which deserves its independence should fight and earn it for itself – a sentiment which is invariably agreed on by all.'

I arrived back in Huntsville later that evening, groomed Browny and collapsed on Davy's couch. I looked up. After the last few days – the Old Sparky museum, running the gauntlet in Houston and now war in Afghanistan – it felt good to be watched over by angels, even if they did have skewed haloes.

CHAPTER 9

Snow from the Moon

I watched the breakfast news on Davy's sofa. The screen was full of graphs and arrows, fronted by immaculately groomed reporters.

'Ninety per cent of Americans approve of bombing specific targets in Afghanistan even if it leads to further threats of terrorism,' read out an anchorman with a silver thatch of hair. He pointed at a heavily shaded pie chart.

'And 90 per cent also approve of how President Bush is handling the crisis,' stated his radiant blonde sidekick.

America was certainly putting up a united and patriotic front. Before September 11 President Bush had often been ridiculed in the press. The Left had been lambasting him for his offhand approach to the Kyoto environmental summit and the Right deemed him too liberal over Mexican immigrant numbers. Now, other than ardent critics and pacifists, he seemed to be receiving praise from most quarters. Even the comedian, Jay Leno, who last month had been lampooning George 'Dubya' as a dim-witted hick, joked that the President was suddenly 'smart now'.

All this war talk made me keen to hit the road again. I dragged myself off the sofa, put on the kettle and pulled on my boots. Davy's angels didn't look as reassuring in the early morning light. I noticed one of them was suspended above the television as if about to crash, a neon Icarus, wings pulsing like a faltering heartbeat.

Within an hour I was walking Browny alongside the busy, mist-smutted Highway 45. It was a nasty stretch to cover, but only lasted for about a mile before branching off east down a woodland path. A timber lorry whipped by, its logs jouncing on the tailboard.

Just as we were about to reach the woods another truck pulled up directly in front of us. This one was a dustbin lorry, its brakes letting off a soprano screech high enough to make Browny's ears spring to attention. Within seconds my mule, normally so steady in traffic, became skittish. As the screech intensified, she panicked.

I whispered to her, but as I moved in to stroke her neck she bucked, lashing out her front hooves. Normally in emergencies I controlled Browny by yanking a chain tight under her chin. This would stop her dead, but I'd neglected to put it on today. Right now, my only means of control was a rope attached to her halter, but this offered little restraint in a high-octane situation like this.

Browny brayed in fright. She bucked again, higher this time, and sawed me towards her, my rein arm as powerless and pliable as a stick of licorice. Then she was off. I gripped her lead rope with one hand and her mane with the other, clinging on with white knuckled fury, but as she accelerated it became too much and I fell. My chin smashed into the dewy ground and I tasted blood in my mouth.

I stood up, slightly dazed. Just for a moment I didn't quite know where I was, who I was, or what the hell I was supposed to be doing. Then I snapped back into focus and saw Browny galloping towards Highway 45. The sack of oats strapped to her pack had slipped and was now dangling on an elastic bungee butting wildly against her undercarriage. The saddlebags cavorted like a dislodged elephant's howdah, spewing out maps, books and tins of soup. I realised in horror that the stretch of road Browny was heading for was a blur of speedy traffic; no driver would be able to slow down in time. I began to run, shouting, swearing, my heart like a trapped animal trying to thud its way out. I ran like a demon but it was still never going to be fast enough.

'Oh Jesus, no, no, no . . .' Browny was already on the road, a blue car coming straight at her. I stopped to watch, gasping for breath, everything grinding down to a strange pace, the car moving as if underwater. Sickness lurched in my guts, my entrails locked in a Gordian knot of anxiety. 'Don't kill her, oh God, please don't kill her.' The prayer was too late but worked just the same. Suddenly the mule was gone, careering headlong into the woods the other side of the highway. A brief toot of horns, a truck swerving slightly and that was it. The clinch in my stomach immediately sprang loose and I punched the air in relief.

I hurriedly picked up all my spilt belongings and set off in search of my beast. I finally tracked her down deep in the woods. She stood stock still, staring at me. Her eyes were dark and unblinking, reflecting the dull forest sun; her saddlebags were completely skew-whiff and covered in foliage and little twigs. I approached her with a handful of grass but she made no move to escape. When I touched her I felt a frisson of electricity as the hair roached along her back. She was breathing fast but otherwise seemed calm.

I repacked the saddlebags, balancing them with great care across the mule's heaving haunches. Then I tied down the feed sack, stretching the elastic bungies over her saddle, tight as veins. 'Whoa up, Brown Girl, whoa there,' I told her. 'I'm not the mule whisperer yet, eh.'

We recrossed the highway without incident, but just before heading down the woodland track a police car drove alongside. 'We've had a couple of calls about your animal,' said the cop in the passenger seat. He was wearing reflective sunglasses and chewing on some gum.

I apologised and told him I never normally walked with the mule near busy highways. I delivered him a hand-wringing patter. How very stupid of me. Isn't Texas wonderful! Yes, I'll walk in the woods from now on. There was a pregnant pause that seemed to last a couple of geological ages as the officer slowly masticated, like a bull on cud. Finally he spat out the gum into his hand.

'Just keep that animal off the road, sir,' the policeman repeated. I felt like telling him Browny was not any old *animal*, she was a mule, but decided it might be churlish. Given the circumstances he had been very reasonable. He even had the decency to call me sir, when cack-handed pillock would have been far more apt.

*   *   *

The next few days were spent walking and camping under towering pine trees as we approached the immense Big Thicket forest. The sun was still intense and the tall, dark conifers provided welcome shade. It was not until we had crossed pretty Onalaska Lake and walked through the blink-and-you-miss-it town of Livingston that the rain came in fierce, warm sheets that tore up the loamy earth and knocked fir cones off the trees.

Browny and I were drenched within seconds, long before I had a chance to put the tarpaulin over the saddlebags. We trudged on miserably, my fogged-up glasses turning the road, the woods and sky all into shades of dirty green. I was hoping to reach an Indian reservation a few miles down the road, home to the Alabama-Coushatta tribe. I had heard there was a campground there, although the thought of sticking up my little canvas dome in this sort of deluge did not thrill me.

Help came in the shape of a holy man. He was leaving his church when he spotted Browny and me trudging along: a shabby, waterlogged circus of man and beast.

'Where are you going, bro?' He walked towards me and introduced himself as Pastor Rudy Martinez. At first Rudy's physical presence was intimidating. He was short, bald, amply muscled and swaggered along as if holding a couple of Shet-land ponies under his arms. His neck was thicker than his head by an impressive margin.

Rudy invited me to sleep in his church, a modern, red-brick building perched on an isolated ridge behind us. It was ideal. I staked out my mule underneath an awning at the back of the nave and inspected my new accommodation. In the church hall there were stacks of plastic chairs and fold-up tables. The walls were lined with biblical quotes and paintings of animals; alligators, panthers, bears and fish.

I unpacked the saddlebags and draped my wet clothes over random pieces of furniture while Rudy brewed up some coffee.

While rummaging for milk in the fridge Rudy explained that his congregation were mainly Alabama-Coushatta Indians from the nearby reservation. He pointed to the surrounding animal pictures.

'Animals are of great importance to the Indians,' he said, switching off the kettle. 'Many of my congregation have tribal names like Jimmy Yellowfish or Vanessa Grey Bear. Whatever their individual animal – fish, bear, raccoon – they believe it is somehow linked to their soul.'

'I hope Browny's not linked to my soul, she'd kick it to bits.'

Feeling the need to display a bit more gravitas, I added. 'Surely it's hard to mix tribal animals with teachings from the Bible.'

'Not really,' replied Rudy, sniffing at the milk cartoon. 'There's always plenty of room for Jesus within the reservation. I'm a Pentecostal preacher. I like my sermons to be very lively. We even speak in tongues sometimes. Like me, the Indians like their religion to be very physical.'

'Have you got any Indian blood?'

'No, no. I'm a second generation Mexican. I was working as a prison warden before coming here.' He stopped to hand me a steaming coffee. 'It was quite a violent job as I often had to restrain people. I didn't like what I was turning into, always throwing my weight around.'

'So you decided to become a preacher?' I asked.

'Yes, I've always had a very strong faith. I wanted to use my energy more positively. I love preaching. It fires me up and means I spend more time with my family.'

Rudy truly did have a pent-up, infectious energy. He found it hard to stand still and would constantly pace the room, gesticulating at random objects, fingers fluttering. On the

rare occasions he did stop his foot would continue to tap as if
to the beat of a fierce imaginary rhythm.

'Are you doing this trip for religious reasons, bro?' he
asked hopefully. 'I figured you were on some kind of pil-
grimage.'

'Not really,' I conceded. 'Only in the sense it's a journey
based on trust.'

'Hey, that's the purest faith possible.' Rudy drained his
coffee cup. 'You want to see the reservation tomorrow? I'd be
happy to show you around. Spend the day, there's a youth
conference in the evening, you'd find it interesting.'

'I'd love to.'

'Good, I think everyone will get a kick out of the mule
too.'

'Oh, yes, I'm nothing without my beast.'

'Look at her now,' Rudy vigorously rubbed the condensation from a window and pointed at Browny. She was tucking
into a patch of tall, flowering weeds. 'I do believe, young
brother, she's grazing on holy ground.'

*   *   *

I knew it was still raining before I opened my eyes. I could
hear it pelting down on the church roof. I stretched, flicked
on the kettle and padded through the church hall to feed
Browny. She stood in a shallow puddle looking at me, forlorn
as Eeyore. Minutes later Rudy appeared with a bale of sweet-
smelling meadow hay. Once he had cut free the bale's wire
wraps Browny's ears pricked up and she tore into it. I decided
to leave her the lot. Unlike horses, which have a tendency to
gorge themselves on hay, mules are more sensible about
calling it a day once they're full.

Accompanying Rudy was Angelina, his sixteen-year-old daughter, who had cascading dark hair and a brassy attitude. 'Cute mule,' she said, observing Browny, before adding: 'Are you going to write a book about your trip?'

'I hope so,' I replied.

'Then put me in it,' she demanded with a toss of her head. 'Once people meet me they never forget me. Interview me at the youth conference tonight if you like.'

'Preacher's daughters,' Rudy whispered affectionately. 'Always the wild ones.'

Rudy dropped off Angelina at school before driving me on to the Alabama-Coushatta reservation. As we headed down the rain-splattered road Rudy explained some of the tribal history. He told me Sam Houston had provided this land to the tribe in the 1850s. The Alabama tribe originated from Alabama itself but, like so many Indians, had been forced to move west by the white settlers. The Coushatta were already established in Texas and the two tribes decided to join forces.

Since then the Alabama-Coushatta have made a living from the land, especially forestry, gas reserves and latterly tourism. Although the Alabama-Coushatta retain some tribal ways, including the election of a chief, they have modernised radic-ally and many of the Indian children now attend schools in the nearby towns of Livingston or Woodville. With almost six hundred members they are now the largest and most prosper-ous reservation in Texas.

A huge sign with the words ALABAMA-COUSHATTA beckoned us in. Underneath it was a picture of a woodpecker-like bird with a long tongue, clearly the tribal symbol. We drove into a compound of modern buildings fringed by the odd wooden cabin. Rudy led me on a tour of the tribal facilities. There was a spanking new gym, a basketball arena with digital scoreboards, a well-equipped primary school, a woodland campground, a library, a health centre and an all-singing-all-dancing HQ.

To finish off Rudy ushered me into a freshly painted room where a group of young Indians were being trained how to deal cards and spin roulette wheels.

'What's all that about?' I asked Rudy after we were back in his truck.

'That, bro, is a potential site for a new casino,' he sighed, steering past a lake with some bobbing kayaks on it. 'Probably the worst thing that can happen here. This is a relatively prosperous tribe but they are not doing as well from forestry or gas as they used to. To my mind a casino may help boost money but it will also lead to gambling addiction, alcoholism and laziness.'

'Have lots of other tribes got casinos?'

'Yes, the gambling rules are very lax on reservations,' said Rudy, steering onto the looping track that led to his church. 'But there is a world of difference between the tribes. Don't be fooled by this place, bro.' Rudy spoke with such intensity his hands momentarily leapt off the wheel. He added that many of the reservations further north were dirt poor and that America's two million native Indians mostly have the highest rates of poverty and unemployment in the country. Almost sixty per cent of the Navajos – the biggest tribe – were thought to be alcoholics.

'So this place is a bit of a paradise?' I asked.

'You could say that,' agreed Rudy with a shrug. 'But it still has problems with drinking and unemployment. I'm not slamming the Indian people. The exploitation they suffered in the 1800s was terrible. But they need to get back on their feet now, especially in a place like this. I don't oppose the casino out of spite. I oppose it as a Christian. I want the best for the tribe. Gambling is not the best. God and self-reliance is the best.'

Before long we pulled up beside Browny who was still munching on her hay. Rudy made me a couple of ham sandwiches and shot off again to prepare a blessing for tonight's youth conference. He said he would pick me up at six. I spent the afternoon writing letters. Outside the rain lashed down, dimpling the puddles in Browny's holy pasture.

*   *   *

The youth conference — at least the part of it I witnessed — took place in the reservation's impressive basketball court. It was so new you could smell the varnish on the walls along with the rubbery pong associated with all indoor sports venues. Ranks of teenagers sat on chairs facing a makeshift podium with a microphone in the middle. The teenagers were not only Alabama-Coushatta members but from visiting reservations as far afield as north Texas and Mississippi.

Rudy read his blessing and then all was quiet as the main speaker, Chance Rush, was called on to the stage. Chance looked young, probably mid twenties. He had a dark, rough-hewn face and a long ponytail that fanned out like a palmetto. Unlike many of the Native Americans in the audience with their neat hairstyles and jazzy clothes, Chance did have a distinctive tribal look about him.

'My name is Chance Rush,' he shouted. 'My grandfather was called Chance Charge an Enemy, but the white man made him change it to Rush. So now I am Chance Rush. But in my heart I am always Chance Charge an Enemy.'

He was already getting a rapturous response from the audience, with much cheering and whooping. Being the only white face in the room I quite irrationally began to feel a little uncomfortable.

'What I want to know is why our people suffer from seventy per cent poverty?' Huge cheers. 'I want to know why we are resorting to building casinos? Why are our people not getting a good education? Why are so many of our people alcoholics? Why?' More clapping. 'I'll tell you why. Because we are always making excuses, can't do this, can't do that. Too many of us hang about in the reservations rather than going to college.

'This is not the way. Our forefathers were warriors, hunters. We are not warriors like them. We have to be different warriors, modern-day warriors, making our mark in fresh ways.

'I used to make excuses about my life. The fact I was poor, or my father drank too much. But when I stopped, that's when I made something of myself. I got to college, built up a business and now try to inspire others. I see some of you out there ignoring me but others will take what I say on board. Won't you?' More howls of adulation and agreement.

'I hear there's a crazy white guy in the crowd tonight, who's walking through our country with a mule.' I shrank into my chair, thinking I would come in for a fanfare of subdued boos. 'Stand up please, the mule man.' Oh bugger it, here goes. Angelina and Rudy pushed me up. I stood smiling nervously, looking about as comfortable as Prince Charles at an Eminem concert.

'This man is following a dream, everyone. An unusual dream, sure, but he's willing to try to walk across our country. I'm not saying you should all do the same but you should all have a dream. Please give him a big hand of applause.' At this stage a young girl in a headdress came over and presented me with a basket made from pine needles. I sat down, surprised, blushing and incredibly touched. Chance carried on for another half an hour, his rhetoric never flagging, the boisterous crowd egging him on.

After he finished all the chairs were cleared away for a disco. Soon Michael Jackson and Kylie Minogue were blasting out. Rudy begrudgingly told Angelina she could dance. 'None of those freaky, show off convulsions, OK,' he warned her. 'Preacher's daughters shouldn't behave like that.' Angelina tut-tutted and swirled her eyes in defiance. I danced with her for a while. She began very demurely before the freaky convulsions kicked in. At this stage I called it quits, being the oldest on the dance floor by at least a decade.

I peeled away and chatted to a group of parents and grandparents. One of the group, Yoma, was a member of Rudy's church. She was a bespectacled, neatly dressed lady in her early forties with a soft voice and a strong knowledge of Indian culture. She pointed at the pine needle basket I had been given which had the tribal woodpecker symbol on it.

'That bird is split into two halves,' she explained to me. 'One for the Alabama and one for the Coushatta. It has four arrows sticking out of it to represent the four winds and the four directions, north, south, east and west.' She pointed at the beak. 'That long tongue is believed to be the ponytail of a warrior the bird has swallowed. The fact one of our people has been swallowed reminds us to keep our humility.'

'It looks a bit like an ornithological yin and yang sign,' I commented. 'Everything is so symmetrical.'

'Oh, yes, Indian people like that sort of harmony,' agreed Yoma, drawing a circle in the air with her index finger. She told me her tribe once believed the world moved in circles. The moon, the sun and the stars were all circles and all spun in circles. Indian tepees, were circular, and even life itself was a circle, with many similarities between a newborn baby and a man on the verge of death. Indian people once moved with the seasons, she continued, but now they all stayed in one place. She herself had always lived in the same place.

'Is it better on the move?' I asked.

'Yes, I think it is,' admitted Yoma, sipping on a plastic cup of orange juice. She thought reservation life had all but destroyed Indian tribal culture. Although the Alabama-Coushatta people had been comparatively well treated, other tribes had been herded west like buffalo and corralled where the white man wanted them. Chiefs like Geronimo fought on, but even brave and elusive warriors like him were so vastly outnumbered they were soon forced to surrender.

'Indian culture was in real jeopardy as early as the 1860s,' stressed Yoma, 'many tribes were being forced to live by a different set of rules. Rules they didn't understand.'

'The 1860s was the Civil War time,' I commented. 'Did the Indians fight?'

'Indians fought on both sides, but very few,' she replied. 'Some even wanted to form their own regiments but were told it was a white man's war.'

Yoma pointed out the most famous Civil War Indian was Ely Parker, a Seneca chief, who was General Grant's military secretary. Then there was the Cherokee, Stand Watie, the last Confederate general to capitulate, long after Lee's army had given up the fight. Ironically it was only after the surrender at Appomattox that it really got bad for the Indians, Yoma told me. The most bloodthirsty of the Civil War generals were still so battle hungry they needed to carry on fighting; but rather than attack fellow white men, they focused on the Indian tribes.

'General Custer and General Philip Sheridan,' Yoma spat out the names like sour fruit. 'Sheridan was the one who said: "The only good Indian is a dead Indian." Men like that treated our people like sport. The Alabama-Coushatta were lucky, still are, but other tribes in the Great Plains were completely ruined.

'There is much misunderstanding of that time,' insisted Yoma, shaking her head. 'Indians are depicted in the Westerns as savages who fought against each other as much as the white man. Of course, some Indians were like that, but most were simply innocent people who lived off the land.

'Custer's Last Stand at Little Bighorn is a classic example.' Yoma flicked her wrist dismissively. 'Today it is seen as a massacre. Pah! It wasn't a massacre. Custer was an arrogant fool – came last in his class at West Point. He went to Montana in 1876 to wipe out the Sioux and the Cheyennes. He turned up with two hundred and fifty men dressed in blue coats and all armed to the teeth.' She stopped and knitted her eyebrows. 'What did he expect the Indians to do, throw him a party? The Indians killed Custer and all his men but it was a fair battle, not a massacre. At Wounded Knee fourteen years later, over two hundred Indian men, women and children were all killed in cold blood. Now that was a massacre. All because they had been dancing, ghost dancing, calling on the spirits of their ancestors.'

Yoma finished her diatribe, a faraway look in her eye. After a long pause, she teasingly asked me: 'Did this ancestor of yours chase us after the war too?'

'Oh, no, he went out to Sudan,' I replied. 'Then ended up as Governor of Malta. Colonel Arthur's career after America was respectable but quite dull. I don't think he was like

Sheridan or Custer, witnessing Gettysburg was enough for him.'

'What about you?' asked Yoma, taking another swig of orange from her cup. 'You obviously like to be on the move.'

'Yes, I suppose so.'

'That's OK. Indian people believe that movement is itself a form of property. It's only now we are in these reservations that we are all a bit lost.'

'It's like Don Quixote,' I said, changing tack. 'A knight with all these romantic quests to pursue. When he's travelling he's half crazy but very fulfilled. When he arrives home as an old man, he gains his sanity but loses his will to live. It's like the reality has killed the dream.'

'For the Indians the dream was always the reality, the two are as one.' Yoma smiled and crushed her plastic cup in her hand. 'The white man only dreams at night, the red man dreams all his life.'

*   *   *

Sunlight filtered through Rudy's office window. No sound of rain. It was time to get going again. As it was a Sunday I wanted to pack up Browny and head off before the congregation turned up. It didn't work out that way. Rudy appeared with a bag full of breakfast burritos and soon after his wife Esther popped in accompanied by Angelina, looking effervescent despite last night's freaky writhings on the dance floor. We all stood outside in the sunshine, munching, the smell of chorizo and egg wafting up from our burritos. Browny watched us with her ears pricked forward.

'I know you want to leave before the service, Tom,' said Rudy. 'But I'd really like some of the Indians to see the mule.'

'Yes, yes,' agreed Angelina. 'We can bless Browny too.'

I wasn't sure how Browny would feel about being blessed but after all Rudy's kindness it was the least I could do. To kill time until the service started at 9 a.m. I scrubbed clean the saddlebags, still filthy after Browny's escape bid in Huntsville.

Before long a group of over fifty members of the Alabama-Coushatta had converged around my restless mule. There was also a small non-Indian posse from the nearby town of Livingston. I positioned Browny's packsaddle and slung her bags on each side.

'Jesus never had no mule,' blurted out a lady in a yellow hat.

'No. Mules don't feature much in any religion.'

'Donkeys do, though,' replied the lady.

'Yes,' I agreed, 'and the Prophet Mohammed rode to heaven on a horse.'

Browny glared at me as if to say, 'Bully for the Prophet Mohammed, purgatory is about my limit, cowboy.'

The congregation now surrounded us. Pastor Rudy approached me and put a hand on my shoulder. Several other members touched my back and the top of my head. I held Browny tight. She was being amazingly stoic considering half the Pentecostal throng were laying their palms on her saddlebags. Oh well, Rudy had warned me he liked his religion physical.

'Please don't touch her face,' I whispered. 'Especially her ears.'

Rudy, who had been uncharacteristically silent, suddenly burst into prayer. 'Dear sweet JESUS! Dear, dear, sweet JESUS!' His flock began to moan and chant Jesus, Jesus, JESUS! I had been keeping my eyes shut in prayer but sneaked a quick look at Browny. Her eyes had sprung wide open in surprise, as if an over-zealous hussar had just rammed his spurs into her ribs. She remained anchored to the spot.

'Lord, bless this man, this pilgrim on his journey.' By now Rudy was whipping himself into a spiritual ferment. 'Lord, bless this mule, this brown mule. Bless these two pilgrims.' In the background was a persistent chorus of Jesus, Jesus enlivened with the occasional JESUS! as if one of the flock had received a nasty shock.

'Bless them, Lord, sweet Jesus, that they make it through this, this, this MISSION! In the name of JESUS! Amen.' Everyone shouted amen several times. Browny nickered with a combination of incredulity and anxiety, a 'what the hell next, boss' look on her face. I pulled her free from the crowd. After hugging Pastor Rudy, Esther and Angelina (who reminded me of her imminent fame), I trudged off down the church path.

'Wait, sir, please wait,' a whey-faced man with a rook's nest of tawny hair sprinted towards me. 'Please take this.'

He handed me a filthy ten dollar bill. 'Take it,' he said urgently, his cornflower blue eyes dancing with excitement. 'Take it for your journey.' He smiled revealing cracked, soiled teeth. He had a tattoo on his neck and several on his forearm. Rudy had told me about him. He was married to an Indian girl and they were both battling with alcohol. They had only recently joined the church.

'That's so kind of you,' I told him. 'But I don't take money from anybody. It wouldn't be right. I accept hospitality, if people put me up for the night, feed me, that sort of thing. But I won't take hard cash.' This was not the first time I had been offered a stranger's money on the journey. It was often by people like this man, people with nothing. They thought

I was homeless, worse off than them and were prepared to give their last nickels and dimes to me. It was as if by helping me they felt they were helping themselves.

The man held out his hand. 'Take it, sir, please, take it,' he insisted, tears welling in his eyes. 'You have to take it.' I was deeply moved by his kindness but backed away.

At this stage Rudy intervened. 'Its OK,' he whispered, putting an arm around the dishevelled Samaritan. 'Tom has enough money, you keep it for yourself, your wife, your baby.'

'Your kindness means more than the money itself,' I told the man lamely. He clenched the note in his fist and stormed back to the church.

'It's OK, brother, he just wanted to help,' Rudy reassured me. 'We're like that down here.' He grabbed my shoulder in an affectionate but vice-like lock. 'I know you're not that religious but we'll keep praying for you. And your mule.'

'Thanks, we'd like that,' I replied, and I meant it.

*   *   *

On our way to the Louisiana border Browny and I spent a night camping in the Martin Dies national park. Although an idyllic setting it was not an especially happy experience. The BEWARE OF ALLIGATORS sign at the entrance got things off to a bad start. Alligators are fine if your name is Johnny Wiessmuller: not if you are a faint-hearted muleteer with a blunt Swiss Army knife. But this was nothing compared with the storm that whipped up soon after dark sending a cascade of magnolia cones and black walnuts raining down on my little tent. To cap it all a park ranger appeared well after midnight and shone a torch through my tent flap. I woke up with a start, brandishing my knife.

Left: Lt Colonel Arthur James Lyon Fremantle: 'a scrawny man, toothy, with a pipelike neck and a monstrous Adam's apple.'

Below: 'The Swiss say mules have odd secret ways, strange fancies, and lurking vice.' This clearly says more about the Swiss than Browny.

The welcoming party at Progresso. From left to right: Loncito, Kevin, Ariel, Brandie, Justin, Fino.

On the road in Texas (the author is the one with the bandanna). Browny has just received new shoes. By the end of the trip she had worn out seven sets – the Imelda Marcos of the equine world.

Browny catching up on the latest gossip: on the way to New York horses, cows, goats and even buffalo charged over to greet her.

Browny ate all types of roadside vegetation; but M&Ms were her absolute favourite.

Mules pay scant attention to road signs.

Sam Houston's statue near Huntsville, Texas.

Pastor Rudy Martinez (far left) and family. Angelina is on the far right.

With Vanessa, a youth leader, at the Alabama-Coushatta Indian Reservation.

Browny liked nothing better than a vigorous roll at the end of a long day, followed by a shower.

Chin and his wife at the Redwood Motel in Leesville, Louisiana.

Soon to be harvested cotton, Louisiana.

'No livestock are allowed in this park,' shouted the torch-wielding shadow, battling to be heard against the wind. 'Please remove your livestock.' *Livestock?* I thought. I have one geriatric mule, not a herd of Longhorn steers.

Considering the wind was howling and I was camping alone on a carpet of pine needles in the middle of a wilderness, I felt the man was being more than a little pedantic. Why couldn't he wait until morning, for heaven's sake? I shouted into the wind about my walk and mentioned that I had got permission to camp here from another ranger earlier in the evening, all of which was true. I also promised I would clear up any mule dung. As we spoke the wind continued to buffet the canvas, threatening to fill out my tent like a spinnaker.

'All right then,' bellowed the shadowy ranger. 'But all livestock out of here first thing.'

The next day Browny and I walked through the community of Jasper. People had been talking about Jasper for the last week. It was a fairly nondescript, rundown sort of town, but in 1998 it had made headlines across the world after the lynching of a young black man by a couple of violent racists. James Byrd, Jr, had been beaten up then chained to the back of a truck before being dragged along a country road at speed. The hateful nature of the murder outraged the community and the world.

The town park had been named in James Byrd's honour. While walking past there I struck up a conversation with Wayne, a friendly black man who worked at a local liquor store. He had tight-fitting dreadlocks and gold-capped teeth.

'The main two murderers were white supremacists from the Houston area,' Wayne explained, as we walked through town. 'They both got the death penalty. One Jasper man was with them too, but he was only an onlooker. He just got a life sentence. It was pretty horrible, all the stir it caused, especially for the Byrd family.'

'Do you think it could happen again?'

'I doubt it,' he mused, spitting out an oyster of green tobacco into the dust. 'It was a very isolated case. Of course there are still too many rednecks and racists lurking about, but not the sort who would lynch someone. The KKK is largely a spent force now.

'People associate this area with racism but other areas are just as bad,' he spat out some more tobacco. 'What about those Rodney King riots in Los Angeles? Stuff is brewing all over the place. It was the bad ass nature of the crime here that caused such upset. Jasper is a nice little place on the whole, but now it's going to be remembered for that lynching, the same way Waco is remembered for that crazy cult.'

'Have you experienced any racism here?'

'Nothing directly,' Wayne replied as he chewed. 'But let me tell you something, I wouldn't walk through Texas with no mule. Don't get me wrong, I like what you are doing. It's real interesting. It's OK for a clean-cut white boy like you, but not so OK for a black man like me. Maybe one day, but not yet.'

I would have liked to talk more, but Wayne had to get to work. He slapped me on the shoulder. 'Watch your back out there, my man,' he warned. 'America can be a dangerous place whatever your colour.'

*   *   *

Two days later Browny and I finally marched over the Louisiana border. We had already clocked up twelve miles that morning, having camped our final night in Texas at a local farmstead.

I was aiming to reach the town of Leesville, meaning a thirty-mile day – the first time Browny and I had tried this. Twenty-seven miles was our record to date. But Browny was champing at the bit, the sun was shining, the crickets chirping and the sky a pure, fresh, cloudless blue. To add to all the glory I saw a turtle cavorting beneath us as we crossed over the Sabine river; for no other reason than its sheer spontaneous beauty I took this as a sign of good luck. Oh, yes, I thought, today my mule and I are unstoppable.

Much as I had enjoyed Texas I liked the fact I was in a new state. I had finally made it through the immense Lone Star, all six hundred miles of it. People still waved and tooted their horns as if in Texas, the pine trees were still as tall as Texas, the people sounded the same too, but I knew I had crossed that precious line and completed another thumbnail of map.

But the one big difference with Texas was that I was no longer hot on Colonel Arthur's trail.

After Houston my ancestor had caught a stagecoach and crossed into Louisiana a hundred miles further north of Leesville than me. He then plied on to Monroe, near to the Arkansas border. It would have meant a huge detour with the mule. However, our paths would soon cross with Arthur again in the historic town of Natchez on the banks of the Mississippi.

Arthur's journey to Monroe does not make for a compelling chapter in his diary. He travels through a landscape 'deserted except by women and very old men . . . the land not fertile, but the timber is fine.' The most interesting part is when he strikes up a conversation about 'the peculiar institution' of slavery in his stagecoach.

Colonel Arthur mentions that his fellow passengers frowned on slavery but considered it a necessary evil to sustain the South's labour intensive cotton harvest. He claims that most Southerners only defended it so fiercely due to the 'meddling, coercive conduct of the detested and despised abolitionists'.

Although Arthur says his companions admit there are many instances of cruelty to slaves he goes on to write: 'But they say a man who is known to ill-treat his Negroes is hated by all the rest of the community. They declare that Yankees make the worst masters when they settle in the South.'

On arrival in Monroe he comes across a group of 'fifty Yankee deserters' who when asked their reason for leaving their regiment reply: 'We enlisted to fight for the Union, and not to liberate slaves.'

Arthur points out that many Northerners were blatantly hostile or at least ambivalent towards liberating slaves. This was perfectly true. He is also right to point out many Southerners looked after their slaves with a degree of compassion. What he is never prepared to do, however, is mention that some Southerners treated their slaves horribly too. Although he keeps saying how distasteful slavery is to an Englishman, he never really backs this up. Rather than conceding that the Union holds the moral high ground over the issue (Lincoln's Emancipation Proclamation had just been issued) he makes it sound as if the Yankees are the only true culprits. Although clearly an observant and at times sensitive man, Arthur continues to accept lock, stock and barrel whatever the Southerners fire at him. Worst of all, he does not once try to see things from a slave's perspective.

But I am perhaps being hard on Colonel Arthur, who was writing his diary without the hindsight of history. He was a twenty-eight-year-old soldier more out for adventure than on a crusade for the truth. What he writes about best are battles, soldiers and everyday observances, rather than about the landscape, the culture or the politics. He was certainly a far tougher, more practical man than I, able to cover huge distances and undergo any hardship. Throughout his three-and-half month marathon he shows few signs of flagging, and remains persistently chipper. The same could not be said for his wimp of a great great cousin.

*   *   *

Colonel Arthur would have been truly ashamed of me as I trudged the last two miles into Leesville. Trying to attempt thirty miles had been a catastrophic error of judgement. Despite being buoyant and optimistic for the first twenty-five miles, I was now suffering from shin cramps. Even more worrying, Browny was also on her last legs. Her nose was bleeding sporadically and her head hung very low: both blatant symptoms of what Justin called 'beast burn out'.

The good news was that Leesville was in sight. On the map it looked like a little place and I was confident we could pinpoint somewhere to camp. It was already dark. Above us some unfamiliar stars spun around a milk-blue slice of moon.

As we trudged on it concerned me that there was absolutely nobody around. I had passed the usual rash of red brick or corrugated churches, a library, some shops. All was quiet bar Browny's clopping and the faint creak of her saddle straps. We were now in the heart of the town and still not a squeak. I finally saw somebody locking up a shop ahead of us and quickened my pace to reach him. Browny sensed my urgency and fell in line. 'Good Brown girl, good girl,' I encouraged her as if she was a child.

'Sir, sir,' after seven weeks in Texas I had picked up this formality. 'Sir, do you know somewhere we can camp for the night?'

The man before us had a big, jowly face and hair the colour of ashes. Considering he had just been accosted by a desperate, bobble-hatted man with a limping mule in a dark, deserted street he stayed remarkably composed. After I explained what we were up to he shook his head slowly, as if watching a tennis rally made up exclusively of high, very slow lobs.

'You know what,' he said dreamily. 'I can't think of anywhere, no, nowhere at all.' *Can't think of anywhere!* I had a huge urge to vigorously shake his jowls.

'All I need is a stretch of grass and somewhere to get water,' I stated as patiently as possible. 'You are a local, aren't you?' The man looked at me blankly.

'This is the centre of Leesville, isn't it?' I asked softly, a slight whimper now evident in my voice.

'Well, it was,' murmured the man, 'but it's pretty much dried up these days. The centre is on the outskirts where the malls are. Another couple of miles down that way.' He pointed towards a distant highway full of fast-food restaurants, garages and motels all heralded with bright signs in primary colours. No, no, *no*! I told myself.

'There is one place with a bit of grass,' he suddenly blurted. 'It's called The Redwood Motel, two or three miles from here. Cheapest in town, no others will let you in. You'll have to go down a busy road though.'

'I can't stay in a motel with a mule,' I said petulantly, my eyes watering in frustration. 'God, we've already walked thirty miles today. Thirty bloody miles.'

'Well, that's all I can think of,' he replied with a look of growing anxiety. He clearly wanted to terminate the conversation right now. 'Good luck.' He retreated, firing nervous glances before ducking around a corner.

This is bad, very bad, I told myself. I was even tempted to doss down in a churchyard but couldn't face unloading Browny and then possibly being told to move on. I also needed somewhere I could find water and pasture. Sod it, I decided, let's try The Redwood.

We struck out down the busiest street Browny and I had yet confronted. There was no pavement so I walked across the lawns of local businesses and the forecourts of garages. It was Friday night, and boozed-up youths made braying noises as they sped past. Somebody threw an empty beer can at me but other than a brief sneer I was too exhausted to respond. Browny was close to collapse. I stopped on a paltry stretch of grass near a Kentucky Fried Chicken and fetched her some water. When I got back to her, she had slumped down. This was the first time I had seen her do this all trip: even at night she always slept on her feet.

Browny drank the water. I was happy to see her nose had stopped bleeding. I took the packs off her and collapsed down beside her. Families chewing on drumsticks and burgers watched us in fascination. This was horrible. Why was this the centre of Leesville? I asked myself. Why was the pretty old part of town deserted and everyone hovering around these soulless glasshouses, these identical rashes of neon, these fast-food shrines honouring only the gods of petroleum and sloth.

Oh, in heaven's name, Fremantle, snap out of it. Focus on your own ludicrous mission and let's get this poor beast some pasture. As Dan Ackroyd in Blues Brothers mode might suggest in a situation like this: 'It's a mile to The Redwood, we've got a half tank of oats, three mouldy carrots, it's dark and I'm wearing a bobble hat. Hit it.'

I levered up Browny and put the bags back on her. She would not stand. I couldn't blame her. I teased her, prodded her gently. 'Hey Browny, hey Brown Girl.' People say mules are stubborn. Mules aren't stubborn. Ketchup bottle tops are stubborn, children without pocket money are stubborn, King Lear is stubborn. Browny, however, at this moment in time is not stubborn. She is utterly unbudgeable. After over ten minutes of increasingly frenzied tactics, whispering, slapping, cooing, bellowing, she is still tent-pegged into the ground. Just as I am about to give up and burst into tears she launches off, obedient as a lamb. I swear that mule knows me too well. She's got my number, as the veteran skinners say, and can call it any time she wants.

We once again weaved the gauntlet of fast-food forecourts and car showrooms, while serenaded by the howls of passing revellers. Finally we reached our Mecca. The Redwood Motel. It did not look very hopeful. All that was on offer was a concrete car park with no cars and more importantly, no grass. The NO PETS sign above reception wasn't a source of unbridled encouragement either. I was in a very fragile state, somewhere between bursting into hysterical sobs or crazed Vincent Price-like laughter. The man behind the counter was Asian. He had a small, angular face with that serene and immensely rare look of someone who is utterly at peace with the world. It was not to last.

'You want a room?' he asked pleasantly.

'Well, er, I have a mule.' I pointed out of the window to Browny who was tied to a railing and tucking into a bed of marigolds.

My Oriental friend did a double-take of such magnitude he knocked over the reception bell.

'What is that?'

'It's a mule.'

I explained what I was doing and the man, whose name I had now discovered was Chin, came outside to inspect Browny.

'Can I touch her?' he asked, laughing.

'Of course.'

Chin moved towards her with outstretched fingers, a bit like a man testing an electric fence. Browny sensed his fear, and got a little jumpy herself, backing off. I felt like a salesman who had just lost his deal. *Bitchy mule, sorry amigo, no room in the inn*. But Chin was captivated by Browny despite her standoffish behaviour. He led me through a back gate at the side of the motel and there before me was a vision to thrill Kublai Khan. It was enough to make a man weep. Well, enough to make me weep anyway. Even Colonel Arthur's granite upper lip might have quavered a little after a day like this.

A sward of lush grass studded with fruit trees and wild bamboo stretched out towards a thick, very English-looking hedgerow. There were cages of wild birds: blue and yellow lovebirds, squawking parrots and a couple of macaws. The cages were large enough for the birds to fly. A wind chime tingled in the warm breeze. It was hard to believe just across the road from this was a modern-day heart of darkness. Mr Kurtz and friends gnawing on a Colonel Sanders and Ronald McDonald combo.

Chin told me it would be fine for Browny to graze here for the night and insisted I take a room at a discount rate. I practically kissed him. Together we unloaded Browny. Chin's wife, a talkative, dark-haired lady with a permanent smile, brought out some iced tea. I fed Browny handfuls of oats. Chin supplemented this with apples and sugar lumps while I lugged the saddlebags into my room.

Room 3 was the height of luxury. A television with a zapper. Hurrah! An enormous clean-sheeted bed with *two* pillows. Hurrah! And perhaps best of all, a cummerbund of paper stretched over my lavatory seat, proudly announcing IN THE INTEREST OF HYGIENE, as if my butt was the first ever to be parked on it. And there I was thinking I'd had a hard day: no Civil War soldier received such blatant molly-coddling. Thanking all my lucky stars I went back outside. Chin was sitting on a bench beneath his aviary of parrots. He was watching Browny.

I sat next to him and soon his wife bought me out another cup of tea. Chin told me he was from Taiwan and had come to Leesville twenty years ago to run the motel. His wife was from mainland China. She had been born at the outbreak of Mao's Cultural Revolution during which her parents were brutally separated. He said his wife's family were all happy when she moved to America, and married Chin. They were excited that she could start a new life, have a go at the American dream.

'I'm proud to be an American,' Chin told me. 'But this garden is my little piece of home.'

He saw me watching his birds. 'Those little silver parrots are called African Greys. Very rare. And that one,' he pointed at an enormous black bird cracking a pecan nut with its beak, 'that can live up to a hundred years, he'll outdo me. Those little lovebirds are my favourite; they stay devoted to one another all their lives. Sing sweeter than any other birds.'

Chin whistled at a white parrot flapping in the nearest cage. It was hanging upside down, its toes throttling the thin bars. 'They are beautiful aren't they, all these birds. They are my snow from the moon.'

'Snow from the what?' I asked.

'Snow from the moon,' Chin replied softly. 'It's an expression my father used when I was growing up. Snow from the moon is something that sounds impossible, unachievable. You've never seen snow from the moon, right?'

'No.'

'But there are some things that mean so much to us that they can become snow from the moon. For me sitting here with my wife, one of my children on my knee, listening to the lovebirds, it's magic. I've worked so hard for it. It's my snow from the moon.'

'Look at you tonight,' he said abruptly. 'You looked so tired and sad and lonely. Now you are sitting here with me drinking tea. Maybe that's the snow from the moon for someone like you.'

Chin took my empty teacup and headed in to join his wife. He told me to stay in the garden longer if I wanted. I walked over to Browny and watched her drinking from her bucket. I thought back to a couple of hours ago when her nose had been bleeding, her legs buckling, my shins smarting, fear in my guts, no idea how to dig us out of it. I was as low as I could have sunk, a roadside wretch. But perhaps it is only when things go spectacularly wrong for us, so wrong we may as well howl at the night, that we can see clearly. Only once outward calamity has been shifted to a sublime, soul-whooping contentment, perhaps it is only then Chin's strange snow reveals itself.

I lay back on a deckchair in the garden. It was late now and the traffic had eased up. After our intense urban experience today it was good to be in this beautiful oasis. I was so at ease here, safe, calm, a fresh breeze on my face. It was as if I could almost sense clouds moving through the night, hear the bamboo breathing, the fruit sweat and the heartbeats of the tiny birds.

I became transfixed by the half moon framed in its aureole of blue light. I watched it for a while and dozed off, a head full of dreams. When I woke Browny was grazing near by, her face lit up in the moonshine.

CHAPTER 10

Mississippi Mules

Browny and I were both shattered and, encouraged by Chin, I decided to stay on for a day at The Redwood. While slobbing in the decadent confines of Room 3 I finished reading Robert Louis Stevenson's *Travels with a Donkey* and Dervla Murphy's *Eight Feet in the Andes*. My treatment of Browny over the last twenty-four hours had been cavalier, to say the least, and I wanted to see if these other travellers had abused their beasts of burden too. I had to salvage my conscience somehow.

I was not to be disappointed. Within pages of Stevenson's account he was walloping his little donkey, Modestine, with savage abandon. It soon became apparent that in comparison to this rangy, devil-may-care Scot, I had behaved as sweetly as a fairytale shepherdess towards my beast.

Stevenson's book charts his twelve-day walk through the wild Cévennes region in the south of France. The restless adventurer was twenty-eight years old and almost broke at the time of his 1879 jaunt. He was also suffering from a lung disease and constantly having to examine his handkerchief for spots of blood. It was a condition that would plague him until his early death in Samoa at the age of forty-four. But Stevenson was a high Romantic, always determined to squeeze the most out of his travels, and this journey was no exception.

He also clearly wanted to squeeze the most out of his hapless donkey. Initially he treated Modestine with a degree of respect but, after some advice from a 'tall peasant . . . of snuffy countenance', who laughed at Stevenson's overly tender attitude towards his beast, the young writer got tough. To be fair, before laying in with his cane, Stevenson tries verbally urging on Modestine. 'Proot, proot!' he encourages her, using the cry of other local donkey-drivers.

Before long 'Proot, proot' seemed to have lost its virtue. As Stevenson wrote: 'I prooted like a lion, I prooted mellifluously like a sucking-dove; but Modestine would be neither softened nor intimidated . . . nothing but a blow would move her.' And, *mon dieu*, did those blows come fast and thick. As the book develops, the author uses such lines as: 'I had now an arm free to thrash Modestine, and cruelly I chastised her.' 'I promise you, the stick was not idle.' 'I . . . struck the sinner twice across the face,' and perhaps most sinister of all: 'there was not another sound in the neighbourhood but that of my unwearying bastinado.'

Stevenson was at times riddled with guilt over his brutality and when he finally parts company with the well-pummelled Modestine, admits, in a rare burst of sentimentality, to shedding tears.

Dervla Murphy treated her mule, Juana, with greater charity as she navigated her 1,300-mile path through the Peruvian Andes in the early 1980s. Her good-natured beast did, however, have to lug much more than Modestine. Not only did Juana carry the saddlebags but balanced Murphy's plucky nine-year-old daughter, Rachel, on her back. The mother and daughter team clearly doted on their nimble-hooved friend and there is no evidence of any thrashing or even prooting.

However, the intrepid duo did cover some remote and perilous terrain. At times this exhausted their mule, especially when the grazing was poor or fodder unobtainable. By far and away the most heart-stopping moment occurred when Juana nearly toppled over a cliff face.

'We watched Juana falling . . . and rolling over and over and over – faster and faster – with no hope of being able to check herself on such a gradient,' writes Murphy. 'Then, miraculously, she came up against the only obstacle on that whole vast slope – a young eucalyptus tree . . . It seemed impossible that she could have escaped serious injury and I found myself praying for a fatal neck-break rather than a smashed leg.'

It turned out Juana was fine, and was soon up and tucking into the surrounding maize crop. Days after this near catastrophe the travellers arrive in the mountain town of Cuzco, their final destination, where Juana is driven off to a local ranch. Murphy even ends up part-dedicating the book to her mule.

These escapades of Stevenson and Murphy made me realise my treatment of Browny, although harsh, was not exceptional. But of all the animal-bonding books in my saddlebags my favourite remained John Steinbeck's *Travels with Charley*. Charley was Steinbeck's elegant French poodle and proved an unexpectedly potent muse for the grouchy Nobel Prize winner. Unlike the youthful Stevenson and the indefatigable Murphy, Steinbeck was in the twilight of his career. At fifty-eight years old, his health already on the wane, he was rather like Don Quixote, off on one last noble quest to put the world to rights. Charley was his Sancho Panza.

To my mind Charley brings out a terrific humour in Steinbeck's writing, not something always evident in his backlog of fine but mostly serious novels. In the introduction to *Travels with Charley* there is an amusing episode between Steinbeck and his third wife, Elaine. Elaine tells her husband before he leaves: 'If you get into any kind of trouble, Charley can go get help.' Steinbeck looked at her sternly and said, 'Elaine, Charley isn't Lassie.'

Charley isn't Lassie, but he does provide (as Browny had with me) a terrific way to break down barriers and meet strangers. The exotic hound is Steinbeck's loyal companion who guards him and helps him stave off loneliness. One of the strongest passages is during a visit to a boozy vet in California after Charley has become seriously sick.

'For Charley is not a human; he's a dog,' writes Steinbeck, 'and he likes it that way. He feels that he is a first-rate dog and has no wish to be a second-rate human. When the alcoholic vet touched him with his unsteady, inept hand, I saw the look of veiled contempt in Charley's eyes.'

After seeing another, more capable vet, Charley made a sterling recovery and stayed with Steinbeck through Texas, Louisiana and the long, non-stop haul back home to New York. They were on the road for a total of four months.

Having read these books back to back I noted certain parallels, other than the obvious animal themes. Stevenson, Murphy and Steinbeck, although radically different as writers, had similar characteristics as travellers. They were clearly very capable of looking after themselves but all loved to throw caution to the wind.

Stevenson perhaps puts it best when he writes: 'For my part, I travel not to go anywhere, but to go. I travel for travel's sake. The great affair is to move; to feel the needs and hitches of our life more nearly; to come down off this feather-bed of civilisation, and find the globe granite underfoot and strewn with cutting flints.'

But the most glaring link between these books is their hopeless addiction to travel, its hardship, its triumphs, its dangers and glorious unpredictability. They are all prisoners of the road. As Steinbeck observes in the opening paragraph of *Travels with Charley*: 'once a bum always a bum.' Even now he was nudging sixty, he conceded that maturity had done nothing to tame his inner gypsy. Steinbeck travelled much of his working life, as did Stevenson and the last I heard of Murphy, now in her early seventies, she was bicycling through Siberia.

Whether mule, donkey or dog, it now became very obvious why each of the three writers travelled with an animal: none of them wanted to travel with other people. They wanted to be alone, fight their own battles; find the gold at the end of their own rainbows. As for the animals, they provide company and a sense of responsibility, but none of them would compromise their boss's journey in the way a fellow human might. Sure, Murphy is travelling with her daughter, but she makes it clear this will be the last time. Why? Because soon Rachel will be old enough to travel with her own friends, make her own decisions. On this trip, Murphy is the one who calls the shots.

All the authors clearly loved their beasts, albeit in very different ways, but this does not stop Stevenson relentlessly thrashing Modestine, Murphy endangering Juana on a cliff face and Steinbeck kennelling Charley when the situation requires it. None of the animals answers back, suggests alternative routes, tells their owners they are being foolish or rash.

It dawned on me I was no different. Despite thoroughly enjoying friends joining me for random stretches, I mostly liked to travel alone, to take my own chances. I respected Browny and treated her as a valued partner but I had already shown I was quite prepared to drive her until her legs buckled and her nose bled. Browny was my Charley, my Juana, my Modestine, whether she liked it or not. I could only hope that she did.

Right now, rolling in Chin's garden, watched by a cage of rare and vibrantly feathered parrots, she looked as happy as I'd seen her all journey. Good, I thought, she deserves this. But just remember, Brown Girl, we've still got two thousand miles to walk. Tomorrow it's back on with the packsaddle and off we go again: the Mississippi awaits us.

*   *   *

For the Louisiana leg I sacrificed my lone star status for a while and joined forces with James Fry, my oldest friend. I was a little worried about James walking alongside me. To say he was in peak physical condition would be stretching the truth and shrinking his waistline in equal measures. As James lumbered out of his yellow cab to greet me on the road out of Leesville, it was clear his promised cabbage-only diet had yet to reap rewards. Either that or he'd eaten one hell of a lot of cabbages. He was huge.

However, I was impressed in other ways. James, a champion smoker, had assured me several weeks ago he had kicked the habit. For a man who had been dragging on roll-ups since the age of sixteen, this was quite something. Usually an evening down the pub with James inflicted lung damage akin to being stuck in a lift with Keith Richards, Marlene Dietriech and Puff the Magic Dragon. The fact he had stubbed out his last Rizla, all for the sake of a week's mule skinning, impressed me greatly. The fact he had gained three stone in the process was just one of those things.

James's other big achievement had been to find me. His only directions were that I was somewhere near Leesville. On arrival in Alexandria, the Louisiana city he had flown in to, he flagged down a cab and delivered instructions on the lines of: 'Drive west, kind sir, in search of a brown mule.' In my last email to James, sent from The Redwood, I had told him that if I needed to piss in the woods at any stage, I would tie Browny to a signpost so she was visible from the road, even if I wasn't. The plan worked a treat and now James stood before me, all sixteen stone of him.

James's cab driver, a small, hunched man with a gap tooth smile, watched Browny graze on the verge and shook his head. 'Man,' he commented, before driving away. 'And I thought I saw some weird shit in LA.'

I gave James a hug, which startled him considerably. As we had known each other since the age of twelve and not once exchanged more than a slap on the back or a firm handshake, it was hardly surprising. America was turning me into a serial embracer. On departing from The Redwood Motel two days earlier I had squeezed the living daylights out of Chin and his wife, a combination of etiquette and heartfelt gratitude. Colonel Arthur would certainly have blanched at such wanton affection, but then my ramrod-straight ancestor found even the crispest of handshakes over-familiar.

Before long James was suffering. While I had not expected him to stride through Louisiana with a gazelle-like grace, I didn't expect him to be grimacing and clutching his shins within the first five miles. When we pulled over for a rest stop at a roadside cafe, he slumped down on the grass, groaned loudly and ordered a colossal battered frankfurter and a slice of treacle tart. He clearly had given up on cabbage. I watched

in awe as his already sizeable girth almost burgeoned before
my eyes.

James told me not to worry. He was determined to make it
across the Mississippi at all costs. He would start eating
sardines and crackers from tomorrow onwards. He explained
he had been going through a rough patch with his new
Gujarati girlfriend, been frantically busy at work (a manager
at London Underground) and his father's health was on the
wane. Now that he'd quit the cigarettes, food had been
James's only solace.

Sure enough he showed quite extraordinary grit. After a
gentle initiation – an eight-mile day, followed by a fourteen
miler – we started clocking up the usual twenty plus. James
limped, hobbled, cursed and continued to eat battered frank-
furters supplemented with local delicacies such as chitterlings
(fried pig guts) and *boudin* balls (globs of seasoned pork liver
and rice). He needed one afternoon off having lost a couple of
his toenails, but apart from this minor hiatus remained formidably bullish. More than anything he enjoyed sleeping in
the great outdoors, looking up at the stars at night as opposed
to the mildew on his East Finchley bedsit.

We were travelling bang through the centre of Louisiana.
This meant we missed out on the sultry Cajun country south
of the state and the wilderness areas to the north which
Colonel Arthur had traversed in his stagecoach. Sadly, we also
bypassed the jazz bars and French quarters of New Orleans:
no city to steer a beast through, even during Mardi Gras.

There was still much to marvel at. We plodded down roads
fringed by wild and spooky swampland where trees, half-
submerged in green water, were alive with the burp and
chatter of wildlife. Camouflaged hunters shouldering rifles
wandered past, off to bag deer, raccoons and squirrels. A
snaggle-toothed catfish farmer of Cajun descent stopped to
hand us both a beer. When I asked if he was originally from

France he threatened to shoot my mule. 'Cajuns originate from Newfoundland and Nova Scotia,' he shouted. 'Not bloody France, that's the Creoles.'

It was an intriguing area that pulsed with a vibrant, at times eerie exoticism. Religious slogans still sprung up from graveyards and gardens. Louisiana was the only state that divided itself into parishes, rather than counties, and we were constantly asked if we 'knew the Lord'. Masquerading as a devout churchgoer was usually the best tactic to keep the sermons brief.

*   *   *

But of all nature's wonders the most arresting sight by far was cotton. Seeing a cotton crop in bloom for the first time ignites the senses with a child-like 'wowee!' James and I were fortunate to catch the harvest in full swing, scurries of snow-white bolls spinning through the bruised evening skies like a miracle. As the harvesters scythed and the tractors carted their bulging trailers, cotton turned the whole landscape briefly white, snagging on trees, lining verges, clogging engines: a fairy-tale weather front.

Colonel Arthur got a little less excited when he spotted the South's most prevalent Civil War crop. He simply wrote: 'I saw cotton fields for the first time.' (It takes a top-brass general or a good battle to whip my ancestor into a literary lather.) Arthur's 1863 diary does, however, strongly insinuate that cotton was not proving to be the vital resource Southerners had hoped it would be. Britain, to a large degree, was the cause of this.

Three years before Arthur's American journey Britain imported eighty per cent of its cotton from the South. Indeed the crop was so lucrative Southern Senator James Henry Hammond had famously declared: 'Cotton is King' and 'No power on earth dares make war on it.' Many Southerners, including President of the Confederacy Jefferson Davis, continued to believe this and thought the British were bound to come on side in order to keep their cotton market buoyant. They also knew Britain, which had the strongest navy in the world at the time, could smash through any Union blockade with ease.

It didn't turn out like that. Rampant stockpiling led to a huge surplus of cotton in Britain before the first shots of the Civil War were fired. Even when its supplies began to dwindle the British government was able to import cotton from India and Egypt, and, as the war progressed, began to trade with America again – this time via the North.

Cotton had not proved the saviour it had been cracked up to be for the South. It is true that loss of trade due to the Union blockade caused some unemployment in the cotton mills of north England, but even here the workers had little sympathy with the Confederacy. The conditions in some of Yorkshire's and Lancashire's factories and mills were atrocious at the time. Child labour was still not uncommon and the jobless workers identified more with the slaves. Some even sent a petition of encouragement to President Lincoln with the words: 'Our interests are identical with yours. We are truly one people . . .'

According to Joe, a farmer who grew a hundred acres of cotton the other side of Alexandria, the crop was not faring well this year either. James and I chatted to him having set up camp on his land one evening.

'We had no rain during the planting season,' Joe grumbled, his hangdog features emphasising his woes. 'Prices have plummeted and now cheap competition from Asia is making things even worse. It's impossible to compete with countries that still pick cotton by hand.'

Joe looked out across his field, carpeted dirty white, like a sheet slept on too long. 'You know in Alabama they have a statue in honour of the boll weevil,' he said sadly, plucking at the straps on his blue overalls. 'The boll weevil is a little bug that wiped out the South's cotton harvest in the 1920s. The statue is to thank the bug for destroying cotton because it forced us farmers to diversify, grow wheat and peanuts and other stuff instead. Not rely only on cotton.'

'These days only five per cent of people in the South work on the land,' Joe continued bitterly. '*Five per cent!* Whether cotton, cattle, wheat, whatever. We'll soon be as industrial as the North. When your ancestor was here, young man, cotton was king. Nowadays, we might soon stop growing it altogether.'

*   *   *

By James's final day he was in acute discomfort but still remained dogged. The Mississippi was luring him on in the same way an Indian sadhu might be drawn towards the Ganges. He was grinding himself into a state of physical meltdown. James wasn't so much a man gingerly stepping out of his comfort zone; he was willingly pole-vaulting himself into a hellish new dimension. He clearly wanted to attain some sort of pilgrim's epiphany. If it meant he had to stagger along like Robert Mitchum with a bad case of dyspepsia, so be it.

We had slept the previous night in a musty cotton pickers' dormitory in a place called Frogmore. It had no electricity, so I used one of my light sticks – tiny batons that when shaken generate a dull green glow – for illumination. We ate some Spam and sardines for breakfast before loading up Browny. That night had been the coldest to date and Browny's saddle-bags twinkled with a coating of crystallized frost.

Soon the sun was up and the morning mist evaporated off the road like softly blown smoke. The landscape was level now, variegated by cotton fields, pasture and clumps of pine and oak. The trees flickered with magpies and wagtails, the little birds' darting flight paths in strong contrast to the slow, thermal-cruising buzzards far above. Hanks of cotton still tossed about in the wind as if controlled by jittery threads.

By lunchtime we had reached Ferriday, a sprawling, depressed-looking town. As we plodded through, James limping wretchedly, we were stopped in our tracks by a flame-haired woman of indeterminate age waving her arms. 'What the hell are you boys doing?' she yelled at us. 'You follow me, now, and I'll buy y'all a drink. What's the donkey want, a bucket of tequila? Man o' man, two men and a jackass, come on, follow me.'

Understandably, James was not too keen on walking even a boot print out of his way, but the flame-haired temptress was not for turning. Fortunately, our drinks were only a matter of yards down the maple-lined road.

Our hostess was called Frankie Jean and she ran a drive-through liquor store. The store was an upmarket tin shack with optics of every kind lining the walls, along with glass-fronted fridges full of beer cans. The wall space below the bar was plastered with Jerry Lee Lewis posters and albums. THE REAL KING OF ROCK AND ROLL, read one. THE KILLER PLAYS LIVE, advertised another.

'You're clearly a bit of a Jerry Lee Lewis fan,' I commented.

'I'm no fan, honey,' replied Frankie Jean, handing James and me a couple of tumblers of iced Coke. 'I'm his sister.'

'Oh right,' I said, unconvinced.

'Hell, I can see you boys don't believe me.' Frankie Jean threw her arms in the air like a preacher reaching the sermon's crescendo. 'Well, I'll just have to prove it to you.'

I tied up Browny to a magnolia sapling before Frankie Jean led James and me into a brick ranch-style home opposite. We stepped over a variety of sleeping cats and blossoming pot plants. The Lewis House, as Frankie Jean described it, is where she had grown up with her firebrand, rock-and-rolling brother, Jerry Lee. The house was a museum in his honour, with a piano in every room and 'Great Balls of Fire' playing in the background. There was the obligatory arsenal of guns hanging from one wall with Bibles and crucifixes lining another. Family photos were juxtaposed with press cuttings and shots of fellow stars: Fats Domino, Elvis, Dolly Parton.

'This here, is John Lennon's pee-yana.' Frankie Jean sat on a stool and plonked out a chord on a set of discoloured keys. 'John loved Jerry. Hell, he worshipped my brother. It was embarrassing. Jerry influenced loads of today's pee-yanists, but none are as good as him.'

Frankie Jean was a captivating and spectacularly indiscreet guide. Much of her comments I suspected were to be taken with a generous pinch of salt. Not only did her sensation-spilling tongue wag about her brother, she also spoke of her adulterous cousin Jimmy Swaggart, once America's most prominent TV evangelist, and another cousin, Mickey Gilley, a country and western singer. Swaggart and Gilley both had little enclaves of the museum dedicated to them as they had both grown up in Ferriday too. Also represented was Frankie Jean's younger sister, Linda Gail, another singer.

'You know sompthing, fellas,' she drawled, picking at her cuticles. 'I'm the black sheep of this family. Linda Gail has been divorced seven or eight times, I forget now. Jerry Lee has been divorced about the same amount. They don't let the grass grow under their feet, those two. And me, I've been married to the same guy most of my life.' She slapped her thighs with a loud crack. 'Hell, fellas, I'm just not keeping up.'

The family had always veered wildly between triumph and tragedy. Jerry Lee's older brother, Elmo, had been killed by a drunk driver at the age of eight and one of his own children,

Jerry Lee, Jr, had also died in a car smash. Jerry Lee's musical genius has often been clouded by a tempestuous private life, most famously when he became engaged to his thirteen-year-old cousin, Myra Gale Brown, at the height of his fame in the late 1950s. He also has a penchant for firing off guns to relieve stress.

'My brother can be a fool,' confessed Frankie Jean. 'I love him so much but sometimes I don't particularly like him, if you get my meaning. Jimmy and Mickey are the same. I love 'em but don't always like 'em. But we all came from a fairly poor Southern family and have done pretty good. You've got to be proud of that.' She stopped and pulled back her long red hair, her voice becoming calmer. 'One thing we all do is love our parents, all the scrimping and saving they did on our behalf. For a while Poppa even had a moonshine still. My folks gave Jerry Lee the chance to prove his genius. And I tell ya, he is a genius, for all his faults he plays the pee-yana like it was a gift from God. Mamma called him the Killer, Linda the Thriller and me the Chiller! Haaa, that just about sums us up.'

Outside at the liquor store Frankie Jean's daughter, Maryanne, a handsome, bosomy blonde in a black singlet, was serving a man in a blue baseball cap. She leant over the bar counter and handed him a Styrofoam cup through his car window.

'That old lech,' whispered Frankie Jean. 'He's a Pentecostal Christian who passes by every day to gawp at Maryanne's boobies. And he's got a wife at home. I swear everyone turns up here to ogle at her, even the Baptists.'

Frankie Jean took James's Styrofoam cup from him and threw it into a homemade recycling bin. She said there were no recycling facilities in Ferriday, so she gave all her foam and plastic to a local taxidermist to use for stuffing. 'I sometimes think,' she proclaimed, 'I'm the only goddarn greeny in the whole of the South.'

James and I signed the Lewis House guestbook and gulped down a couple of Dr Peppers before preparing to plough on towards Mississippi. After pecking Frankie Jean on the cheek I told her: 'That was one of the most flamboyant tours I've ever been on.'

She looked at me through unblinking bright eyes. 'These days, darlin',' she drawled playfully, 'I'm only flamboyant from the knees down.'

*   *   *

James was in a tight-lipped, horizon-gazing trance, all his energies harnessed into putting one foot in front of the other. The silence between us was so intense you could drown in it, but we were good enough friends to understand each other's moods. He chose to deal with his cracked toenails and boiling shins by feeding off the pain. When I was in this state earlier in the trip I had chosen to let my mind fly off into dreamy distractions; James liked to face his pain head on. He opted to pop his mental blisters, while I preferred to bandage mine.

James's teeth-clenching silence enabled me to turn my thoughts back to Colonel Arthur. Meeting Frankie Jean reminded me that one historian had described Arthur as 'a marvellous celebrity spotter'. Indeed, my ancestor was. He not only met Sam Houston and Jefferson Davis but a host of Confederate top brass, including General Robert E. Lee. During his four months in America he socialised relentlessly, ticking off Civil War celebrities with the relish of a child with an autograph album. Colonel Arthur's eccentric looks and good humour made him a popular guest, whether at a cocktail party or sitting round a camp fire.

Meeting Jerry Lee Lewis's sister in the Louisiana boondocks hardly classified me as a bona fide celeb schmoozer.

Jerry Lee was now in his sixties and although still a popular performer, his glory years were behind him. But it was still interesting to compare the movers and shakers of 1863 to those of today. In Civil War times it would have been Robert E. Lee, Stonewall Jackson and Ulysses S. Grant who would have been targeted by the likes of *Hello* and *OK!* magazines.

In that era, where the media still had comparatively limited clout, the soldiers, cops, cowboys and to a lesser extent politicians, were the only real stars. White-bearded, teetotal, non-smoking, devoutly religious Robert E. Lee was the epitome of Southern adulation in sharp contrast to hard drinking, hell raising, piano slaying Jerry Lee Lewis; another type of Southerner altogether. In today's celebrity culture it would be hard to imagine the impeccably behaved General Lee generating much interest, but then again he probably wouldn't want to.

'I've got to stop,' snapped James suddenly, jolting me out of my thoughts. He really did look like he had to stop, his face as sallow as wax. As soon as we reached some grass, he made a comic book 'aarggh' noise, and collapsed as if felled by a sniper's bullet.

We had reached a town called Vidalia on the Louisianan banks of the Mississippi. The immense river bridge was visible now but still a good two miles away. James lay motionless occasionally emitting an agonised gargle.

'Jim, we've got to keep going, mate,' I said tentatively. 'Or else you'll completely seize up.'

'Give me a couple of minutes.'

'Listen, nobody will mind if you don't get over that bridge. Hitch-hike if you like, and Browny and I'll meet you in Natchez.'

'I'm crossing the Mississippi,' he growled. 'End of story.'

'Then we must keep going.'

There was a strained silence. 'You know in that movie *Butch Cassidy and the Sundance Kid*,' I continued. 'There's that bit when Robert Redford has to shoot a tin can to prove his marksmanship. When he stands still he misses it every time, but when he crouches and turns he blasts it to bits. He says something like, "I'm better when I move."' I paused. 'You're going to be better if you move.'

After a brief silence James leaned over and looked at me. 'Sundance got shot to pieces by the Bolivian army,' he pointed out coolly. 'The moral of the story – moving kills you.'

We both laughed. In some ways it was a strange reversal of fortune for James and me. At our Oxford boarding school he had been a star sportsman, in the top squads for rugby, hockey and swimming, while I floundered in the inferior leagues. Other than tennis, the only sports in which I demonstrated any physical prowess were cross-country running and eating toast.

James was also a wow with the girls. I could never understand this because he had the most diabolically uncool taste in music. While the rest of us were air guitaring to The Clash and The Ramones, he hummed along to his box set of Andrew Lloyd Webber musicals. What teenage girl in her right mind would want her precious first kiss accompanied to 'Memory' or 'Magical Mr Mestophiles' playing in the background. Well, lots of them. James made no effort at all to be cool, and as a consequence had queues of hormonal damsels swooning at his then blister-free feet. While I, his oh-so-trendy best mate, would stew in monkish frustration listening to Elvis Costello wail heartbreakingly about thwarted love, revolution and spots.

'I have to say,' I told James, 'seeing you, the original Mr Sporty, conked out like this gives me great satisfaction.'

'I bet it does,' he replied, massaging his shins. 'You may have the will power, you bastard, but you're still a graceless git.' He grimaced as he tried to get up. He suddenly looked rather creaky and old. 'What the hell's happened to us?' he ranted. 'I'm too fat, about to be chucked by my girlfriend and I'm gagging for a cigarette. And you're such a desperado you've been forced to elope with a mule. Where did it all go wrong?'

'It's not that bad, mate.'

'You know what, Tom,' he said, having levered himself onto his feet. 'I want to get across that river more than anything else in the world right now.' He looked fixedly into the distance, his eyes welling with pain. 'It will be something nobody can take away from me. You know what I mean, don't you?'

'Of course,' I judo-chopped him affectionately on the bicep.

He hit me back and gritted his teeth. 'Come on, Sundance, let's move,' he said, shuffling forwards. 'The Bolivians are on to us.'

Vidalia was hideous, an interminable stretch of derelict feed stores, corrugated churches, sleazy-looking motels and identical houses. James had picked up his pace to stay level with Browny and me but he looked worse than ever, walking like a man wearing flippers. I wondered if he was doing permanent damage to his legs but knew there was no stopping him. By the time we reached the river, he was in a state of rickety collapse.

The Mississippi bridge looked intimidating, a multi-lane highway shooting into the horizon with a dragon's back of metal girders stretching either side of it. Browny, for all her sang-froid, might balk at this, I decided. As we broached the riverbank a police car drove past. On a whim I flagged it down in the hope of securing a last-minute escort. The officer was a young black woman in a smartly creased navy blue

uniform. Her nametag read Beverly Metcalfe. She had dancing eyes and a Cheshire cat smile. She looks nice, I thought.
She's bound to help us.

As I explained the situation to Beverly, James ambled on,
waving us off with exhausted Captain Oates panache. Beverly
buzzed her crackly walkie-talkie to get permission to escort
us. Once her superior had approved we were all set. Beverly
explained that she would drive directly behind and that I was
to shepherd Browny as briskly as possible. I immediately set
off over the Mississippi, or Old Glory, the mighty, dun-
coloured river that meandered hundreds of miles north,
carving America almost clean in two.

Within seconds, disaster struck. For some reason Beverly
flicked the whirring blue siren on her squad car roof to life.
The sharp noise and strobing blue light startled Browny,
who pulled away from me. She looked as spooked as Lord
Cardigan's mount must have when facing the Russian guns at
the Charge of the Light Brigade, all bulging eyes and flared
nostrils. I reined her in quickly and Beverly, sensing Browny's
terror, turned off the siren. After we composed ourselves we
pushed on.

Before long we drew level with James. 'Keep going, Jim,
almost there,' I encouraged him. 'How are your toenails?'

'What fucking toenails!' he shouted, managing to laugh
and grimace at the same time. 'Just shut up and keep going.
Get that mule over the bridge.'

The evening had laid on quite a show. It was that time of
day P.G. Wodehouse depicted as nature 'undoing her waistcoat and putting her feet up'. To our right was a half-scuttled
sun, casting blood red shadows over the dark water. Directly
opposite was a fat moon, suspended pale and blotchy in the
blue dusk. Below us the river flowed with a majestic, muddy
languor. In places it whirled into tiny bubbling eddies, before
licking off down currents where the likes of Huckleberry

Finn might once have drifted. I stopped briefly to soak it up: a scene of unalloyed magic.

Beverly had given up escorting Browny and me as we had now pulled far in front. She was now exclusively chaperoning James, whose palsied marching was attracting astounded looks from the passing commuters. James was gamely trying to pick up his pace and tiptoed along like a firewalker, with facial expressions to match. Once I was over the bridge I tied Browny to a WELCOME TO MISSISSIPPI – THE MAGNOLIA STATE sign. A spire of smoke drifted up above Natchez, the historic town that lay ahead, where I would catch up with Colonel Arthur once more.

By the time James made it over the river it was dark. 'That's two mules I've escorted,' quipped Beverly, watching James lean on Browny's neck for support. She took a bunch of photos of us under the Mississippi sign before departing. Erin, an attractive girl with freckles and beestung lips, turned up. She was from the local paper and snapped yet more photos while asking us lots of Why, Who, What, When, Why was that again?-style questions. On seeing James's condition she suggested we stayed at The Natchez Inn, which was only just around the corner. James sighed with relief.

The Natchez Inn was managed by Steve, a Vietnam vet with greying hair and half-mast eyes. Within minutes of meeting us he had furled up his shirt to reveal two bullet wounds on his arm and shoulder courtesy of the Vietcong. 'Gosh,' was the best I could come up with. 'You think that's bad,' I thought James was about to say. 'You should see my feet.' In the end he stayed silent. Fortunately Steve turned out to be a decent, easy-going man who allowed Browny to graze on the motel lawn.

James proudly insisted on helping me unload Browny before hobbling off and collapsing on his bed. After about five minutes of peace an almighty rumpus erupted in the neighbouring room. There was lots of banging on doors and shrieking. 'I'm gonna kill you, you mother******, son of a *****,' someone shouted. 'Not before I kill you, you mother******, son of a *****,' was the not unreasonable reply. Soon the whole place was a war zone, with abuse being thrown by shadowy figures from the nearby balconies.

I dashed out to tend Browny. The poor mule was terrified and running herself ragged around her hitching post. She could deal with most things, but not loud, violent human voices. I moved her to a patch of grass as far from the shouting as possible, petted her a while and then ran over to reception to ask Steve what was up.

'Man, I'm sorry,' he said, genuinely concerned. 'We've got a bunch of guys living here who lay explosives in the swamps all week for the mining companies. It's high-pressure work. They get boozed up as hell on Fridays. Go a bit stir crazy. My wife and I have only just taken over here and we won't tolerate it. I'll tell them to shut up.'

'You're a braver man than me,' I confessed. 'They're threatening to kill each other.'

'Don't sweat it, I've dealt with worse.'

I got back to the room. James was on his bed, prostrate and completely immobile. He began to snigger. 'What's up?' I asked.

'Crossing the Mississippi was one of the best things I've ever done, Tom, it really was.' He clutched his sides to contain his mirth. 'But I've lost my toenails, my shins are on fire, the people next door are about to kill each other and,' he slapped his wobbling belly, 'after over one hundred miles of walking I've put on bloody weight!'

Chapter 11

Natchez

To give him a proper send-off the following morning I treated James to a gut-swelling Southern breakfast of fried eggs, crispy bacon and grits. Grits, I should add, are a culinary legend in these parts; they are to Southerners' tastebuds what Mark Twain's words are to their ears and hickory smoke to their noses.

Grits are tiny, white globules made out of a type of ground maize that are cooked until they soften into a slushy gruel. Southerners love them either plain or mixed with butter, salt, cheese, honey or even garlic. Grits are usually regarded as an offshoot of Indian tribal cooking, but interestingly may well have stemmed from African cuisine. Like other Southern staples of today such as yams, okra and collard greens, grits probably became popular because slaves in the old plantation kitchens enjoyed cooking stuff that reminded them of home.

Whatever their origins, grits have now become a good way of geographically demarking the South – a notoriously hard place to define. Some think of the South as the area below the Mason-Dixon line (which runs from the Pennsylvania/ Maryland border), others see it firmly as the eleven Confederate states that seceded from the Union in the early 1860s, and others, perhaps just as accurately, take it to be any place where grits are always available for breakfast. Then there's not just the South, but the Deep South – broadly encompassing Louisiana, Mississippi, Alabama and Tennessee – where grits are not only always available for breakfast, but served up whether you want them or not.

The first time I ate grits, like most foreigners or Yankees, I thought they tasted like melted polystyrene. But once I experimented mixing them with butter I warmed to their sloppy charms. James clearly loved them and was wolfing them down as if they were Honey Nut Cornflakes. We were breakfasting in a steamy old-style diner in the centre of Natchez, where everybody knew each other but were still prepared to flash a smile at out-of-towners. I loved family diners like this, the food and atmosphere were terrific, and they provided the last buffer of resistance against the flood-tide of fast-food joints spuming across the South.

The only depressing aspect was the number of grossly overweight people. It is well known that America, and especially small town America, has more than its fair share of obesity. I'm no svelte six-packer myself but I was saddened by the sheer quantity of very fat Americans, often startlingly young. The number of obese adults in the US has doubled in the past decade, and the number of morbidly obese – those who are overweight by seven stone plus – has jumped even more. One in eighty American men now weighs over twenty-one stone.

At a table near to James and me were a couple, probably in their late twenties, who were so impressively fleshy that their stomachs could have easily doubled as beanbags. They ate quickly and silently displaying no culinary arousal whatsoever. Down went the fork, then up, quick chomp, then down again, up, chomp, down. It was all so joyless, more as if they were stoking a couple of vast, insatiable engines than enjoying a mouthwatering fry up. James, a picture of athleticism in comparison, ate with the same intensity, but would often stop to murmur rapturously, 'Oh, that bacon's just too good,' or, 'Ah, these grits.' He loved his food and took his waistline as a consequence but for the corpulent couple breakfast offered no Ambrosial glee, it was clearly nothing more than body fodder.

'You know in the Civil War,' I whispered to James, sheltering behind the laminated menu, 'the average Confederate soldier weighed nine and a half stone or less.' I looked furtively around the diner. 'Except for the waitress I reckon everyone here weighs more than that, some probably double.'

'You're right,' said James, spooning in some more grits. 'If the Civil War was today there'd be a lot of cholesterol-bellies about. Easy targets. I'd be a casualty in no time with my gut – be like hitting a barn door.' He paused to chew before adding, 'Was your ancestor a big man?'

'No,' I replied. 'According to reports he was as scrawny as a whippet. That said, in the movie they made about Gettysburg he was played by a large actor in a red tunic. If this had been accurate Colonel Arthur would have been shot in seconds.'

'I'm glad he survived,' mused James, wiping his mouth with a napkin. 'Mind you, if he hadn't, his diary would never have been published, you wouldn't have a mule fetish and I'd still be able to walk.'

*   *   *

Later that morning James, heavy with buttered grits, hitched a lift back to Alexandria and then caught a flight home to London. I was sad to see him go and felt a little empty being on my own again. But there was plenty to keep me occupied. After a typically Southern breakfast it was time for me to explore Natchez, not such a typically Southern town.

First though, I had to sort out Browny. After all the death threats and yelling at the motel I was keen to find her alternative accommodation. I had heard from Two-Bullet Steve that there was a horse-drawn carriage company near by which trundled tourists around Natchez's antebellum mansions. He suggested inquiring whether Browny could be lodged in the same stables as the carriage horses. It proved a good bet, and within an hour Browny was in her own yard, chewing on a nosegay of hay and sniffing over the fence at a black shire horse called Clarence.

I struck up a conversation with Glynn Diehl, one of the company workers. Glynn looked like a cheery rustic from a Hogarth painting, plump, red-cheeked, relentlessly hearty; he also boasted an encyclopaedic knowledge about Natchez. He told me tourism had dried up since September 11 and, if I wanted, he'd got time to tour me around town in his truck.

We started by driving up to the crest of the 200-foot bluff beneath which Natchez, the oldest port on the Mississippi, elegantly perches. The spires of smoke from the nearby paper mills that I had seen yesterday were still just visible. Natchez really was a world apart. One glaring difference to the other towns I'd walked through was the absence of a central square with a Confederate memorial standing sentinel. As Natchez had in turn been ruled by Indians, French, British, Spanish, Rebels and Yankees, it also boasted a subtly cosmopolitan flavour.

'In the 1850s Natchez had more millionaires than anywhere in the South, and almost as many as New York,' said Glynn, staring down on a soupy stretch of river. 'Most of the wealth was from huge cotton plantations. Many of the houses around here made Scarlet O'Hara's mansion look like a gazebo.'

'What happened here during the Civil War?'

'We were damn lucky,' he admitted, pulling on the peak of his red baseball cap.

Glynn explained that as Natchez lay on a straight stretch of the Mississippi it wasn't as strategically important in 1863 as the port of Vicksburg that sat on a kink in the river fifty miles upstream. Vicksburg was a crucial naval hub – described as the Gibraltar of the South – and so the Union desperately wanted it. A terrible forty-seven-day siege took place there, Glynn recounted, which helped take the heat off Natchez. Over sixty thousand feet of zigzagging trenches were dug – one of the first times this attrition style of warfare was tested. Inside Vicksburg soldiers, women and children held out heroically, surviving off a diet of acorns, rodents, frogs and even mule meat before finally surrendering on 4 July 1863. Lots of people died, Glynn concluded, and many Vicksburg residents are still very bitter about it.

'Still!' I exclaimed. 'It was almost a hundred and forty years ago.'

'Well, they consider Natchez a town of traitors as we didn't put up a fight,' explained Glynn. 'They say we made the best of the Union occupation.' He laughed softly. 'That's a little unfair. Sure, some people here flirted with the Union, especially the rich plantation owners, but far from everyone.'

Glynn explained that almost fifteen hundred volunteers in Natchez joined the Confederate army and over five hundred were killed. He insisted that to write off the whole of Natchez as cowardly was disrespectful to those who died. What made the people in Vicksburg so angry, he continued, is that so many of its buildings were destroyed whereas physically Natchez was hardly touched. But Glynn felt Vicksburg was partly responsible for its own decline, and that despite boasting an impressive military park, over the last fifty years it had substituted casinos and shopping malls for history. Natchez, on the other hand, had done everything to preserve its past.

'Sounds almost like a Civil War between two cities,' I stated.

'Aw, not really,' replied Glynn, steering his truck back towards town. 'We're more like friendly rivals. At the end of the day we're all Mississippians. Mississippi comes first. Some of our state's regiments were the bravest in the war. At Gettysburg one regiment – the 11th Mississippi – sustained eighty-seven per cent casualties.' He slit a finger over his throat to make his point. 'They refused to retreat. We're a very war-like state. Even during Desert Storm a Mississippi regiment was the first to arrive to fight Saddam.' We drove passed a church fronted by a tree with red leaves.

'When you look at the Civil War carefully,' he continued, a huge Greek revival mansion now looming into view, 'you realise that most of the common soldiers weren't fighting about slavery or secession. They were fighting because friends from their town or state were and they didn't want to let the side down – simple as that. Only the plantation owners really cared about retaining slavery. That's why the conflict was called a rich man's war and a poor man's fight.'

'Do you think that's right?'

'Sure I do,' stressed Glynn. 'Natchez gives you the wrong impression. Places like that,' he gestured to the mansion we were passing, 'were owned by a tiny elite. Only one per cent of the South had that sort of wealth, the bulk of the Confederate army were just poor farm boys. *Gone with the Wind* has a lot to answer for in that sense. The South was never all mansions and mint juleps.'

'Do you think the South might have won?'

'Hell, yeah, might have,' he said, failing to disguise a brief smile. 'But the chances are if we did, all the Southern states were so goddamn independent and proud we'd have ended up fighting against each other. Before long we'd have all split up, what's the word I'm looking for,' he clicked his fingers in an effort to remember. 'Balkanised.' He repeated the word a couple of times with slow-drawl relish. 'Yeah, Bal-kan-iy-zed.'

'Mississippi sounds especially patriotic,' I commented.

'Sure is,' agreed Glynn, pointing to some Hallowe'en pumpkins stuck on a picket fence. Today was 31 October and pumpkins were everywhere, hanging from shop fronts, gardens and piled outside grocery stores.

'Down here it's not referred to as the Civil War,' Glynn continued. 'It's the War of Northern Aggression. There's still a lot of rancour. Because Vicksburg fell on 4 July – the same day as American Independence – lots of Mississippians didn't celebrate like the rest of the country until very recently. There's been a long mourning process over that war.' He paused, took in a deep breath and exhaled wheezily. 'Hey, enough about fighting. Let me show you another side of Natchez.'

Glynn sped down a succession of sharp switchbacks and before long we were at the riverside again. An overladen cargo boat was chugging under the huge bridge Browny,

James and I had crossed yesterday. Glynn parked his car and jumped out onto a crumbling section of road.

'This is known as Natchez Under the Hill,' he told me, gesturing to a line of bars and cafes stretching down the waterfront. 'Mark Twain wrote this area was full of "riverside riffraff". It's pretty tame now but back in the 1800s people gambled, drank, whored, raced horses, traded slaves, you name it.' Glynn stopped, his expression briefly imagining days gone by. 'But Natchez still has a black sheep side to it,' he added quietly, 'it's still very wild compared to much of Mississippi.'

Glynn mentioned that until recently there had been a brothel in the centre of Natchez called Nellie's Place. Nellie was a great old girl, an institution, according to Glynn, did lots of good works in Natchez but just happened to run a whorehouse on the side. All the authorities turned a blind eye because of her popularity. One summer night back in 1990 she refused to let in a drunken client who, in a fury, doused her in petrol and set her alight. Nellie was eighty-seven at the time and the burns killed her. According to Glynn half of Natchez paid their respects at her funeral.

'Only a place like Natchez would celebrate someone like Nellie,' declared Glynn proudly. 'Oh yeah, we've got the odd problem with divides between the very rich and very poor, with black and white. And, sure, despite its sophisticated look Natchez is supposed to have one of the worst murder rates in America. But most people love it; love its craziness. Compared to all these identical, mall-clogged towns I'd live here any day. Forget the murder rate, at least you feel alive.'

*   *   *

Colonel Arthur's journey into Natchez had certainly been a combination of the lively and the murderous. My ancestor had been forced to sail in a leaky skiff propelled by a 'very

powerful, very vain . . . Negro oarsman named "Tucker".'
Instead of rowing directly down the Mississippi, which was
flooded and riddled with Union gunboats, Tucker piloted the
adrenaline-pumped Colonel and his eight skiff-mates through
a network of swamps and creeks.

'These bayous and swamps,' wrote my ancestor, 'abound
with alligators and snakes of the most venomous description
. . . The distance we did in the skiff was about twenty-eight
miles, which took us eleven hours to perform.'

The Colonel rounded off his long journey, 'by a trudge of
three miles through deep mud, until at length we reached a
place called Vidalia,' where the now exhausted guards officer,
'got the immense luxury of a pretty good bed, *all to myself*
which enabled me to take off my clothes and boots for the
first time in ten days.' You have to hand it to Colonel Arthur,
he is grateful for simple pleasures, never one to moan about
the lack of hot showers or decent pedicurists.

The following morning (15 May) Colonel Arthur crossed
the Mississippi, hired a carriage and made straight for Longwood, the home of a cotton baron called Haller Nutt, two
miles east of Natchez. A 'pretty little town' is my ancestor's
only observation on the busy port as he passed through.
Although Colonel Arthur spent no more than an hour or two
at Mr Nutt's house, I was keen to try and track it down. I was
helped in my quest by a local bookshop owner called Neil,
whom I met while trawling his shelves for information on
mules.

Neil, a strange combination of lank grey hair and youthful
brio, said he knew little of mules but did agree to show me
around Longwood, now a stately home opened to the public.
The morning we turned up at Haller Nutt's old mansion we
were the only visitors. A pearl-encrusted receptionist was
pecking at the keys on a typewriter. She provided a rather

stilted, autopilot tour, and left us to look around at our leisure.

Colonel Arthur had written that Longwood reminded him 'very much of an English gentleman's country seat . . .' Not for the first time, I didn't agree with my erstwhile ancestor. To me it smacked more of a maharaja's palace than of an English country home. With its extraordinary octagonal structure, pagoda-like dome and cypress wood floorboards it was more a fusion of the Orient and classical France. The grounds were studded with luxuriant pine trees and ornamental shrubs, not the sort of hardwoods that would sprout from the gardens of Stowe or Chatsworth.

Compared to the swanky predictability of so many of the other Natchez mansions, Longwood was endearingly eccentric. It was also something of a tragic fairy tale. Before the Civil War Haller Nutt had been one of the wealthiest men in the area. He owned twenty-one plantations throughout Louisiana and Mississippi and eight hundred slaves. Rather than a boastful display of wealth, though, the handsome, urbane Nutt truly wanted to create somewhere aesthetically special at Longwood.

He recruited Sam Sloan, a celebrated architect from Philadelphia, to construct his six-storey, octagonal dream home. Work started in 1860 but in less than a year the Civil War had flared up and Sloan and all his craftsmen fled back north. The basement remained the only part of the house that was ever fully completed. Nutt, faced with haemorrhaging finances and chastised for being a Union sympathiser, died a broken man in 1864. He was forty-eight years old. His family continued to live in Longwood for a while but in fairly wretched circumstances: just one of the many radical shifts in fortune wreaked by the Civil War. With its musty smells, deserted floors and silent, eerie pathos, Longwood is now a strangely moving place: a monument to a shattered dream.

Colonel Arthur notes that: 'Mr Nutt was extremely civil, and most anxious that I should remain at Natchez for a few days.' Considering Haller Nutt's well-known Union sympathies my Rebel ancestor may have wanted to leave before things became awkward between them. However, to my mind, it is more likely the indefatigable Colonel wanted to resume his journey promptly in order to reach Vicksburg before it fell to the Yankees; reports were already filtering back to Natchez that surrender was imminent. The loss of Vicksburg would put my fiercely pro-Confederate ancestor in a tricky spot; he had to crack on.

*   *   *

Before cracking on myself, Neil encouraged me to attend an event at the Fork of the Road, the site of Natchez's old slave market. As Browny was having her third set of shoes bashed on later in the day I had time to kill and jumped at the opportunity. Neil shepherded me through the eastern part of town, with its white brick bungalows and fast-food halls, a very different atmosphere to the grandiose antebellum piles nearer the river.

The only indication of the slave market was a faded historical marker testifying to the fact. A makeshift stage had been set up on a grassy strip on which a portly, full-bearded man in a white robe was delivering a speech. His tongue-straining name (according to my programme) was Mr Ser Seshshab Heter-Boxley. Mr Heter-Boxley spoke of the plight of the slaves who were shipped over from Africa and then sold on to the cotton fat cats of Natchez. He was a good speaker, passionate without sounding bitter, and prepared to criticise the slave traders and the planters who valued slaves for only $1,000 or less – 'We're talking about a human life, people!'

Neil and I sat on the grass verge. We were the only white faces in the hundred-strong crowd except for an elderly lady in a billowy blue frock and a gaunt-faced man in a fedora. Erin, the pretty photographer from the local paper whom I had met crossing the Mississippi, was also mingling in the crowd, snapping away. In time, several other speakers including an eloquent Mississippi congressman took to the stage. He used the word 'hope' with almost comic regularity. 'I hope', 'you hope', 'they hope', 'we all hope', and just occasionally he conceded there was 'no hope'.

After the speeches a band struck up with some old-style jazz, and a troop of six crisply dressed black soldiers in blue Union uniforms marched by. They halted with a click of immaculately timed boots. Seconds later they raised their rifles in unison and fired a salvo into the sultry, ultramarine sky. Once they had lowered their weapons and been dismissed I approached the man who had been barking orders.

His name was Sergeant Major Norman Fisher of the First Mississippi Coloured Regiment Infantry. He was immensely tall, barrel-chested with dark, proud eyes that suggested, 'don't mess with me'. His uniform buttons strained against his top-heavy torso.

'You must have been practising,' I said, 'that six-gun salute was near perfect.'

'Oh, yeah, we take what we do seriously,' he replied. 'In my day job I'm just a postal worker, but when I put on this uniform I like to think I'm a sergeant major.'

Norman explained his men were reenactors of the First Mississippi, a regiment who fought particularly heroically during the siege of Vicksburg. He said he liked to relive the Civil War because his great great grandfather had been a slave on a Natchez plantation who had escaped and joined General Grant's troops in the last push against Vicksburg before it fell on 4 July. Norman told me the rest of his troops were welders, farmhands, one was even an office manager. They portrayed soldiers not only to relive history but more as a chance to escape to another world.

'The manager guy,' said Norman, his face softening into a smile, 'he has to make big decisions and boss people around all day at work. So when he's with us he likes to have other people do the bossing. It's the opposite for me, I do a menial job but here I am an officer. It's a liberating hobby.'

'Are there many black reenactors?' I asked.

'Not that many,' he replied, fiddling with the butt of his rifle. 'The truth is some of the Confederate reenactors feel uncomfortable about having blacks involved. Some are cool, but some are hardliners. Blacks were never officially allowed to fight for the Confederacy and only fought for the Union from 1862 onwards. Some of the Rebels still carry on as if they are fighting that war for real.'

I mentioned that I had seen the film *Glory* in which Denzil Washington and Morgan Freeman portray soldiers of the 54th Massachusetts attempting to storm Fort Wagner, a Rebel-held earthworks near Charleston in South Carolina. The 54th lost almost half its men in the attack, including their commander, Colonel Robert Gould Shaw, but their heroics paved the way for more coloured soldiers to join the Union ranks.

'Yeah, that was a good movie,' stated Norman, somewhat dismissively. 'But everyone bangs on about that one event. The 54th were real brave but they were made up of free slaves, ones already liberated.' He wagged a finger at me. 'Now the regiment we portray were all runaway slaves – now there's a story to be told.'

We got talking about September 11 and I asked him if he felt it had pulled America closer together racially.

'It has in some ways, but it won't last long,' Norman shook his head, while wiping the barrel of his gun with a strip of tallow. 'At Pearl Harbor blacks and whites fought together. After the war we were all chummy for a while but it didn't take long for the old racial tensions to surface again. Now we're almost back to square one.'

'Surely it's not that bad.'

'Listen to me.' Norman moistened his lips and sucked the air in between his teeth. 'During the Civil War there was a Confederate officer called Nathan Bedford Forrest.'

I already knew of Forrest. Born to poverty and largely self-educated, Forrest had a meteoric rise through the ranks from private to lieutenant general. Known as 'that Devil Forrest' by his enemies, he was a formidably brave, competent but brutal cavalry leader, who had supposedly had twenty-nine horses shot from under him throughout the Civil War. Legend has it he also personally slew thirty Union soldiers in hand-to-hand fighting. The prominent historian, Shelby Foote, considered Forrest to be one of the Civil War's two authentic geniuses, Abraham Lincoln being the other.

'Forrest captured Fort Pillow on the Mississippi near the end of the war,' continued Norman, his face hardening. 'Afterwards he ordered several of the surrendering black soldiers to be executed.'

'I agree he could be brutal,' I interrupted. 'But Forrest's defenders say he never issued that order at Fort Pillow.'

'Whether he ordered it or not, he still watched over while the black soldiers were killed,' Norman protested, the sweat glistening on his forehead. 'It was on his watch, he could have stopped it. But even worse, after the war he became the First Imperial Wizard of the Ku Klux Klan. Some people say he pulled out as soon as the Klan turned violent, but that doesn't wash with me. He'd already done the damage.'

'So you don't think Confederates should honour Forrest?' I asked.

'I most certainly don't,' growled Norman. 'Through his actions that man killed and terrorised more blacks than you can imagine. People say that Osama bin Laden is responsible

for the worst act of terrorism in this country. What he did was
terrible but in their heyday the Ku Klux Klan were just as
bad, if not worse. All that taunting and lynching, much of it
never recorded.' Norman softened his voice and smiled
weakly. 'How can things improve if people still venerate men
like Forrest? I'm sorry, brother, but it's gonna be a long time
coming.'

*   *   *

From the Fork of the Road, my head spinning with Norman's
prophecies, Neil took me out to lunch. He plumped for
Mammy's Cupboard, certainly one of the most curious restaurants I've ever seen. It is built in the shape of a huge, black
mammy in a purply hoop skirt under whose tent-like hem sat
the diners. Mammy reminded me of a giant Russian doll, the
sort you can dismantle and find other identical ones inside.
She was another of Natchez's defiantly anachronistic landmarks, pulling in punters since the 1940s.

The place was packed, mostly with elderly, well-dressed
women nibbling on salads and drinking iced tea. The menu
offered plenty of Southern cuisine; catfish, turnip greens and
even chicken fried steaks, which I thought could only be
found in Texas. Confusingly, a chicken fried steak is not made
of chicken at all. It is a piece of breaded, deep-fried beef that
comes dripping in creamy gravy. Texans love it, apparently
eating close to a million daily. The last one I'd had back in
Huntsville tasted like a sun-dried plimsoll, so I unadventur-
ously chose a salad instead.

Over lunch I was keen to sound out Neil on Norman's
comments. I told him about the comparison the tough-talking
reenactor made between bin Laden and the Ku Klux Klan.

'Well, that's a strong opinion,' Neil said, spearing a
tomato. He paused to consider the question. 'I think you've
got to understand, Tom, that in your travels you are going to

hear two very different views. You are going to hear about two pasts and two presents, one black, one white. Of course there is some common ground, but not always. Feelings run very strong either way.'

'But surely things are slowly improving?'

'I hope so, but it's hard to say.'

Neil explained that it was important to understand parts of Mississippi had areas that were 70 per cent black and 30 per cent white. Natchez itself was roughly 50:50. He said people often forget that there is more racial integration in communities like Natchez than in many cities in the North. Even in Washington DC, one of the few Northern cities with many more blacks than whites, he felt there was little mingling of the races.

Throughout recent history, Neil continued, the North has had a more liberal attitude towards the rights of black people but in the South, despite the bitter legacy of slavery and racial violence, there is now often a far healthier blending of blacks and whites. Neil felt Northerners could be unduly hypocritical about race, especially when most of them lived in all-white communities.

'There's a saying that was coined during the Civil Rights period,' commented Neil. 'The blacks joked that in the South it didn't matter how close you got to the whites, just how big compared to them. In the North, it didn't matter how big you got, just how close. There's still something in that.'

Later that afternoon I visited Neil's bookshop again to see if I could uncover more information. After rifling through an assortment of books and articles I discovered that the South was making something of a financial resurgence and that the eleven states of the Old Confederacy (with a population only the size of Germany) now made up the fifth largest economy in the world. Not only this, but now that the South had slowly begun to slough off its image as a land of rampaging, banjo-playing rednecks, Northern blacks were also tentatively returning there to seek work, especially in the major cities of Virginia and the Carolinas.

But not all was so rose tinted. Although hard to believe while in the seductive confines of Natchez, Mississippi itself was at the very bottom of the state leagues for both education and economic output. In his book *No Place Like Home*, Gary Younge, a black British journalist who tours America, notes that the South still has the top five states for infant mortality and three of the top five for both violent crime and people living below the poverty line. Younge stresses that a disproportionate amount of this social meltdown is concentrated in black communities.

On a more frivolous but equally revealing note, I learnt from Younge's book of a striking contrast in black and white culture. In America, the sitcom *Friends* is the fourth most popular TV show for whites, but only ranks at number 118 for blacks. Likewise the number one show among blacks, *Between Brothers*, is 117th for whites. Neil was right. I was hearing about two very different presents, as well as pasts. Ironically on Sundays, the divide was stronger than ever, with 71 per cent of blacks attending black or mostly black churches.

Increasingly confounded by this *Friends* versus *Brothers* scenario I told Neil, who had many black friends, about my latest discoveries.

'Don't forget, Tom, racial divides are not always negative,' he advised me. 'Of course they can be, especially if prejudice or anger are involved. But some cultural divisions are simply a natural way for people to behave. To be at one with their own people.' Neil rubbed his thumb sagely under his chin. 'Remember, even though blacks and whites choose to visit different churches, they are hopefully all praying to the same God.'

*   *   *

From Natchez Colonel Arthur hitched a ride on a carriage east to Brookhaven, before catching a train north to Jackson, Mississippi's state capital. He had decided to bypass belea-guered Vicksburg, which was still heavily under siege. En route he notes the escalating poverty: 'it is impossible to exaggerate the unfortunate condition of the women left behind in these farmhouses,' he wrote. 'They have scarcely any clothes, and nothing but the coarsest bacon to eat.'

My ancestor's train was forced to stop three miles out of Jackson; Union troops had sabotaged the rails and sleepers nearer the city. In fact most of Jackson had already been comprehensively trounced by General Grant's men, who only stayed for a total of thirty-six hours before focusing all their might on Vicksburg. Colonel Arthur is disgusted to witness the still smouldering farms and houses and 'the wanton pillaging'.

Later, while walking through Jackson's dilapidated streets, Colonel Arthur was apprehended by a Mr Smythe, who had 'long gray hair and an enormous revolver'. Smythe does not believe that the Colonel, dressed in his smelly shooting jacket, is a British officer, remarking perceptively that he looks: '*mighty young for a lootenant colonel.*' Smythe, and several other Rebels, became convinced my ancestor was a Yankee spy and kept him under close guard. Colonel Arthur quickly sensed that: 'nothing would relieve the minds of these men so much as a hanging . . .'

My troubled forebear is saved at the eleventh hour by a 'big, heavy man' called Dr Russell, who tells him: 'I'm an Irishman, and I hate the British government and the English nation; but if you are really an officer in the Coldstream Guards there is nothing I won't do for you; you shall come to my house and I will protect you.'

Having been exonerated as a secret agent Colonel Arthur caught a little carriage (which he nicknames the chicken wagon) out to see General Joe Johnson's troops nearer Vicksburg. As he sets off Arthur and his fellow passengers are showered in flowers tossed at them by Jackson's few remaining ladies. On meeting up with General Johnson, my ancestor, still no doubt plucking petals from his hair, notes that all the troops hold the stern, grey-bearded warrior in awe. He is also impressed by Johnson's ability to rough it with the best of them.

'He [Johnson] lives very plainly,' writes Arthur, 'his only cooking utensils consisted of an old coffeepot and frying pan – both very inferior articles. There was only one fork (one prong deficient) between himself and his staff, and this was handed to me ceremoniously as the "guest".'

Arthur only spends a brief spell with Johnson and even as they chat the bombardment of Vicksburg can be heard in the background. Although begrudgingly impressed by the doggedness of General Grant's attack on Vicksburg, no one at the camp has a good word to say about General Pemberton, the Confederate officer defending the port. Arthur notes Pemberton is 'freely called a coward and a traitor,' but then goes on to explain, 'he [Pemberton] has the misfortune of being a Northerner by birth . . .'

While sitting around the campfire on his last night with Johnson's troops, Colonel Arthur is delighted to hear one of the officers remark: 'I can assure you, Colonel, that nine men out of ten in the South would sooner become subjects of Queen Victoria than return to the Union.' This makes Colonel Arthur swell with pride until another officer rains on his parade by stating he would rather serve under the Emperor of France or Japan than under Abraham Lincoln. Arthur simply cannot comprehend anyone preferring these 'infernal regions' to even Union rule.

After hitching a lift on the chicken wagon back to Jackson, Colonel Arthur rode on a train up to Meridian, then over the Alabama border and down to the port of Mobile on the Gulf of Mexico. From here, right up until Culpepper in north Virginia, Arthur almost always rides on steam trains as opposed to stagecoaches and mule carriages. As a result of this his diary loses its addictive, rough and tumble approach and, to my mind, becomes much less stimulating reading. Arthur writes very little about his day-to-day observations and chugs his way from the camp of one top-brass general to the next. He showers his hosts with the usual compliments such as 'most gentlemanly', 'very good looking', 'of venerable appearance' and perhaps his favourite: 'speaks English like an English gentleman'.

The only general who comes in for a mild drubbing is Braxton Bragg, who the Colonel witnesses being baptised at Shelbyville in Tennessee. He describes fey, irritable Bragg, one of the South's most incompetent officers, with the following words: 'sickly, cadaverous, haggard appearance, rather plain features, bushy black eyebrows . . . He has the reputation of being a rigid disciplinarian, and of shooting freely for insubordination.' Although Fremantle notes Bragg is generally unpopular with his men, he concedes that the grouchy General is at least civil to him.

Colonel Arthur's diary does not flag completely in the middle section. In the major cities of Atlanta, Charleston and Richmond he has several fascinating encounters. However, it is only when he reaches Culpepper and begins to travel by a combination of foot and horse on the road up to Gettysburg

that his diary really takes off again. Indeed, the young Coldstreamer's description of the Battle of Gettysburg is deserv-
edly considered a classic. His writing is at its best, fusing
extreme excitement with military savvy. The British historian
John Keegan recently included my ancestor's account of
Gettysburg in an anthology of great military writing, along
with war reports by the likes of Hannibal and Hemingway.

As Colonel Arthur's route zigzags erratically from Brookhaven onwards, I decided to part ways with him until north
Virginia when both his journey and his writing gain momentum. From Brookhaven I would beat the most direct and
mule-friendly path towards Gettysburg, while taking time for
fleeting side trips to Atlanta, Charleston and Richmond, so as
not to lose my ancestor's scent completely.

*   *   *

From Browny's stable, rather than marching northeast up the
Natchez Trace – a scenic antebellum trade route – I decided it
would be quicker to head due east on a minor highway. It
turned out to be plain sailing thanks to Browny. With a fresh
set of shoes and a belly full of hay and carrots the old mule
was clearly raring to go again.

We camped the first night at the back of an Exxon station
with howling dogs and nearby freight trains providing a
haunting soundtrack, while the second night a farmer called
Pop Larkin let Browny and me doss down in his stables.
I nodded off to a lullaby of oat munching and the whisk of
mare's tails. In the morning Pop's spaniel puppy jumped on
my sleeping bag, ripping the canvas and puffing out tufts of
goose down. The wound was easily mended with a combination of needle, thread and, thanks to my dire sewing, masking
tape.

After a pitstop in Brookhaven, once a major recruiting
ground for the Southern army, my ancestor and I parted

company. Browny and I continued plodding east while Arthur veered off north to Meridian before plunging south again through Alabama. Little did I know the Colonel would catch up with us again far sooner than expected: as for the Civil War, it would never really let us go.

PART TWO

The Danish philosopher Søren Kierkegaard wrote a parable about a church whose membership was exclusively ducks. Every Sunday morning the ducks came to church, waddled down the aisle, waddled into the pews and squatted. Then the duck minister came in wearing his duck robe. He stood behind the duck pulpit, took the duck Bible and read: 'Ducks! You have wings, and with wings, you can fly like eagles. You can soar into the sky. Ducks! You have wings!' And all the ducks said: 'Amen!' and waddled home.

Scribbled on a wall at Knibbles Café,
Brookhaven, Mississippi

CHAPTER 12

Trenton's Sky

The remainder of Mississippi had its arduous stretches and at times Browny and I were greeted with suspicion rather than the usual small-town goodwill. Roughly once a day a truck full of rednecks would roar by, its rowdy passengers hurling abuse often followed by an empty beer can. 'Buy a car, you stupid old timer,' they taunted, and a host of considerably more explicit insults. This was all rather dispiriting as was the bland, undulating countryside, the deserted rural stores and the lorries transporting squawking chickens from the nearby factory farms, leaving a trail of skittish feathers in their wake. Only when a couple of girls in an open-top sports car slowed down and yelled out, 'Hey, mister, nice ass!' did I break into a smile.

On the plus side the Mississippi communities where locals embraced the journey were some of the most welcoming to date. In the little town of Laurel we were lucky to meet Wally and Jonelle Damlouji. The evening I bumped into them I noticed Browny had developed a mild saddle sore caused by a chaffing girth strap. With true Southern bonhomie Wally and Jonelle took my mule into the fold along with their three cats, two Afghan hounds and a neighbouring Vietnamese pot-bellied pig.

Wally Damlouji, a swarthy, soft-spoken man with a shy smile, was a first-generation American, who had originally come over from Iraq in the 1960s having secured a place at a university in Kansas. After completing his degree, and marrying Southern belle Jonelle, a fellow student, he set up a kitchen installation company in Laurel. Wally had now retired and the company was run by his capable, goatee-bearded son, Paul. They were, in a sense, the American dream in motion, and Wally, like so many immigrants who had made good, was deeply patriotic towards his adoptive land.

During my stay in Laurel the local vet, a friend of Wally, donated a tub of luminous green goo for me to rub on Browny's sore and within a couple of days her scab had hardened and peeled off. Thanks to this direct action she was now fighting fit again. I, too, felt rested after an indolent spell of writing and reading. In the evenings I played Trivial Pursuit with Paul and his friends on the Damlouji's creaky porch, while ghost-coloured moths danced around in the lantern light.

The trivia was all very American-centred, although there was the odd exception, one of which I remember clearly.

'What is the highest mountain in Africa?' I asked Paul on my last night, reading from one of the question cards.

'Mount Kilimanjaro,' he answered immediately. He knew he was right and reached across for a slice of blue cake.

'How the hell d'you know that, cowboy?' joked Sunny, one of Paul's local friends. 'You're an American. The only mountain you should know about is Mount goddamn Rushmore.'

'Mississippians don't know shit about geography,' said Paul, chuckling. 'They think this little state is the centre of the universe.'

'Hey, Mr Kilimanjaro,' countered Sunny. 'All I can tell you is that I live in the best place in the world. That's the only goddamn geography I need to know.'

*   *   *

Once Browny's sore had healed we marched off east towards the Alabama border. Our first night after the Damloujis' was bizarre even by Mississippian standards. Near the town of Waynesboro a fragile-looking, fifty-something couple, Bubba and Maggie East, pulled over and offered to put us up at their farmhouse. They sketched me a map of how to reach them and within half an hour I had tracked down their front paddock.

Things didn't feel quite right from the start. As I tied up Browny to a fence post, I noticed a large removal van at the back of the house being loaded up with the Easts' belongings. Several people clustered around Bubba and Maggie. There was lots of backslapping and hugging. Emotions were clearly running high. By the time I had finished sorting out Browny, the van and its passengers had driven off and I felt more comfortable about making an appearance.

'Are you sure it's OK for me to stay?' I asked Bubba. I gestured to the remaining boxes the removal team had left behind. 'It looks like a busy time for you.'

At this stage Maggie burst into tears and ran indoors. Bubba sat down on a swinging bench on the verandah and gestured for me to join him. We swayed clumsily back and forth. Bubba, scratching on his forehead, confessed to me that he was in trouble. He had embezzled a six-figure sum from his boss, a local car salesman, whom he had worked with for over twenty years. A few weeks ago, the boss had wised up to Bubba's scam. He had been caught red-handed and put under house arrest. Bubba explained that the only way to help pay back his colossal debt was to sell up the surrounding farmhouse and garden, where he and Maggie had lived all their married life.

Bubba's house arrest meant he would only be able to spend four hours each week away from his new home — a pokey one-bedroom house in the Laurel suburbs — and even this precious time was to be devoted exclusively to church visits. Fortunately Maggie held down a steady job as a waitress and their two children were now both grown up and fending for themselves.

After Maggie had composed herself the three of us sat drinking iced tea in their dismantled kitchen. Bubba and Maggie were clearly both strong Christians, and numerous biblical quotations still adorned the walls. Stuck on the fridge were some family photos, their daughter getting married, their son running a marathon. I was impressed by how loyal Maggie, clearly a sweet-natured soul, had remained considering what had happened.

When Bubba left the room to feed the family dogs Maggie welled up with tears. 'We've got to give away the dogs too, no room for them in the new place.' She sighed, her petite frame shaking with a fierce inner grief. 'My husband's a good, decent man, you know.' She seized my wrist as if it would stop her from falling. 'It was just one stupid mistake. Just one stupid, *stupid* mistake.' There was something heartbreaking about her utter willingness to forgive.

'Yes, I can see that,' I replied, trying to sound encouraging. 'Don't worry. You'll both bounce back.'

Bubba returned. He was holding a camp bed in one hand and a pillow in the other. 'Sleep tight, Tom,' he told me, laying the bed down and puffing up a pillow. 'I promise you I won't steal anything in the night. I've learnt my lesson now.'

We all laughed, although it was functional guffawing rather than anything remotely joyous: laughter in the dark.

'Thank you for letting me stay,' I said, looking around at the boxed-up possessions. 'It was good of you with all, er, *this* going on.'

'Oh, it's fine,' replied Bubba. 'When you've fallen as low as me, it's nice to know I can still help someone.'

Before I turned in for the night Bubba asked if I minded kneeling down to say the Lord's Prayer with him and Maggie. I hadn't knelt to say a prayer, at least outside of church, for as long as I can remember. Anything that provided Bubba with some hope in these wretched circumstances was worth a try. We all genuflected, shy as schoolchildren, then bowed our heads and asked for our trespasses to be forgiven in the still, empty house.

*   *   *

The next day Browny and I made it across the Alabama border. The landscape didn't change that much and nor did the attitude of the drivers. One day, to my fury, a glass bottle flung from a passing truck narrowly missed Browny's hind-quarters. There was an eerie malaise hanging over some of the more poverty-stricken communities we encountered. We were never far from the next burnt-out car, or weed-infested mobile home or backyard full of rusted jetsam.

Another prevalent feature of the surrounding landscape was kudzu. I had seen kudzu throughout much of my Southern wanderings, but in parts of Mississippi and Alabama it reached plague proportions. Kudzu is a triffid-like vine, or more correctly weed, which engulfs just about everything it comes into contact with. Originally it had been imported to America from Japan in the 1870s as a way to combat soil erosion.

For all its benefits kudzu soon became a major pest in the Deep South, running rampant, like verdant scaffolding, through forests and swamplands. The poet James Dickey once described it as: 'a vegetable form of cancer'. Browny clearly agreed with him. Despite the fact kudzu regularly sprouted from Alabamian highway verges, it was one of the only bits of greenery I ever saw her turn her nose up at.

That said, my mule certainly did not starve in Alabama. It was clearly a state where mules were revered. For every redneck throwing beer cans and abuse there were twice the number of kind souls pulling over and treating Browny to apples, carrots, sweet corn and, as a real treat, M&M chocolates, her absolute favourite.

Certainly the most comical aspect of rural Alabama was the roadside bartering. On several occasions a mud-caked pick-up would skid to a halt in front of us. A weather-beaten man, often elderly and clad in blue overalls, would approach. Without any of the usual 'Where you from? What you up to?' niceties he would simply ask: 'How much for the mule?' Before I had time to intervene he would walk up to Browny, rip her mouth open and start feeling her teeth to test her age. 'Got some years on her, but I like her,' was the usual comment while groping around the hapless mule's dentistry. 'I'll give you two hundred/five hundred/one thousand dollars for her.' It would take some time before I could persuade these insistent skinners that my beast was absolutely not for sale.

Despite the sometimes grinding poverty, local people continued to look out for me. They continued to offer me food and shelter, which I accepted, and money, which I always refused. From the look of some of the living conditions I soon realised that Bubba and Maggie were not the only Deep Southerners struggling to make ends meet.

One night deep in the boondocks I secured permission to stake out Browny in a pinewood glade. The nearest house belonged to nineteen-year-old Chip, a heavily tattooed, peroxide-blond ex-con. When I asked to see his parents he laughed bitterly. Chip told me they were both dead, killed in a fire. He had been just ten when it happened. He told me his father had been a drug dealer, who had accrued major debts. The fire had been started by one of his father's rivals and his mother, a drug addict, had been unable to escape from the flames and died too.

Chip explained he had been raised by his 'grandpoppy', a good hearted but soft man, who had been unable to control him through his schooldays. By the age of twelve Chip had been put in a young offenders' institution having stolen guns and money from a local pawnshop. After more run-ins with the law he seemed to have calmed down and now proudly revealed to me that he stacked shelves at the local grocery store. He was clearly still deeply troubled but there was a certain wherewithal and decency about him. He was one of the few people I met who was able to gain Browny's trust within the space of a few hours, using a winning combination of patience and bamboo leaves.

The night I camped near his junk pile of a home, Chip listened to Ozzy Osbourne on his Walkman and puffed on some suspicious-smelling cigarettes with his rangy, saucer-eyed girlfriend, a deadringer for the young Bette Davis.

When Chip was out of earshot she leaned over to me. 'I can see you're a little jumpy,' she whispered, levelling me with her dilated grey eyes. 'Chip may have skull and dagger tattoos on his arm but he wouldn't hurt a fly. Don't sweat it, he's been through a lot but you can trust him.' She exhaled a smoke ring, before adding more cryptically. 'You're lucky you

found us, after those attacks in New York you can't trust a
soul else around here.'

*   *   *

My lowest ebb came on the night of Thanksgiving, 22 November. Browny and I had reached an attractive but languid
village on the road to Grove Hill. Unable to find a place to
camp I was advised to steer my beast to a scrubby patch of
meadow a mile up the road. When I got there the only other
sign of life was a nearby caravan, where I was told a reclusive
hobo called Trenton lived.

The mild weather had suddenly changed and the evening
was bleak and frozen. Fortunately there was no wind and
I was able to spark up a campfire without too much difficulty.
This provided a certain solace but for the first time on the
journey I was stung by an aching loneliness. After all it was
Thanksgiving, a time for celebration, and here I was devoid of
any human company. My travels so far had been so animated
but over the last few days a certain lassitude was taking hold.

I wondered if Colonel Arthur was ever gripped by loneliness. It was unlikely: the rampaging Coldstreamer barely
had time to twiddle his thumbs between adventures, let alone
get caught up in a self-pitying grump. For the regular soldiers
of the blue and grey, however, it was a different matter. They
endured long spells away from their families, with many a
boring and uncomfortable hiatus between the bloody frenzy
of battle.

Sitting by my campfire that Thanksgiving night, I studied
my well-thumbed copy of *The Civil War* by Geoffrey Ward, Ric
Burns and Ken Burns. I knew this book contained several
letters sent by Union and Confederate soldiers to loved ones,
and would provide me with some much-needed company.
I riffled through the pages, occasionally stopping to blow on

my gloved fingers. Many of the letters were poignant but one really caught my imagination.

The letter in question was written by Major Sullivan Ballou, a Northerner from Rhode Island, to his wife, Sarah. It was penned in the summer of 1861 almost two years before Colonel Arthur docked in Mexico. This was a time when many Americans were still treating the war almost as a game, a grand adventure. There was singing and promenading in the streets, girls throwing flowers and kisses to the jauntily dressed troops as they marched by. Few thought it would last long. One Alabama Congressman famously pooh poohed the whole affair and offered to mop up all the blood that would be shed with a handkerchief. Little did he know then that the next four years would destroy almost an entire generation of Americans.

The first major battle of the Civil War, from which Major Ballou wrote his letter, took place in north Virginia. The Union and Confederacy called it different names. The South dubbed it the battle of Manassas, after the local town, whereas the North opted for Bull Run, a nearby stream. After this, many other battles throughout the war were given different names by the opposing sides. The horrific, Tennessee-based battle of Shiloh, for instance, was named after a church by the South, while the North called it Pittsburg's Landing, after a nearby docking station.

On the morning of Manassas, 21 July 1861, hundreds of excited Washington citizens rode out to join the advancing blue army all hoping to witness a Union triumph. Some brought binoculars, picnic hampers, bottles of wine or champagne, as if off to the races or an al fresco opera. Of course, it didn't turn out like that. Despite a strong start, by late afternoon the Northern army was fleeing headlong back towards Washington, its ranks in tatters, pursued by Southerners indulging for the first time in their Rebel yell, a sort of

maniac shouting mixed with a foxhound's yelp. Whipped up
into a chaotic state of euphoria by their victory, the Confederate troops failed to capitalise on their advantage. If they
had pushed on towards Washington, history might have had a
very different outcome.

Manassas claimed over five thousand dead and wounded,
minor casualties compared to the devastation of later battles,
but more than enough to wake up Americans to the potential
horror that lay ahead. The party atmosphere was over. The
war had begun.

What follows is an excerpt from the homesick Major
Ballou's letter to his wife:

> Sarah, my love for you is deathless, it seems to bind me with
> mighty cables that nothing but Omnipotence could break;
> and yet my love of Country comes over me like a strong wind
> and bears me unresistably on with all these chains to the
> battle field.
>
> The memories of the blissful moments I have spent with
> you come creeping over me, and I feel most gratified to God
> and to you that I have enjoyed them so long. And hard it is for
> me to give them up and burn to ashes the hopes of future
> years, when, God willing, we might still have lived and loved
> together, and seen our sons grown up to honorable man-
> hood, around us. I have, I know, but few and small claims
> upon Divine Providence, but something whispers to me —
> perhaps it is the wafted prayer of my little Edgar, that I shall
> return to my loved ones unharmed. If I do not my dear Sarah,
> never forget how much I love you, and when my last breath
> escapes me on the battle field, it will whisper your name.

Major Sullivan Ballou was one of the first men killed at the
battle of Manassas.

*   *   *

Thanksgiving Eve journal, 2001

Sitting by my fire, hickory twigs are crackling under the smudged moon. The billycan is bubbling up a treat. It's so icy sharp out here that Browny's mane is frozen. She looks a bit like that unicorn from Narnia, only fatter, dirtier and a lot less civilised. Of course, Browny can't fly either, the useless lummox. Oh, how I love the old beast though. She's making me laugh right now, the way she's ripping at the briars near the tent, munching like fury. She occasionally stops to look up at me, her breath smoking in the darkness.

I've just spent the evening with an old man called Trenton Smith who lives on the meadow where I'm camping. His home is a caravan no bigger than a garden shed. It's full of junk — a 1999 calendar, a camping stove, a rusty cheese grater and a radio suspended from the roof by a wire. In fact it's so full of junk, so rotten and forlorn, that it has slumped to one side like a torpedoed ship.

The only place to sit at Trenton's is a damp mattress that has little weeds sprouting out from its sides. Some of the weeds are so at home in his stinky lair they have started to blossom, blue and yellow petals shooting out like dreams.

Trenton lives mostly off potatoes and pickles, which he mashes up in a bucket. Occasionally he is treated to some pecan nuts that fall on his roof during gusty nights. 'Same as hobbits dancing,' he tells me. Pecan and pickle potatoes — that's what we ate tonight. Trenton made it sound like the grandest dish on earth. In some ways it was you know. Any meal offered by a stranger to a mule gypsy is special, but this one more than ever because he was just so happy to share it. We drank black tea and a bit too much dewberry wine so forgive my scatterbrain words.

It's Thanksgiving tomorrow, the day Americans celebrate the Pilgrim Fathers docking on the Massachusetts coast in the Mayflower over 350 years ago. It's hard to imagine being the first settlers, striking out in this strange and lonely New World. Of course the Indian people had settled here long before, already at one with the land, happy to worship the trees, the eagles and the buffalo. Anyway, that's another story. Nowadays Thanksgiving is an important day for modern Americans, a time to spend with their families, a time to laugh, gossip, fight, eat turkey and black-eyed peas and celebrate the meaning of home.

Home seems a million miles away tonight and I'm a little downcast. The main reason is because of something I saw in Trenton's caravan. Time has been cruel to him. He has all these pictures of his family on display, pictures of a life he once lived. There are dozens of them — Trenton standing proudly in a suit alongside his parents, leaning against a shiny truck he once drove, kissing a happy, moon-faced woman in a wedding dress.

It's hard to recognise the Trenton of today from these photos Blu-Tacked to his walls. His once bushy hair has receded as dramatically as his luck. He's as lonely as a wolf: his weary, woebegone face reminds me of an unmade bed. The saddest photos are of his young daughter, a pretty girl with sapphire eyes: as a baby, at school, and more recently of her heading off to a party in a spangly skirt. Her face is all over the caravan, watching him. But Trenton never sees her now, hasn't seen her for years, or his ex-wife or anyone really. He'd love to see his family more than anything in the world but they don't want to see him. Thanksgiving is the saddest day of the year in his wobbly caravan.

I don't pretend to understand what caused Trenton's decline. He told me it was some sort of breakdown. He clearly drinks too much but he seems such a gentle soul, as baffled by his shift in circumstances as a buzzing bluebottle suddenly stunned by a windowpane. I've met several characters like Trenton living in caravans and trailer homes throughout my walk in the Deep South, proud souls clinging to the wreckage. Almost without exception they remain optimistic, sure their luck will turn. 'Are you free like us in your country?' Trenton keeps asking me, without realising, or perhaps refusing to realise, he himself is utterly trapped. He wears a baseball cap with the slogan, DIXIE — CLOSEST THING TO HEAVEN. One can only respect his imperishable sense of hope.

Trenton insists that in this life we never know what is going to happen to us, and 'don't let anyone tell you differently, son'. None of us knows, he claims, whether some self-important charlie with the Midas touch or a hobo like him drowning in fate's quicksand. He believes we spin off in all sorts of unimaginable directions, chase dreams and run from demons we never imagined existed. He thinks we've all become far too proud.

At times on this journey I thought I could face this world on my own, a defiant pilgrim. 'Bring it on,' I'd shout at the moon. But that doesn't ring so true tonight, sitting here alone with only my mule and the ghost of Major Sullivan Ballou for company.

Trenton has just walked over to my fire. He's clearly had much more dewberry wine and his face is flushed, twitchy with excitement. He's chewing tobacco now, and when he smiles his teeth look green. With him is a huge fellow called Tony, an old friend of his who has dropped by for Thanksgiving. Tony used to be a boxer. He has bright, unblinking eyes and a jawbone as firm and round as a mule shoe.

I've never seen someone look so happy as Trenton, just to have some company. His Thanksgiving is now complete. A bucket full of potatoes, a bottle of dewberry wine and someone to yarn to about the old times — that's about as good as it gets here. Seeing Trenton's delirious contentment is one of this journey's high points.

I wonder how many people are watching the stars now along with Trenton, Tony and me — astronomers with their feeble telescopes, sailors on their rigging, soldiers, shepherds, lovers? Some looking up, giving flight to their dreams, while others will turn away as if the luminous glitter of the galaxy and its countless possibilities are all a bit much.

Trenton's spotted one star out there tonight, high above the caravan. He tells me it's for his daughter. It's the brightest he can find. I don't know what it's called, probably Cassiopeia or Alpha Centauri Minor or something pompous like that, but tonight it's going to be christened Trenton's Star, and to hell with Galileo and Copernicus.

When Colonel Arthur was out here he probably sat by his campfire wishing on a star too, along with hundreds of other young soldiers seeking reassurance from the heavens. Arthur married a girl called Mary Hall a year after he returned to England, so maybe he named one for her. They never had children, Arthur and Mary: no more branches on the family tree.

But some things are constant and that's what I like about the stars. Of course each generation fears for the next, talks about the good old days as if human advancement only ever creates a legacy of shame, a loss of innocence. But there will always be things to marvel at. I can imagine, in a thousand years, long after Trenton's caravan has sunk in the dust, another group of wanderers sitting by a campfire in Alabama. It will be a Thanksgiving Eve and they will look up at the night sky, each pick a star, and pray for someone far away.

CHAPTER 13

Any Colour You Like

By the time I steered Browny into the historic town of Selma I was dirty and footsore. I decided to take some time to explore and, more self-indulgently, treat myself to a night tucked up in fresh linen. I checked into the Graystone Motel, lured by its semi-literate billboard that bragged $29 SINGAL ROOM, CHEEPEST IN TOWN. The other big advantage of the Graystone, other than a chance to scrub my foetid clothes in a bathtub, was a generous patch of clover for Browny to graze out the back. The friendly Indian couple that ran the place took an instant shine to my beast and kept an eye out for her while I was sightseeing.

SELMA – FROM CIVIL WAR TO CIVIL RIGHTS read a banner near the visitor's centre. A CITY WITH A THRILLING HISTORY. There was no disputing this. In 1860 Selma's dark, fertile farmland had been at its cotton-producing prime, making surrounding Dallas County the wealthiest area in all Alabama. Once the Civil War broke out Selma retained its prominence by becoming a key munitions hub. The Union army only wrested control of the city as late as 1865, after a spirited but fruitless defence action by that ever-controversial Confederate, Nathan Bedford Forrest.

However, Selma's main claim to fame came a full century after Forrest's last battle. Tourists today tend to visit the city, not for Civil War reasons, but to see the Edmund Pettus Bridge where the groundbreaking 'Bloody Sunday' Civil Rights protest march took place in the summer of 1965. This peaceful event famously turned ugly after a posse of Alabama troopers laid into the five hundred or so marchers.

The troopers clad in gas masks and helmets used tear gas, clubs, bullwhips and even cattle prods to turn back the crowd. The marchers eventually retreated but not for long. Television footage of the troopers' violence shocked America and two weeks later three thousand defiant protesters, including Martin Luther King, marched across the bridge again, this time unmolested. Many of them kept going as far as Montgomery, over fifty miles east, sleeping in cotton fields en route.

'Bloody Sunday' proved pivotal, a quantum leap in the previously sluggish road towards racial equality. In the march's aftermath President Lyndon Johnson pressed Congress to pass the Voting Rights Act and today, over thirty-five years after the Selma bridge incident, this part of Alabama has more black-elected officials than almost any other part of America.

Walking around Selma now, though, it was easy to see the tension had not entirely diffused. While the historic central district appeared neat, tree-lined and prosperous, with a healthy blend of races, the predominantly black east side, beyond the River Alabama, was run down and depressed looking. There was clearly no happy mingling of colour or class here, no classical mansions interspersing the drab stores and tumbledown shacks.

Back in the rain-soaked city centre, very near the Pettus Bridge, I paid a visit to the Voting Rights Museum to see what light it could shed on Selma's complex past. The first exhibit that leaps out at visitors is a notice board entitled 'I Was There' with messages from people who had attended the 1965 march. 'Thank you Selma' read one Post It. 'The struggle continues' warned another in shakily written felt pen. Near by were photos of state troopers muscling in on a group of black marchers, the whole scene blurred by tear gas.

Apart from the many black Civil Rights campaigners there was a wall dedicated to some of the whites that had lost their lives while championing racial equality. These included James Reeb, a Boston preacher, who had been clubbed to death in Selma by a gang of white racists and Viola Liuzzo, a pretty Detroit mother of five who had been shot dead while travelling in a support truck between Selma and Montgomery.

The most disturbing room displayed a historical gallery of racial violence. A caption above some grainy, black and white photographs claimed that between 1889 and 1918 over 3,200 black men, women and children had been lynched in the South. The lynching was often carried out for reasons as spurious as a black man being 'uppity' or looking at a white woman in the 'wrong way'. One snapshot showed two young black men hanging from a tree branch. In the foreground is a mob of spectators, some of them pointing and laughing at the dangling corpses. 'STRANGE FRUIT' reads the caption.

*   *   *

Soon I'd had of enough of all these grim images and headed out back towards the foyer. Here, a sturdily built black girl with a Marge Simpson hairdo and a beaming smile approached me. Her name was Arlethea Pressley and she worked as a reporter for the local newspaper, the *Selma Times-Journal*. She had heard about my mule walk and had been tipped off by the museum staff as to my whereabouts.

Arlethea offered to show me around town while conducting the interview. We jumped into her hatchback and she steered alongside the river towards Brown Chapel where Martin Luther King had made several speeches. It actually turned out that I quizzed Arlethea far more than she did me.

Arlethea explained that at the time of the Selma–Montgomery march her grandfather and mother had both been employed as cotton pickers on a local farm. Although they both joined the start of the march they could not go all the way to Montgomery, as their employers would have fired them. Arlethea stressed that although the march was important, Civil Rights had been in motion long before that violent summer of 1965.

'It really all goes back to when the Civil War ended,' she said, parking behind a yellow school bus near the Brown Chapel. 'Free slaves were supposed to be given forty acres of land and a mule. It didn't always turn out like that. There was still terrible mistreatment of blacks after the Civil War, especially in the South. The formation of the Ku Klux Klan followed by the Jim Crow laws that encouraged segregation and racial superiority – all that stuff.'

Arlethea explained that it wasn't until 1955 when Rosa Parks, a seamstress living in Montgomery, was arrested for refusing to give up her bus seat to a white man that the tide really started turning. Mrs Parks's arrest caused a furore. Then in the early 1960s the Freedom Riders, a small group of campaigners, both black and white, travelled through the South deliberately flouting the segregation rules. They made a strong impact too but Arlethea still conceded that Bloody Sunday is when the floodgates really came down.

'So has Selma finally purged all its demons?' I asked her, as she locked up the car.

'It's still got its troubles but it's certainly come a long way,' stressed Arlethea, setting off down the deserted sidewalk towards Brown Chapel. 'Even George Wallace, the Governor of Alabama at the time of the 1965 march, finally apologised for some of his negative comments about black people. He died recently and probably realised how harsh he'd been. He was known as a real old redneck, but I admire him for admitting he was wrong. Then,' Arlethea rolled her eyes dramatically, 'there's Joe Smitherman. Quite a character. Self-made man and very old school. He was mayor here for thirty-six years on the trot. Just recently he lost the election for the first time and Selma now has James Perkins Junior, its first black mayor. I guess that's progress.'

We now stood in front of Brown Chapel, an unremarkable twin-spired red brick church. Arlethea tried the door but it was locked. A bust of Martin Luther King's head, with the words 'I HAD A DREAM' underneath it stood on a plinth near the chapel facade. Were it not for this modest monument nothing about Brown Chapel stood out, it was like a hundred other churches I had seen across America.

'It's not much, is it?' said Arlethea, echoing my thoughts. 'But that's the point. Doctor King was the champion of ordinary people. These days, people say the blacks have won equal rights and should stop complaining. I can only sympathise with that up to a point. You've got to remember just forty years ago black people round here were treated like second-class citizens. They attended separate schools and were led to believe they could never make it to college. Constantly being told you are the underdog takes a long time to get over.'

Arlethea walked over to King's bust, moving her hands as she spoke to emphasise her words. A pair of mocking birds, pecking around in the churchyard opposite, spotted her and flew off towards the river.

'You have to remember, Tom,' continued Arlethea, 'that the Civil Rights movement was not sparked by a violent grass roots revolution. It was very different to that.'

Arlethea believed events like Bloody Sunday had in fact been generated by a small, dedicated group of largely edu- cated blacks who got fed up with the paternalistic attitude of the white elite. She felt people like Martin Luther King wanted to show that black people were no longer prepared to be patronised and could stand on their own two feet. She admired King's patient, non-violent tactics as opposed to the more aggressive sabre-rattling approach of radicals like Malcolm X, who also spoke at Brown Chapel on several occasions.

'Equal rights was the real driving force,' stressed Arlethea. 'Not violence, or revenge. King was saying, hey, we blacks are able to contribute just as well as you whites, sometimes even better. He was fed up with black subservience.' She jumped back into the car. 'Hop in, Tom, I want you to meet somebody else.'

Arlethea returned to the office of the *Selma Times-Journal*, made a couple of calls and then shuttled me over to Selma's Live Oak cemetery, splashing her little car through the puddles. Hairnets of Christmas decorations and fairy lights arched over Selma's main drag. Church bells occasionally peeled. A mile out of the town centre Arlethea slowed down and pulled up on a dirt track by the cemetery gates. The overcast afternoon coupled with the dark, moss-drenched oaks gave the place a spooky atmosphere. We walked past several stone angels and a sombre monument in honour of 150 unknown Rebel soldiers. Near the cemetery centre was a bust of a fierce, neatly bearded man erected on a plinth fringed with a miniature Confederate battle flag.

'That,' said Arlethea, pointing at the sculpted metal head, 'is Nathan Bedford Forrest. Ruthless KKK grand wizard or dashing Confederate cavalryman, depending on your point of view.'

'Yes, I've already heard a lot about him,' I replied.

Arlethea told me this little statue had caused enormous controversy within Selma. When she joined the newspaper as a rookie over a year ago, the statue had been her first big story. Due to Forrest's links with the KKK, many people thought it was not right to honour the contentious Confederate in a town that was over 60 per cent black. However, other traditionalists argued that Forrest had been instrumental in Selma's defence in 1865 and saved it from being completely ransacked by the Yankees. The debate heated up to such a degree the statue became the focus of the world media.

'I had all sorts of people phoning me,' remembered Arlethea. 'I couldn't believe it. Press from England, Australia, Asia all going crazy over a statue. I suppose I could understand the passions up to a point. People either detest Forrest or respect him. Several locals even slung a rope over Forrest's head and tried to pull him down but he was too heavy. Then others would come and leave flowers.'

Arlethea said it became a very complex and drawn-out issue. Racially it wasn't clearcut either. A few of the local whites agreed that Forrest was a monster and that the statue should be moved or destroyed while a few black townsfolk urged Forrest's enemies to be tolerant and encouraged 'heritage not hate'. Arlethea herself didn't like Forrest but accepted that history couldn't be changed. As long as the statue was tucked away in a cemetery rather than a prominent position in town — initially it had been erected in the grounds of Selma's mayoral office — she wasn't too bothered. She thought the story attracted far more media attention than it deserved.

After receiving a call on her mobile Arlethea told me she had to dash. She had arranged for a local historian, Alston Fitts, to complete my tour of the cemetery and he was due to arrive any minute.

*   *   *

Sure enough, just as Arlethea was leaving Alston appeared right on cue. He was a genial-looking man with a slightly stooped posture and swept-back white hair. As he cautiously walked my way he reminded me of a turtle treading gingerly over some sharp coral.

Alston knew Selma intimately. He had written a history of the town and clearly loved the place. 'There's not many cities that commemorate an important Civil Rights march every year,' he said in his gentle drawl, 'and hold a Civil War reenactment too. It's fairly amazing.' Since he moved to Selma in 1978 Alston had been doing his utmost to ease the city's racial divides. It wasn't always easy. Alston had got fed up with all the brouhaha over Forrest but equally he felt too many people deified Martin Luther King. He longed for Selma citizens to seek a less confrontational middle ground.

'King was undeniably a great man,' said Alston. 'I respect him hugely but he wasn't perfect. He had a weakness for the ladies and certainly had his paramours. Of course he died tragically young, shot in his Memphis motel, but he shouldn't be put on too big a pedestal.' Alston stopped to flick some foliage off one of the graves. He looked up at me and smiled. 'Personally I like my heroes a little flawed. I prefer Doctor King as a human rather than some sort of superman.'

There was one particular grave Alston wanted me to see. Chicaning his way through the damp headstones he soon

Civil War reenactors in Natchez, Mississippi.

With James and Frankie Jean Lewis in Ferriday, Louisiana.

The controversial statue of Nathan Bedford Forrest in Selma, Alabama.

DEFENDER OF SELMA
WIZARD OF THE SADDLE
UNTUTORED GENIUS
THE FIRST WITH THE MOST

I HAD
A DREAM

DR MARTIN L.
KING JR.

Martin Luther King memorial in Selma, Alabama.

Kim on top of Stone Mountain, Atlanta, Georgia.

The world's one and only double-barrelled cannon in Athens, Georgia.

Monument in honour of all the mules and horses killed and injured in the Civil War, outside the Virginia Historical Society, Richmond, Virginia.

Becky Vail with an exhausted Browny, near Sweet Briar, Virginia.

Browny surveying the scenery near Harpers Ferry, West Virginia.

Roger Hughes in his Coldstream uniform ready to face the sleet on the battlefield at Gettysburg, Pennsylvania.

Browny sporting a tarpaulin to fend off the rain in New Jersey.

Amish mule team, Lancaster County, Pennsylvania.

Walking over the George Washington Bridge into New York City.

The last few steps into Central Park, New York City.

Tributes and flags near Ground Zero, New York City.

reached it, an almost brand new monument in honour of one of Alabama's black heroes, Ben Turner. Alston had spearheaded the fundraising campaign to secure Turner a place in this tranquil and selective cemetery.

Ben Turner's life was certainly a remarkable one, Alston explained, as we admired the monument. Born into slavery in 1825, young Ben spent most of his teens working on a plantation near Selma. At the time slaves were forbidden to teach themselves to read and write and if caught doing so were likely to receive thirty-nine lashes: it was felt education would give slaves ideas above their station. To remedy this Ben hid a spelling book under his cap, which he covertly referred to when he had the chance. Before long the intelligent young teenager was literate.

When his plantation employer got into financial trouble Ben was sold on to a lady called Susan Gee, whose family owned the swanky St James's Hotel in Selma. For years the energetic slave ran a carriage service picking up passengers from steamboats and ferrying them to the hotel foyer. Then, during the battle of Selma in 1865, Ben's mules and wagons were seized by Yankee troops. He soon volunteered for the Union army and marched with them all the way to Georgia.

Following the Civil War Ben returned to Selma and set up a livery stable and a saloon with a friend. He quickly became the richest black man in Dallas County and a leader among newly freed slaves. In 1867 he joined the Republican Party and was soon elected to Congress, the first Alabamian black man ever to be so. He only served one term during which he pushed for greater Civil Rights to be granted to former Confederates and for bills cracking down on the then fledgling Ku Klux Klan.

After his stint as a Congressman, largely spent in Washington, Ben Turner returned to Selma and bought a plantation north of town. He continued to play a low-key role in local politics but focused primarily on farming. The agricultural recession of the 1890s hit him hard. To make things worse an illiterate farmhand accidentally poisoned his cattle. Soon after this Ben suffered a massive stroke and, tragically, was almost bankrupt when he died in 1894.

'Ben Turner's is an inspiring story despite the sad ending,' said Alston, rubbing his palm over the monument. 'A slave managing to wind up owning a plantation, it's practically a miracle.'

Alston looked down affectionately at the inscription. 'When I set up this monument in Ben's honour I wanted it to be a bi-racial project,' he stated quietly. 'We had a good cross-section of blacks and whites attending the unveiling and I was real proud. It felt like a step in the right direction. So many Selma events seem to polarize the races, this one united them. Ben Turner would have liked that.'

*   *   *

Over breakfast the following morning I flipped through a newspaper article that Arlethea had left me. It made for especially relevant reading. Dating back almost a month, it covered a race-centred story at Auburn University, Alabama's biggest campus, some one hundred miles east of Selma.

The story focused on the suspension of several students for posting racially insensitive material on a website. Accompanying the article was a photograph of two of the students dressed up for a Halloween party, one in a white Ku Klux Klan cape holding a gun towards another student with a blackened face and a noose over his head. In the background is a Confederate battle flag, clearly being used for provocative rather than historical reasons. The article noted that of Auburn's 22,500 or so students, roughly 1,600 are black.

Reading between the lines it was clear this was a tasteless but very isolated incident that had tarnished a university with generally decent racial dynamics. As one of the university's spokesmen said: 'Auburn is not a racist institution; it is an institution that houses some racist individuals . . . Something like this definitely overshadows all the good things that are happening.'

After finishing the Auburn piece I flicked through the most recent copy of the *Selma Times-Journal*, dated 29 November, with a headline that brought things swiftly back into contemporary focus: 'ALABAMA MAN FIRST TO DIE IN AFGHANISTAN.'

The story concerned Mike Spann, a young soldier from the nearby town of Winfield, who had been killed in action during a prison riot north of Kabul. A follow-up piece indicated that US troops now had the Taliban on the run, although bin Laden's whereabouts were still uncertain. Somehow it all seemed impossibly far away.

After breakfast, stuffed with too much grits and newsprint, I slung on Browny's saddlebags and set off north. Selma had been a stimulating environment but I needed to press on. I was hoping to reach Atlanta, via some three hundred miles of country roads, by Christmas.

*   *   *

Over the next ten days Browny and I had a wonderful run of luck and clocked up the miles relentlessly. In Plantersville I was put up in the local fire station and dined on chicken stew cooked by the fire chief's wife. In the pine forests of Minooka, just as I was about to stick up my tent in the local cemetery, I was taken in by Chris and Ginger Senn, ex-blues band musicians, who reminisced about once jamming with B.B. King in Memphis. While I sipped Jack Daniels, Browny feasted on the weeds amid the cemetery tombstones.

Browny's most sociable night was as a guest at Skipper Stables near Vincent, where she was able to hobnob with some premium halter horses. These elegant creatures (one topping a million dollars) were groomed every day, shampooed twice a week and manicured once a fortnight. They were the beauty queens of the equine world, with Naomi's mane, Elle's posture, Claudia's fetlocks and Kate's cheekbones. Needless to say, Browny, who had now sprouted a yak-like winter coat, looked utterly out of place.

Before long we had bypassed Anniston, a town with the dubious honour of storing some of America's chemical weapons, and were soon tramping into the Appalachian foot-hills. It was a beautiful parcel of land with brown, crisp leaves swirling in the wind, old men raking up pecans and an ambient whiff of bonfire smoke. The only soundtrack was the hoot of owls and the occasional roar of a freight train. Fairy lights twinkled in the farmyard porches and plastic elves and reindeer began to decorate the suburban gardens.

On 10 December we crossed into the state of Georgia, where a signpost heralded: GLAD THAT GEORGIA'S ON YOUR MIND. This was a prescient warning because Georgia was soon much more on my mind than I'd bargained for. Just across the border in the little town of Tallapoosa a man in a grey, Confederate uniform was waiting for Browny and me. He was heavy-set with a thicket of black hair that was receding in clumps, like velvet on a deer's antlers. He was holding up a Confederate flag, the size of a bath towel.

'Mr Fremantle, I presume,' he announced amicably, stretching out his hand. 'My name's Billy. I'm a great admirer of your ancestor's diary.' Billy also turned out to be a member of the Sons of Confederate Veterans, attached to a branch called Forrest's 28th Escort.

'Nathan Bedford Forrest?' I asked.

'Of course,' Billy replied. 'Who else?' Here we go again, I thought, there seemed to be no escaping the ubiquitous Confederate horseman.

Billy was certainly proud of his Southern genes. He told me his great great grandfather had lost a leg defending Atlanta from the Yankees while two other ancestors had fought at Gettysburg. He asked if he could help me in any way and whether I would mind if he marched with me for a while. I told him I had no problem with him joining with me, but made it clear I would prefer it if he wore civilian clothes and furled up the Confederate flag.

'I understand you are proud of your heritage,' I told him. 'But this trip is really just a simple mule walk through America. I don't want it being misinterpreted.'

Billy seemed a bit taken aback by my stance. I sensed my reluctance to fully embrace the Confederate cause had stalled his initial camaraderie.

'I respect my ancestor,' I explained. 'But I don't agree with everything he writes. Please understand I'm not Colonel Arthur. He was here over a hundred and thirty years ago.'

'Yeah, okay,' he replied, a little dejected. 'But I'll still come and walk with you. It will give me time to explain why the Confederate flag should not be seen as a symbol of slavery but of Southern pride.'

Sure enough, as I was loading the mule the following morning Billy appeared in his beat-up jalopy. I was glad to see he was in mufti; he had also thoughtfully brought us both some breakfast.

Before we walked off, Billy opened up his car boot and delicately unfurled an old Georgia flag as if it were a precious tapestry. Billy told me that Roy Barnes, the freshly elected Governor of Georgia, had now banned this flag – which was dominated by the Confederate battle emblem – and replaced it with a new, 'politically correct' one. He pulled out the new state flag from his boot. It was mostly navy blue with a host of little symbols fringing it.

'This is the *updated* flag,' sneered Billy, jabbing a finger at it. He reminded me of an outraged schoolboy poking at an unwanted toy. 'It looks like it's designed by a damned committee.'

'It does look pretty awful,' I agreed, 'but I suppose it's still the state flag.'

'If there had been a vote about it, I would have accepted it,' growled Billy. 'But Roy Barnes just steamrollered it through without asking anyone. That's what's annoyed me. So I'm fighting to keep the old one.'

At this stage, Billy chucked the new Georgia flag on the ground and stamped on it. 'That's what I think of this,' he fumed, pounding it with his boots. 'It's an insult to our heritage.' Browny backed away, nostrils twitching in anxiety.

Fortunately Billy soon put both flags back in his car boot and off we marched through Tallapoosa's drizzle. We were in the hills again. Mist hovered over the crest of the road while a light breeze cuffed at the conifer spires. Occasionally a timber lorry would overtake us, straining up the hill, but other than that we were alone with the rain, the mist and the odd squawk of woodland birds.

Billy continued to lecture me about flags. He told me that he used to love the TV show, 'The Dukes of Hazzard', in which two hillbilly brothers tore around in a car with a Confederate flag on the roof.

'The Duke brothers were rebels, good ol' boys who did as they pleased,' explained Billy. 'Boss Hogg, the pompous lawman who chased them, represented government interference. That's what the Confederate flag stands for, the right to stand up for yourself. The Civil War started because the Southern states wanted to play by their own rules without Northern interference. It wasn't because of slavery.'

'But slavery was strongly linked up to all that,' I insisted. 'I can understand your pride in the flag and I have no problem with it being flown at battle reenactments or at Confederate memorials, but I can also understand why many people, especially blacks, don't like it flying in prominent places.'

'Most don't mind,' Billy corrected. 'It's only the NAACP, a group of black radicals who stir everything up.'

I pointed out I had seen a recent poll in which at least 50 per cent of black Southerners viewed the Confederate flag as a racist symbol. I had also heard that the flag had largely become defunct straight after the Civil War. It wasn't until the mid 1950s when certain pro-segregation campaigners started waving it again that it became a familiar symbol once again.

'That's not the whole story,' stressed Billy. 'There's a huge percentage of people who view it only as a source of historical pride. Nothing to do with race.' He was becoming quite rattled, his cheeks colouring. 'I'm not racist, I'll try my best to help anyone if they deserve it. Any colour you like.'

'Sure, I can see that,' I agreed. The atmosphere became a bit heavy between us. 'Hey, what do I know, I'm from England, for heaven's sake,' I said, and we both laughed.

We had been walking for roughly six miles and Billy, after a strong start, was starting to limp. He was clearly out of shape but plodded on doggedly. Although we didn't see eye to eye on many things I rather liked him. I felt his role in the Sons of Confederate Veterans provided him with a sense of pride in what was clearly quite a tough life. His father had been a career soldier, a veteran of the Second World War, Korea and Vietnam, whom he respected greatly. Billy was currently unemployed flitting in between menial jobs in restaurants. He was married with a young son, whom he spoke of with great affection.

'The army wasn't for me, I didn't have the heart for it,' confessed Billy, as we walked into the little town of Buchanan. 'But I'm very patriotic like my dad. I think John

Walker, that American guy who fought for the Taliban, should be shot for treason.'

'Really,' I countered. 'He was only twenty. I think he was just naive and stupid. He deserves prison but surely to kill him would be pretty harsh.'

'Hey, I'm just a hard-line conservative,' muttered Billy. 'I think Jane Fonda should be shot too, for her pro-communist stance during Vietnam.' He stopped, sat down on a patch of grass and rubbed his calves. 'This is where I split.' He grimaced as he prodded an ankle. 'So have I convinced you about the South or do you think it's a Lost Cause?'

'Come off it,' I interrupted. 'The South is one of the most generous places I've ever travelled. I don't dislike it at all. I just think it's still possible to respect your history and your values, without always waving a Confederate flag. That's all I'm saying.'

'We'll have to differ on that,' he concluded, as we shook hands. 'Good luck on your walk. It's been a pleasure. You know you're lucky to have an ancestor like Arthur. I hope you appreciate him.'

*   *   *

I could see what Billy meant about Arthur and mostly I did appreciate him, but there were odd times when he acted as more of a curse than a blessing. The day after my walk with Billy was one such instance.

The morning started well. The sun was up, Browny was moving with uncharacteristic speed and I was only three days' walk from Atlanta, where I would treat myself to a week's rest over Christmas. Then a huge, diesel-belching truck pulled up alongside and shattered my sanguine mood. On the flank of the noisy vehicle all sorts of political slogans had been scrawled, mostly insulting Roy Barnes, the Governor of Georgia, who had instigated the new state flag.

'Hey, Tom,' shouted the driver leaning out of his window. 'My name's Elijah. Billy told me about you. I want you to sign a couple of copies of your ancestor's diary. I'll see you up the road.'

Before I had a chance to say a word, Elijah roared off up the conifer-lined highway. About half an hour later I saw his white van again. The other thing I noticed was a substantial old Georgia flag hanging from a long steel pole nearby.

'Ha, Tom, there you are,' Elijah shouted. He was a wild-looking fellow, with an impressive paunch and energetic mannerisms. He presented me with a couple of hardback copies of *Three Months in the Southern States*. I signed them on the front page and handed them back.

'How do you like the flag, eh?' pressed Elijah, pointing up at the huge pole. 'Great huh.'

'Looks, er, big.'

'Oh, yeah,' sighed Elijah with pleasure. 'I'm putting them up all over Georgia. I hate that new excuse for a flag. Damn Roy Barnes. He thinks the old flag is to do with slavery, but it ain't. It's heritage, that's what it is.' Here we go again, I thought.

Elijah led me over to the back of his van. He had dozens of 24-foot poles and a mini-cement mixer, which he used to erect his beloved old Georgia flags. He was clearly a man with a mission.

'I'm going to stick these up all over the state,' he repeated. 'Yessir, I sure am.'

He handed me several large flags. I thanked him but told him they would weigh down my beast too much, which was perfectly true. Elijah was friendly enough but had quite a manic glint in his eyes and I thought it wise to push on before I got on the wrong side of him. He offered to cook me a barbecue lunch but I told him I had to dash in order to set up camp before dark. He took several photos of Browny and me before we set off again.

'Your ancestor was a great man,' he shouted out, as Browny and I walked away. 'He loved the Confederacy.' As with Billy, I sensed Elijah thought I would be some sort of quasi-Confederate reincarnation of my ancestor. He was probably a bit disappointed by my subdued response to his flags.

I had made a lucky getaway, but it wasn't over yet. That night I discovered Elijah's business card in my coat pocket. I hadn't even looked at it when he had handed it over in the morning but now it grabbed my complete attention. 'Editor', it read, and was surrounded by little Confederate flags. Elijah clearly ran some sort of pro-Southern magazine. I suddenly panicked that he might use Browny and me for old Georgia flag propaganda.

That night I was lucky to be put up by a local family near a place called Dallas and asked to use their computer. I winged off an email to Elijah, polite but firm, explaining that I respected his point of view but I did not want my trip used for political purposes. I was English, I wrote, the Georgia flag issue really had nothing to do with me. The next morning I had a slew of strong, at times mildly abusive emails from Elijah's supporters plus a couple of good-natured ones apologising for their friends' anger.

My favourite abuser was a man who lived in Charleston. DON'T STOP HERE! warned his message headline. I quote his following words verbatim.

Sir!
I have read about your trip across our Country! I also saw the email you sent Mr Coleman requesting that your picture not be used if it

had the true Georgia flag! You Sir have some nerve, travelling through our Country but ashamed be seen with our flag! I live in South Carolina and I asked Mr Coleman to tell you I would show you around the Charleston area! Well I'll show your mule around but you are not welcome! Your ancestor was a very good man but you got left out of the old gene pool! You Sir need to bypass the South and head on up North!

A Confederate American!

After having a good chuckle (the mule gag really was a good one) my cowardly nature took over and I suddenly became a little scared. I anticipated a posse of flag-waving Southern crackers, incensed by my wishy-washy attitude, out for my blood. Then I put things in perspective. People like Elijah were not dangerous: opinionated and proud, yes, perhaps even a little obsessive, but dangerous, no. In fact I was glad I had taken my stance. If I hadn't I would have been endlessly fêted by trenchant-willed Confederates all the way to New York. Much as I applauded people honouring their Civil War ancestors, still living like them seemed a bit much.

*   *   *

The following day, keeping half an eye out for Elijah's white van, Browny and I forged on through the drizzle to the historic Kennesaw Mountain. The twin peaks stood out for miles like tiny, supine breasts on the pancake-flat horizon. I parked Browny at the visitor's centre and quickly yomped up part of the mountain path, admiring the split rail fences where the Confederates had slowed down General Sherman's advance in the spring of 1864. I seemed to be the only visitor, other than a solitary crow cawing from a skeletal beach tree.

The woodland foliage steamed like compost under foot, exacerbating the haunted atmosphere.

Having descended back down to Browny, I marshalled her into the nearby community of Kennesaw where I struck up a conversation with AJ, a smartly dressed Indian man. AJ let me graze Browny outside his home while I explored the town. As we chatted he told me he had come over from England in 1979 and never looked back.

'I love America, there's so much opportunity here,' he enthused, as so many other immigrants had during my walk. 'The only thing I miss about England is Ipswich Town Football Club.'

When I asked AJ what there was to see in Kennesaw, he recommended taking a look at Dent Meyers store, which had a large collection of Civil War books and memorabilia. He told me Meyers was something of a local celebrity, who supposedly walked around with two loaded revolvers on each hip, and had an exhibition of KKK memorabilia at the back of his shop. He liked to call himself the Wild Man.

'Some people say he's a genius, others say he's completely bananas,' said AJ. 'With my skin colour I've never gone near his place. Don't pick an argument with him or he'll just throw you out. Just browse around and listen.'

'How come he's tolerated?' I asked.

'Oh, Dent Meyers is like a snake,' explained AJ. 'Leave him alone and he'll hibernate with his like-minded friends. But poke him and he'll bite. He's clearly not the nicest guy in the world but at least you know what to expect with him. He's never bothered me.'

Fascinated and slightly jittery, I made a beeline for Wild Man's Store, using my raincoat hood to shield off the rain. Amid all the smart glass-fronted shops, Wild Man's was an easy place to spot with a variety of Confederate flags splashed across its facade. I pushed open the creaky door and bundled in. The first impression was the smell. It was fusty, and slightly sour, the sort of whiff that sometimes comes from very old books. It wasn't difficult to identify Wild Man. He stood directly opposite me sorting through a box of clothes.

'Hope you didn't get too wet,' he said pleasantly, taking a look at my dripping coat. Apart from a revolver jutting from each of his hips, he didn't look that sinister. He had long, grey hair, which despite being ringed by a bandanna, stuck out all over the place like a freshly rubbed spaniel. His eyes were rheumy and half asleep. Rather than looking like a ragged Confederate foot soldier he looked more like a washed-up folk singer.

As AJ had advised I steered past him and began to browse. At first it all looked inoffensive enough. Civil War chess sets, uniforms and a massive collection of books lined the shelves. There were some fairly tame cartoons pillorying Bill and Hillary Clinton but it didn't take long to spot the true nature of Wild Man's cluttered grotto. Further in, a T-shirt hanging from a coat hanger read: 'Goon Goon, Black Babboon, Worthless Thieving Coon'. Attached to this was a hand-written message to Wild Man, sent from somebody telling him to keep up the good work.

A glass cabinet contained KKK penknives and several booklets championing white supremacy. It wasn't only blacks that were targeted. One of the displays showed a map of Japan with the words, 'One Bomb Was Not Enough' printed over it. All this was before I had even reached the main collection of KKK memorabilia at the back of the store. This was fronted with a sign warning NO MEXICANS, NO BLACKS, NO DOGS. Just to labour the insults the words

NO DOGS had been crossed out and DOGS OK written in its place.

It was all pretty nasty stuff. It amazed me how blatantly Wild Man had mixed up the Civil War with his messages of racial hatred. In amidst the guns, the KKK hoods and the laminated white supremacy tracts were statuettes of Robert E. Lee and posters proclaiming 'Don't Blame Me, I Voted For Jeff Davis'. I'm quite sure staunch Confederates like Billy and Elijah would have been appalled with General Lee being included in this Miss Haversham-like den of animosity. It was this sort of baleful nonsense that soured all of the nobler aspects of the Confederacy. It interested me that Wild Man had no derogatory posters or cuttings about bin Laden. Perhaps he was too busy with the Civil War to even notice another one was underway.

But far worse than any of the exhibits was listening to the conversation struck up inside the store. While I perused the shelves, a young gimlet-eyed skinhead with tattoos all over his face walked in accompanied by a grossly overweight man who looked like Tweedledee. The two of them engaged in a foul-mouthed conversation, with Wild Man occasionally joining in. The word 'nigger' was liberally peppered around, usually preceded by an expletive. Before long I just wanted to get away, sickened by such hate-fuelled language. While I hadn't expected Wild Man's to be a cosy environment, full of cheery souls drinking café latte and reading *To Kill a Mockingbird*, I hadn't expected it to be quite so venomous.

Part of me wanted to confront them, but I didn't have the courage. Anyway, was it really worth it?

I finally sneaked out of Wild Man's and made tracks back to AJ's place to reunite with Browny. After all the fusty unpleasantness of the store it was nice to be out in the open air with my mule, an animal who cared not a jot about class, or creed or colour.

I'd seen Browny's expression as she watched human beings shout death threats at one another or throw cans and bottles from truck windows. I'd seen her look of patient disbelief as I dragged her over bridges or as human fingers grappled with her teeth to gauge her age. I'd seen her 'what is it with these people' shrug, her ever-perceptive mule's eye view and, you know what, I've come to the conclusion she is convinced the human race is bonkers.

CHAPTER 14

Amazons In Atlanta

'Every time I look at Atlanta,' wrote Southern commentator, John Shelton Reed, 'I see what a quarter of a million Confederate soldiers died to prevent.'

By the time Browny and I had penetrated Atlanta's outskirts I began to see what the humorous Professor Reed meant. On first impressions this was not a place basking in moonlight-and-magnolia Southern charm. In fact from a distance the city that hosted the 1996 Olympics owed far more to the soulless sprawl of Houston than the antebellum mystique of Selma or Natchez. Still, I didn't care that much. It was nearly Christmas, I'd clocked up fifteen hundred miles and a local family had offered to stable Browny and feed me. I couldn't have cared if I was in downtown Sodom and Gomorrah, at least I could stop walking for a while.

As it turned out my mule and I had really struck it lucky. I had expected to be holed up in one of the city's manicured gated communities. I couldn't have been more wrong. We ended up as guests of Rodney and Emily Cook, friends of my cousin Eddie, who owned what must surely be the only farm in Buckhead, a plush, western suburb of Atlanta.

The Cooks lived in a distinctly rustic enclave of Buckhead, a world apart from the ambient mansions and malls. Their home was a magical barn that had been converted into a Russian dacha with tall, conical spires and Gothic windows. The view from the sitting room panned over a landscape that was half *Lord of the Rings*, half Home Counties with a dash of the Orient thrown in. Towering bamboo plants festooned the horse paddocks while angels and stone pillars sprouted from the overgrown lawns.

Other than the odd garbled phone call the Cooks knew next to nothing about me, and even less about my beast. Now here I was, rumpled and bewhiskered, defrosting in front of their log fire while Browny cavorted in her freshly bedded adjoining stable.

I soon discovered Rodney, a tall, urbane entrepreneur and his attractive, raven-haired wife, Emily, lived not so much in a social whirl, but a full-on yuletide twister. The night of my arrival, with only two lumberjack shirts to my name, I was trussed up in a black tie and a pair of Rodney's shiny brogues. These shoes were so big for me I had to wear three pairs of worsted socks just to keep them from slipping off. I looked like a cross between James Bond and Rumpelstiltskin.

Next thing I knew I was transported into a lavish hall to celebrate the birthday of a venerable family matriarch called Mamma Jo, who, despite hitting ninety years old, wore heels sharp enough to throw at a dartboard. She had the legs of a woman thirty years younger, and I'm sure was quite capable of doing the cancan. I toasted Mamma Jo's health, tapped my foot to the jazz singer and told tall tales about mules to the assembled glitterati. Hey, I decided after my second glass of champagne, I could get used to this.

And so the week progressed. Browny feasted on lush meadowland and was spoilt rotten by the Cooks' many guests handing her mulish treats. I slept in a bed brimming with plump pillows, ate like a Viking and sat under a defoliating spruce tree singing carols while English and Alexandra, the Cooks' young daughters, opened their presents. It wasn't home, but it was the next best thing, and took away some of the inevitable heartache. The Christmas spell, despite such practicalities as organising Browny's fourth set of shoes and my visa extension, was strangely dislocated from the rest of the trip. I was able to slough off my ancestor-chasing, mule-skinning identity, and briefly resume a more familiar life.

*   *   *

Atlanta was not a beautiful city to explore but it was an interesting one: a mongrel metropolis caught between its historic past and rampantly progressive future. In fact the city only began its life in the late 1830s as a railway junction (before being christened Atlanta it was known, rather grimly, as Terminus). The fledgling city was all but torched to the ground in 1864, firstly by retreating Confederates, followed by a Union force under General William Tecumseh Sherman, a man many Georgians still love to hate. The small part of the city that survived the war was later ripped down in the name of modernisation, and now astonishingly not one Civil War building remains downtown.

Atlanta's many detractors write it off as a snakepit of greedy Johnny Come Latelies, a once noble city that has sold its soul to freshly won greenbacks. During my visit it was clear that, despite some harsh poverty in certain precincts, this was a city on the make. Not only was it home to the headquarters of Coca-Cola, CNN News and a host of other mega businesses, but its airport was now thought to be the busiest in the world. 'If you die and go to hell,' one local told me, 'you will probably have to change planes in Atlanta.'

Fortunately Rodney, something of an architectural aesthete, revealed to me a side of Atlanta that was easy to overlook. In between the skyscrapers and glitzy malls, he opened my eyes to some classical beauty amid the urban beast. He gave me a tour of the Fox Theatre, with its Moorish-style interior and star-spangled ceiling, and pointed out the World Athletes Monument, an attractive structure fringed with five bronze figures holding up a globe, which Rodney had helped secure for the city prior to the Olympics. He ushered me around some of Buckhead's more elegant mansions and revealed Bullock Hall to the far north of the city, a rare architectural survivor of the Civil War.

'So why is Atlanta so unpopular?' I teased Rodney that night, as we drank mulled wine in front of the Cooks' ever-roaring fire.

'Some people say it's a city that's anti-South,' he replied, reaching down to stroke Tara, the family collie. 'They say it's forgotten its past. You have to remember, Tom, the bitterness of the Civil War was caused more by poverty than violence.'

'Poverty?'

'Absolutely. The South was in an economic mess for over a century after Lee's surrender. It wasn't until the 1960s that we got back to the same levels of wealth we had in the early 1860s.'

Rodney emphasised that in Atlanta General Sherman was still a hate figure. After trouncing much of the city in the summer of 1864 Sherman had notoriously marched to Savannah on the Atlantic coast, during which his men twisted railway tracks (known as Sherman's neckties), burned homes and pillaged farms. The episode is still talked about with disgust by rural Georgians although Rodney conceded that Sherman, like so many Civil War leaders, was basically a decent man who knew harsh measures were sometimes necessary to win.

'Sherman realised the Southern army would not crack,' stressed Rodney. 'So he took the war to the civilians. It was a nasty thing to do, but an effective one. Ordinary people saw the destruction here, not just soldiers. It left a strong legacy of mistrust. In truth, Sherman's men could probably have behaved much worse.'

'Sherman would be surprised to see Atlanta today,' I commented.

'Yes, corporate Atlanta is thriving now,' explained Rodney, prodding the fire with a poker and sending up a shower of sparks and soot. 'Trouble is many Southerners associate big business more with the North. They see it as threatening the morality of a traditionally rural culture. They're suspicious, and perhaps a little envious too.'

'I've always lived here,' he continued, refilling my mulled wine. 'Both Emily and I had ancestors who fought with the Confederacy. I'm very proud to be a Southerner but I'm proud to be an Atlantan too. Although I hate much of its modern architecture I'm glad it's a progressive city.'

'So it's getting better then?'

'Lord, yes. When I was a child some Ku Klux Klansmen burnt a cross in our garden.' Rodney briefly grimaced at the memory. 'We had a black housemaid at the time. I was outraged she had to witness such a hurtful thing. I'm glad Atlanta has a more tolerant, multicultural side to it now.'

'Some say it's almost too PC, don't they?' It was well known that during the Olympics Atlanta had done its best to erase any traces of the Confederacy for fear of causing umbrage.

'This city sometimes suffers too much guilt over its past,' admitted Rodney. 'Critics now say it's a sterile place, a dull place. Pah!' He laughed softly. 'Think about it. The writer Margaret Mitchell lived in Atlanta. She died here too, run over by a taxi soon after completing *Gone with the Wind*. Martin Luther King was an Atlanta baby. Ted Turner has a home here, and Elton John. Tom Wolfe even set his latest novel here. It's a happening place, exciting, always in a state of flux.'

I told Rodney that I had heard the bibulous writer James Dickey once lived in Atlanta. Although primarily a poet, Dickey's best-known work is the novel, *Deliverance*, which focuses on a group of city slickers being terrorised by violent rednecks in the wilderness of north Georgia. It was subsequently made into a disturbing film in the early 1970s, with a memorable duelling banjo soundtrack. To avoid unnecessary paranoia I deliberately hadn't seen it prior to my walk. It would be the equivalent of checking into a remote hotel and discovering the only other guest is Jack Nicholson with a bad case of writer's block and a loony grin.

'Yes, Dickey lived here,' Rodney said, throwing another log on the fire. 'It's said he based *Deliverance* partly on his own trips to the wilderness. He admits many of the hillbillies he met were friendly but in the book, which was fiction, he turned them into maniacs. He could spin quite a yarn. That's the South for you. Sometimes it's not quite as scary as it's made out to be.'

*   *   *

On my last day in Atlanta I visited Stone Mountain, supposedly not only the largest chunk of exposed granite in the world but the largest bas-relief sculpture too. Neither of these statistics thrilled me that much, but I still felt compelled to take a look. Stone Mountain was after all a major Confederate shrine with Robert E. Lee, Stonewall Jackson and Jefferson Davis carved on its colossal flank, all of them riding off as if to face the Yankees one last time.

My guide for the morning was a friend of the Cooks called Kim Wall. Kim was a lissom, rose-cheeked Amazon who stood almost a foot taller than me. She was a fashion model and actress who was thankfully kooky rather than vain. She was also completely outrageous, and would suddenly burst into a string of hilarious and very loud impersonations – her grandmother, Dolly Parton, a pack of baying hounds – to the amusement, and sometimes alarm, of the surrounding tourists.

From a distance Stone Mountain, for all its geological grandeur, was a bit of a letdown. The holy trinity of the Confederacy, hewn into the centre of the huge, domed mountain, were quite hard to even make out. Lee, Davis and Jackson may have taken up three acres, but on an outcrop of stone this big they were dwarfed. They looked more like a small fossil or the faded imprint of a signet ring.

Kim and I took the cable car up the mountain, which gave a bird's eye view of the three carved horsemen. As we trundled closer I could see that each of the riders held a hat over his heart in an honorary salute to the Confederacy.

'Yah know,' announced Kim, in her rich drawl, her voice a Deep South equivalent of Dame Edna Everage, 'when all the sculptors finished this carving,' she pointed downwards, 'they had a dinner party on General Lee's shoulder – over twenty of them. They used a table, plates and everything. That's how big it is. Not the sort of place you'd want to drop your cutlery.'

The fact Lee's shoulder had served as an al fresco dining room helped to explain the carving's vast dimensions, even if visually it still failed to overwhelm me. By far the most impressive view came when we reached the peak of Stone Mountain. I followed Kim as she sashayed her way to the edge, dodging the odd stunted pine tree that sprouted from fissures in the rock. A frigid wind ripped into us as we looked over Atlanta's pale, extensive suburbs.

'The main guy who did the Stone Mountain carving gave a talk at mah school once,' said Kim wistfully. 'He was the same man who carved Mount Rushmore in South Dakota. I can never remember his name. Real shy, had a bad stutter, but real interesting too. Must be a funny sort of job, hanging from a mountain, chiselling big men with beards all your life.'

'No odder than strutting down catwalks.'

'Or strutting about with mules,' riposted Kim, with a snort of laughter. As we walked back towards the cable car she added: 'You know at night they have a laser show here. They bathe the carvings in light and play Dixie mixed with pop music. It's a bit gimmicky. I wonder what that old sculptor would make of it all now?'

'I wonder what Robert E. Lee would make of it all,' I said. 'Do you think he'd consider the South is still worth fighting for?'

'I sure do, honey,' proclaimed Kim, in her lovely, butter wouldn't melt in my mouth purr. 'I'd sure fight for it.' She raised her fists and began to playfully shadow box with me, to the mounting anxiety of our fellow cable passengers. 'You can take the girl out of Georgia, mah dear, but you can't take Georgia out of the girl.'

*   *   *

Although Kim had largely been larking about with her shadow boxing, during the Civil War there had been many real life Amazons willing to lay down their lives for the South. Nobody knew this better than Colonel Arthur who had met a female soldier while in a train carriage heading into Atlanta.

In typical Coldstream-speak, my ancestor described the young warrior as 'goodish-looking' and that 'she wore a soldier's hat and coat, but had resumed her petticoats'. He mentioned that the cross-dressing Confederate's gender was common knowledge to her Louisianan regiment, but they had no problem so long as she fought bravely and conducted herself properly. Arthur added: 'she was not the only representative of the female sex in the ranks.'

According to records over four hundred women, both in blue and grey, are thought to have fought in the Civil War. A few saw themselves as modern-day Joan of Arcs while others simply wanted to be with their husbands or lovers, and endured all the horrors necessary to fight alongside them. Many were simply wildly eccentric.

Secrecy was usually the key to their success, and the majority of the women soldiers were exposed only when wounded or killed. It's now well known that a Confederate husband and wife team were both slain at Gettysburg during Pickett's Charge, while an Iowa soldier was so upset on being found out to be a girl that she killed herself. A group of hot-blooded Southern belles even tried to organise a whole regiment, the Mississippi Nightingales, but their petition was denied.

Of course official non-fighting women also attended the battlefields. Nurses, cooks, laundresses and water carriers all played vital, often heroic roles, on both sides. Naturally there were whores too. Indeed in 1863 over five thousand soiled doves (as prostitutes were sometimes known during the war) were thought to be operating in Washington DC, while many others offered their services at the army camps across the country.

Venereal diseases were a constant problem for the North and South – between 1861 and 1865 nearly 100,000 cases of gonorrhea were recorded in the Union army – hence the

saying, 'For one night with Venus, a soldier would spend a
lifetime with mercury' (the most common VD treatment at
the time). The euphemism 'hooker' was also spawned during
the Civil War, named after Joe Hooker, a Union officer famed
for his leniency towards female camp followers.

But the woman Colonel Arthur encountered on his
Atlanta-bound train was not a nurse, a laundress, or a soiled
dove. She was undoubtedly a soldier. The historian Walter
Lord goes as far as guessing her identity to be that of Loreta
Janita Velasquez, the daughter of a Cuban aristocrat, who was
known to have been fighting in that area during Arthur's
travels. Loreta's military career is formidable. Shortly before
the Civil War she had married an American merchant. Her
husband immediately joined the Confederate army in 1861
but was dead within a year. Grief-stricken Loreta swore
revenge for her man and disguised herself as a Rebel officer in
order to fight the Yankees. She was know by the splendid
name, Lieutenant Harry Buford.

Rebecca D. Larson in her book, *When a Rose Is Not a Rose*,
provides this charismatic description of Loreta: 'She cut her
dark hair short and glued on a false mustache [sic] and goatee.
Loreta spoke in a deep voice, walked with a masculine
swagger, and even spat on the streets. She flirted with several
young women to complete her disguise.'

Loreta first served with an Arkansas regiment but after
being wounded in 1862 transferred to the 21st Louisiana,
which is when my ancestor would most likely have met her.
Later she was wounded again by a shell blast near Corinth in
Mississippi but managed to persuade the operating surgeon
not to reveal her identity. Once her wounds were healed she
was involved in a number of risky cloak-and-dagger style
forays, delivering supplies to Confederates in Canada.

After the war Loreta married a wealthy Southern major
and travelled extensively in the interior of Latin America.

When her elderly husband died in Venezuela, she is believed to have settled down with a third husband in Salt Lake City, where she gave birth to a son. Whether her wanderlust was sated here is uncertain. There are no further records of Loreta's life in Utah and her adventurous trail finally runs cold.

Following his encounter with Loreta (or another woman of similar appearance) Colonel Arthur spent only three hours in Atlanta during which he snatched a quick siesta at the nearby Trouthouse Hotel. On his connecting train to South Carolina he described the countryside directly east of Atlanta as, 'well cultivated . . . this part of the Confederacy has as yet suffered little from the war.' The upbeat Colonel would never have guessed that in just over a year Atlanta would be in ruins.

CHAPTER 15

The First Submarine

Browny and I left Atlanta three days after Christmas, full bellied and revitalised. After all the jollity and home comforts of the Cooks' farm it was tough resuming the long march. Frustratingly on our first day we didn't even walk far enough to make it out of Atlanta. The gridlocked roads made progress tortuous and that night was spent in a stable in Alpharetta, one of Atlanta's eastern suburbs.

Still mollycoddled by the springy, lemon-scented bed I had been slumbering in for the past week, it was a bit of a wrench roughing it again in the stable's hayrick. Thankfully this was more than compensated for by the thrill of returning to the great outdoors: the sharp night air, the sweet smell of dew and minerals, the reassuring chomp of Browny grazing and the stars dancing up above.

As expected it soon turned radically colder. The iciest snap took hold on New Year's Eve and, according to passers by, was unlikely to let go again until the following week. Serendipitously Browny and I had reached the university city of Athens, some seventy miles east of Atlanta, shortly before the snow began to fall. Acting on a recommendation from a friendly cop we weaved our way through the campus to the College of Veterinary Medicine. This was probably the only place likely to take in a homeless beast and her shivering sidekick in the closing hours of 2001.

After a brief explanation about my walk the college staff agreed to help out. One of the trainee vets marshalled Browny to a stall where she was barracked between a sour-faced donkey with a bandaged leg and a raffish-looking gelding with an eye patch. I had plans of bringing in the New Year in style but, having walked twenty-five miles that day, I simply tossed Browny some hay, toasted her health with a Lucozade slammer, and wimpily fell asleep long before the midnight hour. Some cowboy I was turning out to be. That said it was great to wake up early the following morning without a mule kicker of a hangover.

With the glacial turn in the weather I decided to keep Browny under cover for the next couple of days and jump on a Greyhound to Charleston on the South Carolina coast. Charleston was not only a chance for another furlough; it was highly pertinent to my journey. Colonel Arthur wrote an extensive chapter in his diary about the historic port, and the first shot of the Civil War had been fired at Fort Sumter near by its seafront on 12 April 1861 at 4.30 a.m.

On the bus I squeezed in next to a large, ravaged-looking woman sipping furtively on a whiskey bottle. As we trundled east I flipped through some back copies of various news-papers. It made for gloomy reading. Several mosques across America had been vandalised in the aftermath of September

11, bin Laden's whereabouts were still unknown, India and Pakistan were at each others throats again, as were Israel and Palestine and, hold the front page, so were Liam Gallagher and Robbie Williams. I woke up in north Charleston late in the afternoon having fallen asleep on my boozy neighbour's shoulder.

From the frigid gloom of the Greyhound station I took a crowded city bus – in which I was the only white passenger – downtown where, in vivid contrast, just about everyone appeared to be white. It looked as if Charleston was less of a cultural hotpot and more of a mixed salad; its different ingredients wary of blending too closely. As there was no backpacker hostel (why doesn't the South have any of these?) I checked into a pristine but soulless motel. I threw down my rucksack on the bed and looked out of my window, where snowflakes fell, soft as ashes, onto the wide, moonlit street.

*   *   *

The next morning Charleston was still dusted with a carpet of fine flakes. With its colonial parks and church spires it was a city that lent itself to snow. It looked intoxicatingly lovely and I tramped happily towards the sea breathing in the pure, damp air. Then something struck me: there wasn't a soul around. Where was everybody? Where were the tobogganists? The children hurling snowballs? That happy frisson of communal excitement associated with freshly falling snow?

At the tourist centre I got my answer. 'This is the worst fall we've seen in years,' a nervy, grey-bouffoned lady at reception told me. 'The schools are closed. All the government offices are closed.' She pointed at a fax on her desk. 'Bitter Storms Herald New Year,' read the smudged letters, 'Worse to come.'

I could hardly believe it. A slightly chilly day enlivened by a few fluffs of snow and the whole of Charleston had simultaneously pulled an Edvard Munch scream and battened down the hatches. The approach of this mildly unruly front was being treated as if the legions of Mordor were advancing on the city. Fortunately it was still possible to tour Fort Sumter, about the only tourist attraction in Charleston still prepared to brave these supposedly fiendish elements.

'We're not used to snow here,' apologised the lady, sensing my confusion. 'Further north, up in Virginia, they have snow-ploughs and all that. But here we don't even have shovels. We hardly ever see a snowflake.'

I made my way over to the jetty to catch the ferry to Fort Sumter. The brick fort, which from the seafront looked nothing more than a squashed black hat, sat on a tiny island roughly three and a half miles away. The wind was whipping up a bit and the borscht-coloured sea had turned wild and choppy. The twenty or so passengers sat grimly facing each other in the lower deck listening to the taped commentary as the ferry yawed its way towards the open sea.

The deadpan voice on the tape informed us that as early as the 1700s Charleston was something of a sybaritic honey pot, full of grand homes and theatres – the largest city south of Philadelphia. Cotton, rice and even indigo flourished in the inland plantations.

'That damned machine doesn't tell you about the slaves,' harrumphed the man sitting next to me. 'The fact they often outnumbered the planters by ten to one.' I soon realised my irascible shipmate was a far more informative source than the 'damned machine' he talked over. His name was George, a bald but regal-looking maths teacher, who spoke with fruity, consonant-rolling assurance.

'Those Charleston *fat cats* had the highest *per capita* income in the country once,' George informed me. He put ludicrous emphasis on certain words. 'They may have been super rich but slavery had made them *lazy*. Everything was done for them. They were the ones who wanted to secede so badly, not the *wretched* farm boys who made up most of the Southern army.'

'A rich man's war and a poor man's fight,' I said, echoing the words I had first heard in Natchez and many times since.

'*Exactly!* South Carolina was the first state to secede in 1860 and the last to take down the Confederate flag from its state house, just two years ago now. Charleston is a beautiful place but kinda *superior*, don't ya think?'

I told him I hadn't really been in the city long enough to form an opinion. George seemed rather down on the South and I asked him if he was a Yankee.

'God no,' he replied. 'I'm from *Virginia*. Them *Yankees* were just as bad as us. They won the war and then *emancipated* millions of slaves. Just like that. Most of the slaves were illiterate, didn't know any other profession and then suddenly had to fend for themselves. It was very badly handled. A *disgrace*. Maybe if Lincoln hadn't been shot it would have been better, but who knows. The Yankees have no reason to be all *worthy*.'

It soon became clear that broaching any aspect of the Civil War would inflame George in the same way ladling water on hot rocks heated up a sauna. If I probed much longer I sensed smoke would start to pour from the old teacher's ears. I stayed silent for a while. A child sitting near by pointed up at a couple of pelicans gliding over the ferry.

'So why have you come on this tour, George?' I asked him finally, my curiosity having got the better of me.

'I'm researching the American Revolution,' George said, his voice softening for the first time. 'More revolutionary battles took place in South Carolina than any other state. Now that's a war we Americans can be *proud* of. We beat you guys, you *Brits*, through sheer cunning and bravery. You had more men and better weapons but we *whupped* you.' George slapped me hard on the arm. 'Then we *whupped* you again in the war of 1812.' With this he began to recite some tuneless doggerel about General Andrew Jackson sinking the British fleet at New Orleans.

'But why come to Fort Sumter?' I interrupted swiftly. 'It's pure Civil War here, isn't it?'

'Know what, young man,' spat George, his temper simmering up again. 'I wish to hell I hadn't come here. The Civil War always makes me mad. It was horrible, *horrible*,' George rolled his 'r's with more passion than a Hispanic soap diva. 'Why are Americans still so caught up in it? Four years of *carnage*. It was a horrible thing that we should put behind us. *Horrible*.'

Before George's blood pressure could overcook again, the pelican-spotting child shouted: 'Dolphins! Look, look, dolphins.' Many of the passengers, including George and me, bustled over to the starboard side to catch a glimpse of the grey fins breaking through the waves. A man in an orange baseball cap began firing his camcorder. A quiet, unspoken camaraderie fell between all of us at the sight of something so beautiful and unexpected. The droning commentary about Charleston continued in the background but nobody seemed to be listening any more.

Feasting his eyes on the jaunty fins George broke into a smile. 'Now would ya look at *that*,' he announced, giving my collarbone another comradely thwack. 'Beats the hell out of war, huh, even the ones where we *whupped* you Brits.'

*   *   *

When we docked at Fort Sumter our tour guide did finally materialise. He was cocooned in a black sou'wester and all I could make out of him from under his hood was a pair of steamed-up glasses. The weather had taken a turn for the worse and we all huddled up in the lee of the pentagonal fort's ramparts. Our spectral guide stood beside a cannon barrel clapping his mittened-hands together as the snowflakes swirled around him. His melancholy voice was barely audible above the sea wind.

The gist of his commentary went something like this. By the April of 1861 Fort Sumter was the only Union installation of any value in the South that had not already been seized. Major Robert Anderson occupied the little fort with the eighty-five men under his command. When Anderson refused to surrender the Confederate General Pierre Gustave Toutant Beauregard – a French-speaking Creole who ironically had been taught about artillery by Anderson at West Point – ordered the fort to be fired on. Legend has it the first retaliating Union shot was fired by Abner Doubleday, who went on to achieve fame as one of the founders of modern-day baseball.

Miraculously, not one soldier was killed as the two batteries blasted the hell out of each other (sometimes using flaming cannon balls) for over thirty hours. Finally, the beleaguered, outgunned Anderson surrendered to his old pupil on the insistence he could fire a 100-gun salute before lowering the Stars and Stripes. During the salute one of the Union cannons exploded and killed two soldiers with 'friendly fire' – the first casualties of what would become America's bloodiest war.

After a while, George and I slunk away from the guide to explore the fort. 'What that guy *didn't* tell you,' said George, somewhat grandly, 'is that after the war Lincoln was due to attend a ceremony at Fort Sumter.'

'What sort of ceremony?' I asked.

'He was going to re-erect the Stars and Stripes over Fort Sumter on 14 April, the very day it had been taken down at the start of the war,' enthused George as we clambered over the battlements. 'But, guess what, Old Abe decided he was too busy to travel that far. So instead that night he goes to Ford's Theatre in Washington. Where – *bam, bam* – a certain Mr John Wilkes Booth shoots the poor bastard. If he'd come here to raise the flag history may have been different,' he paused for breath, 'although Booth might well have picked him off later.'

We were now on top of the ramparts being buffeted by an implacable sea wind. I tried to imagine Colonel Arthur when he toured the fort in early June 1863, no doubt dashing about asking lots of pertinent questions about cannons. I have been neglectful of my ancestor's comments at this point because his chapter on Fort Sumter is one of the most tedious in his diary. This is probably just my own ignorance. To any Civil War scholar or ballistics boffin it no doubt offers the sort of exhilarating exposé Pepys' diary provided on seventeenth-century London or Alan Clarke's on Tory party peccadilloes in the 1980s.

But no matter how hard I tried, sentences that began: 'They weigh 14,000 lb, throw a solid shot weighing 129 lb, and are made to traverse with the greatest ease by means of Yates's system of cogwheels,' were not exactly page turners. Later on Colonel Arthur's writing returns to form when, on meeting General Beauregard in Charleston, he reveals the vain Creole's hair is almost completely grey, not due to the pressures of war, but because the Union blockade has prevented him receiving any fresh hair dye.

When George saw me referring to my ancestor's diary, he naturally began to quiz me on it. '*Man o' man!*' he shouted as we walked back to the boat. 'So you're related to that Brit with the red jacket in that Gettysburg film. The guy who drinks tea with General Longstreet.'

'The very one,' I replied pompously. It seemed most people knew Arthur not through his diary but through his brief but sartorially unmissable cameo in a four and a half hour feature film.

'Well, I'll be *dogarned*,' George slapped me on the back, almost provoking minor whiplash. 'And now you're following him on a frickin' *mule!*'

'You know, George, for someone who hates the Civil War you certainly know a lot about it.'

'Yeah, far too much,' he conceded, as we walked down the ferry gangplank. 'The American Revolution is my main love, my wife if you like. The Civil War is more like a fascinating but *sinister* mistress. I try to cast her away but she always lures me back: and every time I go back I feel *horrible*, *guilty*.' He paused and flashed me a smile. 'Tomorrow you're going back to your mule and me, well, I'm going back to my wife.'

*   *   *

Before catching the bus the next morning I conducted a whistle-stop tour of Colonel Arthur's Charleston. The downtown hotel where he had stayed was long gone, but St Michael's, one of America's oldest churches, where he worshipped on the Sunday after his arrival was still in immaculate condition. With its impressive white spire, musky smells and sturdy pews it was a lovely spot to sit and conjure up images of my ancestor at prayer, or perhaps George Washington or Robert E. Lee who had also worshipped there at different times.

Afterwards I wandered through Charleston's stately, palmetto-lined streets and admired the many attractive houses painted in pastel colours. I peered into the old slave markets, but they were shut up and deserted. This was not the case in 1863 when Arthur had witnessed a slave auction here. The experience clearly made quite an impact on him:

'The Negroes – about fifteen men, three women, and three children – were seated on benches, looking perfectly contented and indifferent,' wrote Colonel Arthur. 'I saw the buyers opening their mouths and showing the teeth of their new purchases to their friends in a very businessman like manner. This was certainly not a very agreeable spectacle to an Englishman, and I know that many Southerners participate in the same feeling . . . And I think if the Confederate States were *left alone*, the system would be much modified and amended . . .'

Colonel Arthur strongly maintained that slavery was already fizzling out in the South without the need for Northern intervention. He also believed, presciently, that to suddenly emancipate all the slaves at once, as the British had recently done in Jamaica, could lead to major social unrest. Yet he still persists in viewing the Charleston planter classes through rose-tinted spectacles, without ever questioning the undoubted cruelty and indolence of its less moral members. Whether my ancestor turned a blind eye to all this, or simply refused to believe it, we'll never know, but it can make for an infuriatingly one-sided commentary.

After his visit to the slave auction, Colonel Arthur spent much of his time in Charleston looking out to sea. Nowadays only occasional warships grace Charleston's harbour but in 1863 it was a crucial naval base. During Arthur's visit there was much talk of ironclad ships, which both the Union and Confederacy had already experimented with. Once perfected, it was clear these ironclad bruisers would make mincemeat out of any wooden ships. Arthur realised that the navy was modernising before his very eyes.

My ancestor also witnessed two Rebel steamers successfully run the blockade, while another, the *Ruby*, he spotted burning in the distance having run ashore. It interested me to learn that on average the Union only managed to stop one out of every six Rebel blockade runners. Without any preventative measures at all, though, many more vessels would have chanced it, so the blockade still provided a vital function for the Union. In fact it was largely the North's sustained naval dominance, both in rivers and seas, which finally won them the war.

While standing on the Charleston seafront my ancestor had one especially interesting conversation with a Confederate captain by the name of Tucker. Tucker tells my ancestor that he 'expects great results from [a] certain newly invented submarine . . .'

To my delight I discovered an exhibition at the Charleston Museum focusing on a Civil War submarine. Not any old sub either but the *H.L. Hunley*, the first submarine in history to sink an enemy warship. The *Hunley* achieved its groundbreaking feat roughly ten miles from the Charleston coast, only eight months after my ancestor's visit. From the exhibition it soon became clear that despite its success in destroying the Union sloop USS *Housatonic* the *Hunley*'s history is rather a tragic one.

The submarine was the brainchild of a Louisiana lawyer and devout Confederate, Horace Hunley. With help from mechanics and money men Hunley built his submarine in Mobile, Alabama, in the spring of 1863. On completion, the iron-hulled *Hunley*, which was powered by a crankshaft turned by seven men, was transported to Charleston, as a secret weapon against the Union fleet. The omens were not rosy from the start. On one of its preliminary runs the *Hunley* sank, probably swamped by the wake of a passing steamer, and five of the crew drowned.

Undeterred by this accident Horace Hunley took control of the sub himself. Disastrously, due to a loose flood valve the vessel sank again, killing Hunley and all of his seven crew members. By this stage General Beauregard was reluctant to allow more trials with the seemingly jinxed *Hunley*.

However, a mechanical engineer, George Dixon, persuaded the flamboyant Creole to let him have one last go. After several leak-free trial runs, Dixon decided to take his chances. On the night of 17 February 1864 Dixon and his heroic new recruits cranked their way into the Atlantic, deployed their torpedo and blew the entire aft of the *Housatonic* to pieces. The sloop sunk soon after, and put the *Hunley* into the history books. Tragically, for reasons that are still uncertain, the *Hunley* sank on its way back to shore with all her eight crewmen going down with her.

In her turbulent history the *Hunley* claimed the lives of twenty-one Confederates, who manned the doomed sub at different times. However, it is a testimony to the determination of the Southern war effort that the little submarine came to exist at all. It was way ahead of its time – built a full seven years before Jules Verne even wrote *Twenty Thousand Leagues under the Sea*. Now, after 136 years in the water, the *Hunley* is back on dry land, having recently been excavated by a team led by the adventure novelist Clive Cussler.

The skeletons of the eight crewmen who died that winter night in 1864 were all found at their stations in the sub. As I write this there are plans to honour the dead men by burying them in Charleston alongside Horace Hunley and his crew. They certainly deserve it. As Robert Neyland, one of the excavation team said: 'The *Hunley* is to submarine warfare what the Wright brothers' airplane is to aviation. It changed the course of naval history.'

*   *   *

Later that afternoon I bussed westward on snow-chocked roads, ready to resume my mule walk the following day. From the Greyhound station at Athens I took a roundabout route

back to Browny's stable, passing a concert hall, where the
blues singer Robert Cray was billed to play later in the
month. After Charleston's prim elegance, Athens had rather a
funky feel to it with lots of student cafes blasting pop. One
such place boasted on its doorway: 'Athens – Hometown to
REM and the B52s – The World's Best Bands'.

Far more interestingly to me, Athens was also home to the
world's only double-barrelled cannon. One of the university
vets had told me I must see it if I had an interest in the Civil
War. I located the curious-looking cannon outside the city
hall, ice crystals glinting on its twin barrels. Underneath it
was a historic marker that explained its bizarre history.

The cannon had been designed by John Gilleland, a local
dentist and a private in the Mitchell Thunderbolts, an 'elite'
Dad's Army-style unit. Cast in an Athens foundry, the revolutionary weapon was intended simultaneously to fire two balls
connected to a chain that would mow down the enemy
somewhat as 'a scythe cuts wheat'. The four and a half foot
cannon was tested in a nearby field in April 1862. The test was
spectacular, if nothing else.

According to Richard Irby Jr, one of the balls left the
muzzle before the other and, 'the two balls pursued an erratic
circular course, ploughing up an acre of ground, whipping
through a corn field and mowing down some saplings before
the chain broke. The balls then shot off in different directions,
one killing a cow and the other demolishing the chimney on a
log cabin.' Not surprisingly the spectators fled. Although a
failure as a weapon it now remains an object of curiosity and
affection within Athens.

As I walked through the snow back to Browny, I pondered
on the extraordinary nature of the American Civil War. The
first double-barrelled cannon, the first enemy-sinking submarine, the first war in which hot air balloons were used (for
reconnaissance purposes), one of the first uses of attrition-

style trench warfare (during the siege of Vicksburg), some of the first mass concentration camps (at Andersonville in Georgia 13,000 Union prisoners died from sickness and starvation), and the first and only American in history to be charged as a war criminal (Andersonville's commander, Henry Wirz, who was hanged in 1865).

On a more positive note it is also the only war where a bullet spawned life as well as death. At the 1863 Battle of Raymond in Mississippi a minié ball reportedly passed through the reproductive organs of a Rebel soldier and seconds later penetrated a young lady standing nearby. Miraculously she became impregnated and nine months later a child was born. According to some reports the minié ball mother and the soldier later married and had two more children by the conventional method.

It all sounds hugely improbable, but in a war that wreaked so much death and destruction it's perhaps understandable this tale of new life surviving against all the odds has stood the test of time.

CHAPTER 16

Hooves of Thunder, Feet of Clay

Browny and I plodded north through puddles of icy slush. It felt good to be off again, to enjoy the therapeutic clop of mule hooves and the vanity of solitude. In fact solitude was becoming increasingly hard won now we were out of the boondocks. From Atlanta onwards the tongues of inquisitive locals were often wagging long before our arrival. 'You're the Englishman, aren't you?' they would shout from their porches. 'And *that* must be Browny.'

The capacity for pastoral gossip never ceased to amaze me. Much of it was terrific stuff. A South Carolina newspaper reported that I was a Frenchman walking around the world while one local police station received a nervous call warning of 'a suspicious-looking man with a donkey'. But my favourite gossip revolved around sightings of other travellers far more unusual than me. In Athens there had been reports of two septuagenarian cowboys riding horses from Florida to Alaska, in Abbeville a zealous Catholic pilgrim dragging a cross twice his size had recently struggled through town. But my favourite by far featured a traveller called Goatman.

Stories about Goatman had been circulating throughout much of the South, but they were all so conflicting and implausible, that I tended to dismiss them. Then I reached Calhoun Falls, where a twinkly, snow-haired local historian called Wilton Anderson flagged me down. At a diner fringed with cock-eyed deer antlers, Wilton produced a scrapbook of Goatman cuttings and let me rifle through them as he narrated the legendary gypsy's story.

Goatman's real name was Chess McCartney. Sparked by the book *Robinson Crusoe*, wild-haired McCartney spent almost half a century drifting around America pulled by a goat-drawn wagon. He is thought to have trundled through every one of the US states barring Hawaii and Alaska. McCartney even requested to spend a night at the White House but was politely turned down by President Carter (possibly on the grounds there were already enough goats in the West Wing).

As with all nomads, much of the information on Goatman was colourful but vague. When he died in his Georgia nursing home in 1998, some said McCartney was 97 years old, and others 107. Whatever the truth, he is thought to have retained his gypsy lifestyle and fifty-odd billy goats until well into his nineties. He had been married once and had a son, Gene, who had predeceased him by six months.

McCartney, who from his photographs resembled an ethereal Gandalf-like character, had eked a meagre income selling postcards of his wagon. He looked like someone saddled with the poverty of another century, but happy to be so. Despite attracting ridicule from certain quarters he was a popular figure described by one of his friends as 'a caring man, very pleasant, though his language is sometimes on the edge'. 'He had a serene quality, like he knew something the rest of us didn't,' commented another.

'I visited Goatman shortly before he died,' Wilton told me, blowing the steam off his coffee. 'He was a fine, God-fearing old man. Bright little eyes. His critics were just jealous. They saw a man whose life was free and simple and they resented it. It's a shame, but I'm not sure America would tolerate someone like him now.'

*   *   *

I possessed one shaggy mule rather than fifty goats, but thankfully America was still tolerating me. Throughout January I continued to camp at ranches, fire stations and in the tiny community of Whitmire, deep in the Sumter forest, I bedded down in a greenhouse infused with jungly warmth, and full of drooping, fit-to-burst tomatoes. Browny was well cared for too. At the Gaston family ranch near Lando she lodged with Jaybo, a tubby goat; at a rare breed farm near Stanfield, she grazed alongside two very elegant antelopes (zebras and ostriches roamed near by) and at Van Wyck near the North Carolina border, she briefly rubbed shoulders with a bison.

The latter incident was especially memorable. Browny and I pitched up at the remote Mediterranean-style farmstead of Andrew and Margarita Pate, well after dark. I roped Browny to a fence post and bashed on the door. There was nobody home. Strange, I thought, earlier in the day I had been told they were expecting me. It was a cold night and I was keen to sort out Browny fast. After waiting almost an hour, watching pairs of roosting mallard splosh into a nearby pond, I decided to walk back down the Pates' long, swervy drive and ask the neighbours where they might be.

I returned twenty minutes later, none the wiser, only to find the whole family surrounding Browny. It was soon clear they had no idea who I was and were rather unsettled to find a semi-house-trained mule ripping into their lawn. To his eternal credit, Andrew, a calm, lanky doctor with a sense of quiet authority, ushered his wife and children indoors and rose to the occasion. Fortunately he vaguely remembered something about my mule trip from a local paper. He suggested setting Browny loose in some fenced parkland to the rear of the house.

'Just one thing,' Andrew said as we tramped across the frozen grass. 'Dakota lives in the park too.'

'Dakota?'

'A buffalo,' he explained casually.

'A buffalo!'

I told Andrew my knowledge of buffalo psychology was thin, but I expressed some concern about Dakota being territorial.

'Oh, don't worry,' he insisted. 'He's old and lazy, he won't trouble your mule. He'll enjoy the company.'

I bowed to Andrew's superior grasp of husbandry and unleashed Browny into the seemingly deserted park. We leant over the gate and watched my mule roll in some dirt near the water trough. All was quiet for a while, no sign of Dakota. Then a rumble, like distant thunder, permeated the night. Browny's head shot up, her eyes popping with cartoon-like intensity, and off she blazed like a Derby contender up the fence line. Hot on her fetlocks was Dakota. The hulking beast displayed alarming agility, jinking his way through the oak trees, and to my horror began to gain ground on the retreating Browny. It soon became obvious it was not violence that gripped the speeding bison, but passion. The mechanical impossibility of such a coupling did not deter him: my mule had clearly kick-started the old behemoth's libido.

In unison Andrew and I leapt into the paddock to retrieve our respective animals. It had never been easier to catch Browny. She stood stock still, unashamedly pleading to be rescued. I led her back to the lawn, pulse racing, her mane almost static with fear. Meanwhile the spurned Dakota sulked off, heavy-hoofed, back into the park's misty woods.

'Sorry about that,' puffed Andrew, his short breaths visible in the dark. 'I'm surprised Dakota had so much, well, you know, vigour.'

Andrew explained that the elderly bison had once had four female companions. Several years ago during a summer storm a bolt of lightening had killed them simultaneously as they were sheltering under a tree. Dakota was the only survivor. With his harem gone, the lonely beast now craved company: fellow buffalo, seventeen-year-old mules, he clearly wasn't fussy.

Back in the family kitchen Andrew fed me some hot gazpacho. He apologised that the house was full, but said I could sleep in his garage. He handed me a copy of a magazine called *BisonWorld* and a blow heater and left me to it. I bedded down on Browny's saddle mats and read some buffalo trivia.

I learnt that at the time of Columbus America boasted up to sixty million buffalo. Although hunted by Indian tribes (who often stampeded them en masse over cliffs or into snow drifts in order to kill them), their numbers were always sustainable. Then came the big push west by immigrants and fortune hunters in the mid 1800s. This, coupled with the advent of railroads through the Great Plains, led the buffalo (whose hides and tongues now fetched high prices in New York and Washington) to be hunted almost to extinction. General Sheridan, who actively championed the slaying of Indians, had a similarly uncharitable attitude to buffalo. '. . .

kill, skin and sell till the buffalo are exterminated,' he encouraged hunters. Not surprisingly, numbers plummeted from millions to a pitiful three hundred or less.

Ironically it was a taxidermist cum zoologist, William Hornaday, who, realising the devastating plight of the buffalo, spearheaded a campaign to save them. By the turn of the century many buffalo reserves and ranches had been established and numbers slowly picked up. Now, Dakota, I was happy to learn, is one of some 150,000 buffalo that thrive in modern-day America.

*   *   *

On every long journey there is a moment where interest in your surroundings falters and all that matters is the need to move, to progress, and fast. On crossing the North Carolina border the day after the Dakota incident such a moment hit me. I simply wanted to steam my way up the map. Colonel Arthur shot through this section of America and I would do the same.

I started tramping furiously north, my quest to reach Gettysburg turning as blinkered as Captain Ahab's pursuit of Moby Dick and, ultimately, almost as disastrous. In a burst of introspective lunacy I unwittingly set about pushing my mule to breaking point.

As a result of this heightened urgency North Carolina, the Tar Heel state, passed in a blur. Some locals told me it was known as Tar Heel because of its dark, clay soil, others because General Lee had once complimented a local regiment on gamely sticking in its heels during a Civil War battle. Initially, though, North Carolina had been wary of the war, being the last of the eleven Confederate states to secede from the Union in 1861. But walking down any Tar Heel road today it was still very clear I was in the South. At the first diner

I reached in the sprawling town of Monroe a sticker on the door proclaimed: 'American By Birth, Southern By The Grace Of God'.

Southern hospitality was still alive and kicking too. Throughout much of North Carolina I was passed from the home of one accommodating stranger to the next. In Albemarle, Jim and Marilyn put me up in a bedroom full of Marilyn Monroe dolls before ushering me on to Liberty where Sheila and Edwin set up a special wooden corral for Browny in their garden. They in turn pointed me towards the barn of dazzling Abby Jones, who rode a horse like Boudicca, and fed me peanut butter cheesecake.

I didn't hang about though. Every day I urged Browny on. Twenty miles. Twenty-four miles. Twenty-nine miles. It didn't matter. We walked over russet-coloured fields, combed ready for the next tobacco crop. I spotted blue jays and raccoons and one morning thrilled at the sight of a beaver in a creek bed, its tail dragging behind it like a large, dark tongue. I ate catfish in The Three Stooges honky-tonk, full of back-woodsmen with pirate smiles and bought myself a cowboy hat from a Piggly Wiggly store. The weather stayed dry, the cold sun peeking through clouds of pale denim. Keep moving, I told myself, got to keep moving.

On Groundhog Day (2 February) when Americans predict the end of winter by means of a groundhog's shadow, Browny and I reached Virginia. That evening I learnt the shadow of the famous hog (who lived in Punxsutawney, a small town in Pennsylvania) was still visible, meaning spring was at least six weeks away. But nothing could stop us now. Fired by the thought of the Blue Ridge Mountains we pressed on through Danville, famed as the last Capital of the Confederacy, and on to Chatham, where a jolly, tobacco-spitting farmer with a raspy voice sheltered us from a hailstorm.

The following evening, though, at a park in Altavista, our luck turned spectacularly for the worse. Browny, usually so confident on bridges, had a turn. I should have seen it coming a mile off but it had been a long afternoon and I was cold, jaded and ignorant of my mule's discomfort. The War Memorial park where I had secured permission to camp was accessible only by means of a wooden bridge with railings on either side. As I navigated Browny across the first narrow ramp a dog began barking at us. Browny freaked, snagging one of her saddlebags against the side of the bridge. Clutching her lead rope with bruised knuckles I watched impotently as the bag's stitching ripped apart, spewing my belongings into the stream below. 'Whoa, Brown,' I shouted, before adding more desperately, 'Stand still, you old bitch.'

After much stamping and nickering Browny calmed down. I coaxed her onto the grass the other side, staked her and spooned out a portion of oats. Feeling sick and light-headed, I sat down on a park bench. Seconds later I threw up. The dog was still barking and I rose to shoo it off, a desperate-looking collie with a greying muzzle and crippled back legs. 'Go on, get away.' The dog howled, a terrible, plaintive, why oh why sound, not quite of this world. 'Git, you mongrel.' It howled again, a sound so forlorn and grief stricken that I couldn't bear to shout any more. I threw the dog a biscuit. It snatched it and hobbled away on its ruined paws. I gathered my kit and curled up in my four-season sleeping bag without even bothering to put my tent up. In the morning the stream was scabbed with ice.

I mended the ruined saddlebag with some rope, but it was far from perfect. We trudged on miserably through the cold, hoping to get beyond the large city of Lynchburg before dark. It was not to be. Browny had developed a mild limp and her nose was clogged with phlegm. Just as we infiltrated the city limits her pace began to slacken drastically and her head drooped. I urged her on, hoping to find her some decent pasture for the night.

Lynchburg was far bigger than I anticipated. As darkness fell we were still right in the thick of things, snarled in a Friday night gridlock. The tapering verge was hard to walk on and I ended up leading Browny onto a grassy strip running between two jammed highways. All the cars now had their lights on. A truck transporting a large mobile home drove so close I was forced to duck. The driver shouted abuse and waved a fist at me. Browny was deadbeat, and I knew we would have to stop.

In the distance I saw a motel. Worth a try, I decided, and made a beeline for the gaudy DAYS INN sign. On arrival the receptionist was clearly dubious but sensing my despair said she would make an exception. I was allowed to stake out Browny on the grass beyond the car park, next to a conifer spinney. I unloaded her, fed her and collapsed on my bed.

All was quiet until shortly before midnight when all hell broke lose. Opposite the Days Inn was a bowling alley. After it closed swarms of revellers were decanted into the night. Before long several trucks were using the motel car park like a speedway track, screeching around corners and shouting 'wheyheeey'. Near by two rival gangs of youths chanted abuse at each other and several half-hearted fights broke out. I dashed out to placate Browny in my flip-flops. She stood in the shadows, calmly surveying the ambient high jinks.

Soon the police arrived: roughly a dozen of them in black, padded uniforms. They swarmed through the car park and then the motel, occasionally yanking suspects from rooms. I sat on a tree stump next to Browny supping on a hot chocolate. After things had settled down a couple of the police approached me. They asked what a mule was doing in the middle of Lynchburg. I apologised and told them my story.

'That mule is the least of our troubles,' said one of the cops. 'But get her out of here first thing tomorrow.'

*   *   *

Early next morning I consulted my map of Virginia. From Lynchburg I realised I was only fifteen miles from Sweet Briar, which I had marked with a yellow fluorescent marker. It suddenly dawned on me a friend of Rodney's from Atlanta had told me I might be able to stay at an artists' colony near there. Browny and I desperately needed a place to rest up. Sweet Briar, on the fringe of the Blue Ridge Mountains, would surely be perfect.

Later that evening we limped up the drive of the Virginia Center for the Creative Arts hoping to camp in its mountain-fringed grounds. As it turned out the VCCA had been expecting us, and had a spare studio for me to sleep in. After sorting out Browny in one of the outlying sheds I was led down a long corridor into a dining room full of artists, writers, composers, musicians and songwriters. I sat down at one of the tables with a plate of lasagne and a glass of red wine, hoping to decompress a bit. Soon I was amidst a sea of inquisitive bohemians. Never in my life have I undergone such a grilling.

'Can I paint Browny? I've always loved donkeys' eyebrows.'

'A song about Browny, now there's an idea. *This mule was made for walking, and walking's what she'll do, one of these days this mule is gonna walk all over you.*'

'I'm going to do for mules what Hemingway did for bulls. Lead me to Browny now. I feel a Pulitzer brewing.'

By the end of the meal I was so punch drunk and disorientated by all the banter that I struggled to remember where I had parked Browny. I found her sitting on a clump of pine needles in the moonlight. She seemed strangely listless.

Tomorrow I would have to call the vet. The good news was that Swanny, the VCCA's affable groundsman, agreed to fix Browny's ruptured saddlebag.

I woke early and used a payphone to call around. I didn't have much luck with vets. The only person on hand was Becky Vail, a local farrier. She turned up half an hour later, a muscular lady, with frayed, purple braces and forearms as sinewy as celery. She had a row of pens in her top pocket like a TV doctor.

Becky circled Browny watching her intently. Various artists walked past us on their way to their studios to paint, write and play piano. The Blue Ridge Mountains silhouetted the horizon, spread beneath a scarf of pink, fissured cloud.

'What the hell you been doing to this animal?' said Becky sharply, rubbing Browny's ribs.

'What do you mean? What's wrong with her?'

'Well, I'll tell you straight,' replied Becky. 'She's lame, skinny and plain worn out.'

I looked at my mule and realised she really didn't look her best. As Browny paced up and down the VCCA lawn, she appeared stiff and brittle, as if she needed oiling. Worse still, a tendril of lettuce-green snot dangled from her right nostril. What a bastard I've been, I thought. Over the past week I've treated her like some sort of disposable, long-eared flunkey.

Guilt-ridden, I explained to Becky about the walk. The fact Browny had clocked up roughly two thousand miles, through a variety of mercury-busting heat in Texas to blood-chilling winds in Virginia. This did mollify the formidable farrier a little but she still gave me an earful.

'Right, let's get some facts straight,' announced Becky, flicking her braces. 'I'll look after this mule for you until she's fit. That might be one week, it might be two.'

'One week!'

'Shut up and listen! Browny needs to shake off that limp and she needs feeding up. Virginia's got a drought at the moment, worst for two hundred years. That mule ain't been getting good enough grazing. You've got to feed her more hay and more sweet oats. Got it?' I nodded. 'You've walked her into the ground. She's tough, but she ain't invincible. You've got to let her rest up more. The odd day here and there ain't enough.' I nodded again. 'Now I wanna help you. So I'll take her away, treat her and you can call me in a few days.' I nodded, shook Becky's calloused hand and gave Browny a farewell hug.

*   *   *

So that was that. While Browny was undergoing a makeover at Becky's I was stranded in a studio in the Blue Ridge foothills. Oh well, there were worse places to kill time than with Cuban pianists, short story writers from Vermont, film-makers from Washington and an exuberant and motley coterie of songwriters. Grand views, fine food and stimulating company: the perfect pitstop for a weary skinner.

What was really refreshing about the artists' colony was hearing some alternative points of view. So far on my walk, despite the occasional voice of dissent, most people had eulogised George Bush. I thought Bush had dealt with the September 11 aftermath competently enough, but not to the extent he was beyond criticism. At Sweet Briar, for the first time, I heard people openly question the extent of the bombings in Afghanistan; the fact that the war was spreading far beyond just the Taliban.

Although I had been deeply touched by the decency of individual Americans and impressed by the country's unity, sometimes it worried me how unquestioning its population could be collectively. Predictably, other travellers had tapped into this long before me, as I discovered while flicking through some books in the VCCA library.

In his travels in the 1830s I discovered the French writer Alexis de Tocqueville became obsessed with America's 'tyranny of the majority'. It is one of the main themes of his classic *Democracy in America*. De Tocqueville railed about the shocking 'oneness' of American thinking, its lack of eccentricity and its dread of rocking the status quo. More recently the Wales-based writer and Lincoln biographer Jan Morris struck on a similar theme. 'As individuals modern Americans seem to me almost miraculously free of arrogance and chauvinism,' she wrote, 'but as a nation they have never lost that sense of superiority, and the instinct for interference that goes with it.'

The Australian author, Tim Flannery, perhaps puts it best. He argues that America has always been a nation of immigrants, who seek inclusion, not separation.

'In a sense American popular culture has to be a superglue,' writes Flannery, 'and to do that it must appeal to the lowest common denominator. [It] has no choice but to be a mass culture, from baseball and football to hot dogs, Coca-Cola, McDonald's, baseball caps, pop tunes and Hollywood movies. It will always be superficial, full of self-reference to big-screen clichés . . . and to a consensus news media. That's why it appeals to everyone . . . and that's why American popular culture is now a global phenomenon.'

This 'oneness' in American thinking did have its redemptive side as I found out one night while watching the news in the artists' TV room. One bulletin covered a report that showed over seventy-five per cent of Americans had donated in some way to the September 11 appeal. This, at least to me, seemed an extraordinary act of positive solidarity. Following this report there was a flashback to a ceremony commemorating the Twin Towers victims. A tearful girl in the crowd held up a banner with the words: 'We're all Yankees now.'

Somehow, however contemporary the news, whatever the subject, the Civil War was never far away. I suppose this was to be expected. It was, after all, the war that defined America. Before the conflict people were prone to say 'the United States are'. After 1865, more often they said 'the United States is'.

*   *   *

Thankfully for most of my time at Sweet Briar it was love, not war that was on my mind. Fully aware that a dishevelled bum like me was unlikely to allure many members of the opposite sex, I had long discarded any hope of romance on the road. Jack Kerouac may have managed it, but he never had to chaperone a cantankerous brown mule.

So when Margo appeared, it was quite a surprise.

Margo was a New Yorker, a children's author with a soft, confident voice. She was petite, with cascades of gold hair and smiled like she had just heard the first joke ever told. She liked to say: 'That's just crazy' and her perfume smelt of summer.

The VCCA was a strange environment to find romance. All the various artists spent the day in their studios: the pianists in large rooms with fine acoustics, the artists in well-lit studios and the writers in quiet hideaways, empty but for a desk and a bed. In the evening they would all meet up for an evening meal and afterwards often took it in turns to perform their work – reading poetry, exhibiting art or playing music. My first night Ariacne, a nineteen-year-old pianist from Havana, wowed us with her haunting voice. Then came a screening of *The Life and Times of Hank Greenberg*, a charming film directed by a wild lady called Aviva, about the first major league Jewish baseball player.

After watching Hank wallop his final home run I got chatting with Margo. I found some of the Sweet Briar residents a bit clannish, but it was clear Margo was independent and didn't fall into any clique. In the evenings we played Scrabble and ping pong together and flirted innocently. Then, out walking in the grounds one evening, stoked with too much wine we fell into a clumsy embrace. I'd been embraced by so many Americans – Bible-thumping evangelists, hirsute ranchers, matronly housewives – but this was the first time I chose to hang on for more. Margo's cold fingertips on my face felt like balm, like some strange reward.

Sometimes it's only when you've been touched in the right way that you realise how lonely you've been.

*   *   *

Unfortunately my time at the VCCA was short-lived. After four days I needed to vacate my little studio. Sweet Briar had been a spell of undiluted lotus eating and put fresh fire in my belly, but it was time to reunite with Browny. 'I've never been jilted in favour of a mule,' joked Margo. She gave me a book by Flannery O'Connor and agreed to meet up in New York in a month or so. On leaving the VCCA was a large sign that was only visible on the way out. In big letters it read: THE REAL WORLD.

Back at Becky's farm the prognosis was not good. Browny still needed to gain weight and had failed to lose her limp. 'You can't take her yet,' Becky told me. I decided this would be a good time to catch up with Colonel Arthur again and make a brief side trip to the nearby city of Richmond. If Browny was not fit on my return to Becky's, so be it, I would be forced to carry on walking without her. Becky had agreed to transport Browny north in a trailer if this was the case — but only once she was fully healed.

After a hopelessly sluggish journey in a Greyhound (America surely has the worst cross-country bus service in the world) I only ended up spending two days in Richmond, once the principal capital of the Confederacy.

Richmond is a place that reaffirms William Faulkner's maxim: 'The past is never dead. It's not even past.' It was here that Robert E. Lee, ever loyal to Virginia, agreed to serve the South, having only recently turned down Abraham Lincoln's offer to command the entire Northern army. It was also here that the Tredegar Iron Works, which greatly impressed my ancestor, provided essential munitions to the Rebel war effort.

More recently it was in Richmond that a statue of the black tennis champion and local hero, Arthur Ashe, caused controversy. Ashe's monument was erected on a boulevard already honouring five Confederates: Davis, Lee, Jackson, swashbuckling horseman J.E.B. Stuart and the naval commander, Matthew Fontaine Maury. Although planned as a sign of reconciliation, some Richmond locals viewed it as unfair on Ashe to include him with the Confederate statues, while others said it was disrespectful to the Confederates to put Ashe alongside them. Whatever the opinions, Arthur Ashe's statue is now part of Richmond's history.

But for me, Richmond is the city in which my ancestor met the President of the Confederacy, Jefferson Davis. Colonel Arthur visited Davis in his private home, which is now part of the Museum of the Confederacy, on the evening of 17 June 1863. During my tour I found the revamped home to be rather a dank, joyless sort of place, with the odd portrait of

Davis lining the walls. His face looked pinched and severe, with stern eyes and a finely primped goatee.

My ancestor described Davis as: '. . . looking older than expected. He is only fifty-six, but his face is emaciated and much wrinkled. He is nearly six feet high, but is extremely thin and stoops a little . . . he looked what he evidently is, a well-bred gentleman. Nothing can exceed the charm of his manner, which is simple, easy and most fascinating.'

Arthur chats with Davis about the desperate poverty in Mississippi (home state of Varina, Davis's second wife). After his interview my ancestor realises that Davis — who fought with distinction in the Mexican War — would clearly have preferred to serve the Confederacy as a soldier than as its president. He also notes that Davis, in his days as a young cotton plantation manager, had a reputation for never mistreating his slaves.

Despite being a reluctant president, Davis remained a steadfast believer in the Confederacy right to the end. Indeed he never officially surrendered. After fleeing Richmond and then Danville, he was finally caught by Union troops travelling south through Georgia (according to some reports disguised in a woman's headscarf). He was then taken in leg irons to Fort Monroe in Virginia where he was held for two years. On his release he lived in Canada, where he wrote his memoirs and outlived all his sons.

History hasn't always treated the first and last President of the Confederacy kindly. Walter Lord notes Davis could be bitter if he didn't get his way (he and General Joe Johnston particularly despised each other). 'Davis was basically stiff and cold. He had no humor whatsoever,' writes Lord. 'Above all he was obstinate.' Even Varina, while championing her husband's strengths, conceded he 'has a way of taking for granted that everybody agreed with him . . .' However, Davis also has his champions, including Civil War historian Shelby Foote.

'Davis was an outgoing, friendly man . . . and had an infinite store of compassion,' pointed out Foote. 'These misconceptions about Davis are so strange that it's as if a gigantic conspiracy was launched. It was partly launched by Southerners, who, having lost the war, did not want to blame it on the generals, so they blamed it on the politicians and, of course, Davis was the chief politician.'

Davis certainly had a near impossible job leading the Confederacy. It was hardly surprising Arthur noticed how stressed he looked. The President had already led a tough life, losing his beloved first wife, Sarah Taylor, to malaria and plagued himself by facial pains, eventually leading to blindness in one of his eyes. The loss of the war failed to break Davis, however, and his last public speech to a group of young Southerners, shortly before his death in 1889, shows a commendable willingness to forgive:

'The past is dead,' he said; 'let it bury its dead, its hopes and its aspirations; before you lies the future. Let me beseech you to lay aside all rancor, all sectional feeling, and to take your place in the ranks of . . . a reunited country.'

Jefferson Davis's funeral was attended by a quarter of a million people, the largest ever held in the South.

*   *   *

More than anything in Richmond I was determined to visit the Virginia Historical Society. Although it boasted a trove of Virginia's richest pickings (including a a portrait of 22-year-old Pocahontas) there was really only one thing I was interested in and, in truth, I had come to see it on behalf of Browny.

Standing outside the Society's stately facade was a statue of a war horse. Unlike most equine sculptures this horse appeared on the verge of collapse. It was a truly miserable specimen, scrawny and downcast. The dying animal's head sagged pitifully, one of its rear hooves tilted upwards while its tail hung as limp as frayed rope. Underneath the rider-free animal was an inscription:

IN MEMORY OF THE ONE AND ONE HALF MILLION HORSES AND MULES OF THE CONFEDERATE AND UNION ARMIES WHO WERE KILLED, WERE WOUNDED, OR DIED FROM DISEASE IN THE CIVIL WAR

It strikes just the right note. To sculpt a prancing stallion breaking through the enemy ranks would have been just another fanciful monument to an often over-romanticised war. Most horses and mules fared horribly between 1861 and 1865, suffering on a par with the human casualties, and many of them, like their masters, through starvation and disease. To learn more I trawled the Historical Society's elegant hallways and flicked through a variety of books.

Horse casualties were far more severe than mules (of the 1.5 million equine casualties, probably less than half a million were mules). Horses tended to be more in the thick of the fray whether ridden in cavalry skirmishes or by tenacious officers at the head of their troops. Mules toiled more in the background, lugging guns, ammunition, food and equipment. Their tough, nimble hooves could also deal with rough ground far better than horses.

Mules were of vital importance to both the Union and the Confederacy. At the beginning of the war Kentucky was the chief mule-producing state of the Union, whereas for the South the Tex-Mex area boasted the largest population. Physically, these beasts were chalk and cheese, Kentucky mules being huge and powerful whereas the Tex-Mex mules were considerably smaller, the result of a cross with a Mexican mustang.

The Union managed to maintain a fairly steady supply of mules to the battle lines but, as the war dragged on, the overstretched Confederates became more dependent on horses to pull their supply wagons. Losses could be horrendous. During the battle of Chattanooga in the winter of 1863 an estimated ten thousand Union horses and mules fell to their deaths transporting food over treacherous mountain paths. After the same battle a similar number of Confederate mules perished from disease, exhaustion and drowning while slogging back and forth with supplies in the heavy mud.

The Civil War posed major problems with the disposal of dead animals. Equine corpses were clearly much more troublesome to bury than their masters. On rare occasions birds of prey, if they were not scared off by gunfire, would help clean battlefields. But more often than not the rotting carcasses would linger, exacerbating the possibility of disease and infection.

Keeping the animals healthy was a persistent challenge. The army of the Potomac – over 140,000 men strong in its heyday – used to march with almost 50,000 mules and horses. The rations required for the animals were immense. For example, in the spring of 1864 a total of 450 tons of feed was needed every day to supply all the beasts (one fifth hay, the rest grain). On General Sherman's devastating march from Atlanta to the sea, over 20,000 mules and 15,000 horses were used to lug equipment.

Mules had been used effectively in several conflicts prior to the Civil War, especially during the Mexican War and for quelling the rebellious Mormons in Utah in 1857. During both the First and Second World Wars tens of thousands of mules played an invaluable role in the battlefields of Europe. Only as late as 1956 was the last US Army mule unit disbanded, and even today three mules are kept at West Point Military Academy as mascots. But, for now, the American army has no serving war mules. That said, in the recent conflict in Afghanistan local mules were utilised by the US troops to transport supplies over the mountains. In this nuclear age it is perhaps heartening that the humble beast of burden still has a role to play.

Through history, however, not all soldiers approved of mules. General Ulysses S. Grant, while fighting as a young officer in the Mexican War, once railed: 'I am not aware of ever having used a profane expletive in my life, but I would have the charity to excuse those who may have done so if they were in charge of a train of Mexican pack-mules . . .'

General George 'Blood and Guts' Patton was not a fan either. He famously shot dead a couple of obstinate mules that were blocking his army from crossing a narrow bridge in Italy during the Second World War.

As Secretary of War in 1850s America, Jefferson Davis distrusted mules so much he actively encouraged experimenting with camels instead. In many ways it was a sound idea. As Emmett M. Essin in his book *Shavetails and Bell Sharps* writes: 'Camels could each carry seven hundred to twelve hundred pounds of supplies, day after day for thirty to forty miles.' A camel's carrying capacity was at least double that of other beasts of burden, claimed the author, and like the mule it could thrive on limited water and rough vegetation.

However, Essin concludes that despite their lugging skills, 'most soldiers and packers despised camels . . . Their odour was overpowering and totally unlike the sweet musky smell of mules. When packed they groaned, bleated, snarled, and wheezed in a noisy manner. By comparison mules' neighs were like fine music.' The author goes on to criticise camels for their biting, life-threatening kicks, trickiness to load and general 'ornery' nature. Mules won the day.

The one instance of a camel being used in the Civil War was by a Confederate Colonel during the siege of Vicksburg in May 1863. While humping the Colonel's baggage the unfortunate beast was soon picked off by a Union sharp-shooter. The only Civil War animal tale more fantastic than this centred on, not surprisingly, General Beauregard. According to one source the flamboyant Creole officer trans-ported his own dairy cow by train from New Orleans, as, due to gut troubles, he claimed he couldn't drink the milk of any other beast.

As usual the animals that stole the Civil War headlines were not mules, camels or cows – but horses. Perhaps the most famous of all these is Robert E. Lee's horse, Traveller. Lee used other horses in battle – headstrong Ajax and the skittish Lucy Long – but Traveller, a calm and beautiful grey gelding, was his favourite. Traveller only blotted his copybook once. During the second battle of Manassas in 1862 he was spooked by Union fire and lunged, breaking a bone in Lee's rein hand. But other than this, his sang-froid remained impeccable.

Traveller died of lockjaw in 1871, nine months after lead-ing the funeral cortege for his master. His story did not end here though. Traveller's bones were initially interred, then shifted for several decades into a taxidermist's shop, before being displayed at the Virginia Military Institute in Lexington where students inscribed their initials on his skeleton. When the bones began to wear away they were finally laid to rest in the Institute's chapel beneath a granite tombstone. Today, visitors leave carrots and sugar lumps in Traveller's honour.

Stonewall Jackson's mount, Little Sorrel, is also on display at the Virginia Military Institute, but in the museum. Unlike Traveller, Little Sorrel was stuffed and now boasts glass eyes and upholstered hair. The horse received mixed reviews during the war. One observer wrote him off as 'a dun cob of very sorry appearance', and another as 'a plebeian looking beast'. However Jackson, never a great horseman, described riding him 'as easy as the rocking of a cradle'.

Little Sorrel survived a bullet wound early in the war and bolted only once, when Stonewall was shot riding him at the battle of Chancellorsville. His dotage was spent touring country fairs across the South where diehard Rebs and souvenir hunters clipped hairs from his tail and mane. By the time he died, aged thirty-six, the venerable horse was nearly bald.

The sun was setting over Richmond now. I shut my research books and took a final photo of the statue of the dying horse, now glimmering in the red dusk. It was gratifying to think some respectful soul had gone to the effort of producing this monument to slain and wounded horses, and especially pleasing that the less celebrated, but equally noble mule, had not been overlooked. It was a bleak, honest and moving work of art that, for once, fully united the affections of both the grey and the blue.

*   *   *

Back at Becky's farm, Browny was still below par. I toyed with visiting nearby Appomattox, the site of Lee's final surrender, to provide my mule with more recovery time. Becky told me I could stay with her but I was becoming demoralised by my lack of progress. I decided to head off the following day, hefting my gear in a rucksack. As agreed, Becky promised to transport Browny up to me in Culpepper in a week's time.

It has to be said walking along the road without my beast by my side changed the flavour of the journey completely. The toots of car horns and the waves from passing drivers almost dried up completely. I was just another drifter trudging my way north. If I didn't realise it already, I did now. As Robert Garza had observed on the first night of our journey, Browny was the star of the show and I was just the sidekick. My only consolation was – if no further hiccups occurred – she would still have been by my side for over 95 per cent of the trip.

I struggled on through the town of Charlottesville, where I saw the statue of local worthy Captain Meriwether Lewis and his fellow explorer Captain William Clark, whose expedition from St Louis to the Pacific in the early 1800s is probably the greatest journey of discovery ever undertaken in America. The city was abuzz with talk of the expedition's upcoming two hundredth anniversary.

I slept one night at the tiny community of Crossroads camping near a thrumming sewage plant, and in comfortable contrast spent an evening in Madison Mills at a house where Thomas Jefferson once ate dinner. Over steak and chips I was delighted to learn from my hosts that Jefferson passionately advocated walking. Indeed he even believed that horse riding made the human body lazy. Like car-loathing Wilfred Thesiger two centuries later, the dynamic third President of America believed a good walk the only proper way to stretch legs and mind.

By the time I reached Culpepper I have to confess a car would have been most welcome. My right knee was pinking, three of my toenails had turned black and one of my teeth had broken after crunching on a rock-hard muesli bar. My rucksack-laden shoulders made me appreciate Browny far better, and I had only been carrying fifty pounds, whereas she normally lugged well over a hundred. I couldn't wait to be reunited with her, especially now New York was less than five hundred miles away. Even if all my toenails fell off in the process, I knew we could make it now.

PART THREE

Because we are also what we have lost.
    Seen on a wreath at Ground Zero, New York

CHAPTER 17

Gettysburg

Once in Culpepper I checked my emails at a local vet's office. One was from Lana, a horsy friend who, on hearing of Browny's exhaustion, wanted to have her say. She recommended I read a book called *Tschiffely's Ride*, about a Swiss adventurer, Aimé Tschiffely, who rode from Buenos Aires to New York in the 1920s.

'Tschiffely's two horses swam rivers, braved jungles, deserts and busy towns for over two years,' wrote Lana. 'They trotted across the finishing line in New York in good shape. Tschiffely knew his onions. But, you! Six months and your mule is half dead. What are you like?'

Lana had the decency to add that I could have been worse. She cited an excerpt from a book called *Coryat's Crudities*, in which Thomas Coryat, a happy-go lucky Somerset traveller describes his 1608 tour around Europe. Coryat, a joker in

King James's court and a champion 'legge stretcher', was also something of a buffoon. Near the start of his journey at the outskirts of Fontainebleau, Coryat's horse begins to lag. The eccentric wanderer viciously engages his spurs but still no luck. At this stage Coryat's travelling companion, known as Master I-H, rather drastically chooses to stab the horse in the rump.

'He drew out his Rapier and ranne [sic] him into his buttocke near to his fundament,' writes Coryat, 'about a foote deep very neare.'

This doesn't help propel the horse either and the two travellers end up washing the poor animal's skewered hind-quarters in a nearby fountain. Unsurprisingly, some local bystanders become 'extreame cholericke' and the two men are fined six French crowns. Coryat, who is famed for intro-ducing the fork to England, later died of a fever in 1617 having walked all the way to India.

'Moral of the story,' wrote Lana. 'Don't stab Browny in the arse with a rapier.'

Considering the most abuse I had ever inflicted on my mule was some robust chivvying, I felt all this was a little rich. Anyway, there was no need for any swords as when Becky dropped off Browny she was champing at the bit. After thanking Becky profusely — without her skill and generosity the trip would have been severely jeopardised — I struck out with Browny on the road to Gettysburg.

We were now hot on Colonel Arthur's trail again. It was at Culpepper that my ancestor shunned steam trains and took to the road with the Confederate army, often on horseback. Like so many of the horses and mules that would converge on Gettysburg, Colonel Arthur's mount was far from healthy. Near Winchester — a hotly contested place that changed hands seventy-two times throughout the Civil War — he wrote:

> my animal was in such a miserable state that I had not the
> inhumanity to ride him; but, by the assistance of his tail,
> I managed to struggle through the deep mud and wet.

This sounded equivalent to nobly refusing to ride piggyback
on your grandfather, then opting to dangle from his coat tails
instead.

In West Virginia I set up camp at Harpers Ferry, a dramatic,
ghostly town set on a steep hill on the confluence of the
Shenandoah and Potomac rivers. I staked out Browny in a
clearing where Stonewall Jackson had rounded up record-
breaking numbers of Yankee prisoners in the spring of 1862.
Of greater interest, though, was the site of the arsenal which
John Brown, the firebrand preacher and abolitionist, raided a
year and a half before the Civil War began.

Brown, a wispy bearded, fierce-eyed man (at least from his
picture in the Harpers Ferry museum), had hoped to arm the
slaves and spark a black rebellion. The outcome was less
romantic. The only casualty of his raid was a free slave who
was accidentally shot. After a brief clash Brown and his gang
surrendered to a small force of US soldiers, led by none other
than Lieutenant-Colonel Robert E. Lee (before his days as a
Confederate). Brown was later tried and hanged in nearby
Charlestown, transported to the gallows on a mule-drawn
wagon. Six of his men were also executed.

Brown's uprising at Harpers Ferry had been a crushing
failure. Indeed much of Brown's life had involved lurching
from one doomed enterprise to the next – sheep farmer,
preacher, businessman and finally ill-fated revolutionary. And
yet, it was just before facing the noose that Brown sealed his
immortality. He approached the gantry with great dignity,
believing to the end that 'the crimes of this guilty land will
never be purged away but with blood'. His prophecy was to
prove only too true.

In death Brown, while still loathed by many, became a martyr to the anti-slavery cause. The writer Henry David Thoreau drew parallels with Brown's hanging to Christ's crucifixion and referred to him as 'an angel of light', while Herman Melville called him 'the meteor of the war'.

Brown's raid, along with Harriet Beecher Stowe's big-selling, anti-slavery novel, *Uncle Tom's Cabin* written seven years before, were both major catalysts leading to those first shots at Fort Sumter. Some would even go as far as calling John Brown and his followers the Civil War's first true casualties.

*   *   *

These days Harpers Ferry is also the headquarters for the Appalachian Trail, a popular wilderness path, over two thousand miles long, that stretches between Georgia and Maine. Browny and I had cut across the trail before in Virginia but hadn't joined it as a sign had warned: ALL PETS FORBIDDEN. To remedy this at Harpers Ferry, I wanted to cross over the River Shenandoah and walk along a north-bound canal towpath, which had a more lenient policy towards beasts. Sadly the footbridge across to the canal, with its dozens of steep steps and spectacular backdrop of cliffs, proved impregnable for Browny. Watching jealously as posses of hikers made their way over the swirling current, I wondered what to do next.

Suitably stumped, I had only one option, to head further into the hill country of West Virginia.

This was perhaps the first time I had properly stepped out of the South. Although still below the Mason-Dixon line, the state of West Virginia only came into existence in 1863 as a pro-Union segment of Confederate Virginia. It surprised me that my usually news-hungry ancestor didn't mention this in his diary. The splinter state was formed just as Colonel Arthur was travelling through the heart of Virginia and must have been an explosive topic of conversation. That said, Arthur was on his way to one of the biggest battles in history; he perhaps felt he had bigger fish to fry.

Without doubt the highlight of my two-day westward detour was Shepherdstown. With a bustling college, a fat, green river that glinted and burbled in the sunshine, and a cafe called The Lost Dog, it launched itself, at least on first impressions, to very near the top of my American small town hit parade. That night I slept in a hayloft, intoxicated by rich, dusky smells and serenaded by the coo of doves and faraway bells.

From Shepherdstown it was only a morning's stroll into Maryland where Browny and I pitched up at the town of Sharpsburg, near the Antietam battlefield. Remembering Cory's history lesson in Texas the day after September 11, there was one place I was especially keen to see. I left Browny grazing at a local fire station and hotfooted it to Dunker Church, a tiny white building dwarfed by a sweep of jaundiced pasture. A historical marker reminded me it was here that soldiers in blue and grey downed arms, tended their wounded and swapped tobacco after 17 September 1862, the bloodiest single day of the war.

I was further interested to learn that prior to Antietam one of General Lee's written orders – carelessly dropped by a Confederate officer – had been found on the roadside by a Union soldier. Without this vital information falling into enemy hands, one wonders if the resulting battle would have wreaked such unprecedented carnage.

Whether wandering around the tranquil Dunker churchyard or the fringing scenes of conflict at Bloody Lane and Burnside's Bridge, Antietam really does have a haunting quality. Unlike some of the other Civil War arenas, diluted by nearby Dairy Queens or shopping malls, Antietam remains

impressively stark. 'Some battlefields have a sense of redemp-
tion, almost a softness about them now,' wrote one guest at
the visitors' centre. 'But Antietam is still raw.'

The isolation and the howl of the wind across this bleak
and spooky landscape got to me a bit too. I didn't stick
around. Colonel Arthur never visited Antietam but it is the
one place on my journey I felt in the presence of ghosts.

*   *   *

The following morning Browny and I crossed the Mason-
Dixon line into Pennsylvania. We were beyond the Rubicon
now: the South was truly behind us. The sun radiated a
spring-like thaw and I was happy to sleep rough as I weaved
through the wooded, ripe-smelling hills towards Gettysburg,
helicopters on their way to Camp David thudding overhead.

This far north the one thing that really astonished me was
the number of mobile homes. I had expected them in parts of
the Deep South, but now that I was less than four hundred
miles from New York they still seemed surprisingly wide-
spread.

What fascinated me about these grey, neat, soulless buildings, peppered across so much of America, was their utter
lack of mobility. These were not footloose and fancy-free
cabins soon to be carted off to their next destination: they
were homes with roots, often passed down through families.
One attractive mobile where I stayed in south Virginia had
even been kitted out with an extension and, yes, a con-
servatory. By now it probably boasts a mock Elizabethan
balustrade and marble fountains.

The different types of mobile home reminded me of
drinkers at a bar. Some were proud locals with no intention
of uprooting, others dreamily talked about moving on but
never got round to it, while a few had simply gone to seed,
slumped forever on a barstool, their pride drowned, their

grid reference no longer of any importance. Only very rarely in America was a mobile home ever actually on the move. It was all a far cry from the thrusting frontier days Colonel Arthur witnessed in 1863.

However, there was one aspect of my ancestor's journey that still really struck a chord with me today. Ever since I had reached north Virginia I noticed certain people had become very dismissive of the South. Some were purely having a lark while others were not. The latter were mostly genteel, slightly stuffy types whose opinions had nothing to do with political morality and everything to do with smugness. They would say things like: 'My dear, you *walked* through Alabama – I wouldn't even drive through *there!*' or 'The South's just an embarrassment, it's worse than the Third World.' When I asked these people if they had ever been to Mississippi or South Carolina, they would usually reply, 'Lord no, *never.*' Or, 'We did go to Natchez/Charleston once, very charming for a day, but that was *quite* enough.'

To my surprise I often became passionate in my defence of the South. When Colonel Arthur spoke of the 'foolish, bully-ing conduct of the Northerners' I had thought it was just another of his uppity anti-Union rants. Then I realised there really was a clutch of blatantly sniffy Northerners who, even today, spoke of the South, mostly the Deep South, with genuine derision. These urban savants were as blinkered and vitriolic towards small town Louisiana as a Tennessee hillbilly would be towards Philadelphia. It suited both parties to believe in the stereotypes.

If a Southern-bashing debate really got out of hand I enjoyed quoting a popular phrase I had read: 'The South is a place,' I would insist. 'East, west, and north are nothing but directions.' Even though my tongue was firmly in my cheek (making my English accent even less decipherable than usual),

I think for once Colonel Arthur might have been proud of me.

*   *   *

Once we had descended the hills of south Pennsylvania, Browny and I drifted into Gettysburg on the evening of 16 March on a road as straight and narrow as a canal. A journalist from the *Gettysburg Times* had agreed to let us use his home, on the north lip of the town, as a base. This was good news as it meant I could scrub up and look my best to meet Colonel Arthur. Well, not *the* Colonel Arthur, but the next best thing.

Sure enough, on my first morning in Gettysburg a man in a red tunic, a black cap and an ornate gold sword at his side appeared as I was feeding Browny. My mule was tied to a washing pole, exploring her lush new suburban surroundings. She looked up at the radiant guardsman in astonishment.

'Ready for battle?' Colonel Arthur asked, snapping to attention.

Roger Hughes, a marketing consultant from Nottingham who now lives in Florida, has been portraying my ancestor at Civil War battle reenactments for the past decade. He had generously driven over a thousand miles from Orlando, in full uniform, in order to give me a tour of the battlefield.

Roger and Colonel Arthur certainly had similarities. He not only boasted my ancestor's boundless energy and curiosity but an authentic moustache, tweaked at both ends into minute pointer's tails. Colonel Arthur would also have approved of Roger's English accent which had yet to be tinged by Florida's harsh vowels.

However, Roger, who enjoyed a pint, was plumper than the consumptive, Ichabod Crane physique of my ancestor. He also had several decades on Arthur, who had only been twenty-eight years old at the time of his American journey.

That said, Roger bore an uncanny resemblance to photos of my ancestor in his later life, when the Coldstreamer had fleshed out a bit and his pop eyes were less pronounced. Roger, I should add, knew more about Colonel Arthur than any man alive.

The other difference is that my ancestor never possessed a red sports car with an engine roar as loud and throaty as a Tiger Moth. This was Roger's pride and joy and our means of touring the battlefield.

'Here is where Arthur entered Gettysburg with the Confederate army,' explained Roger, as we cruised through the battlefield half an hour later. 'It's called the Cashtown Road.'

'Oh, yes,' I shouted above the snarling exhaust. 'I remember from his diary.'

I had first learnt of Roger in a *Vanity Fair* article about reenactors at Gettysburg. After exchanging emails the pair of us met briefly in England during one of Roger's visits to his Nottingham-based mother. It was just prior to my departure for Mexico.

'I wanted to check you weren't a nutcase,' Roger told me at the time. 'Likewise,' I had replied. I had half expected him to be some sort of Colonel Blimp in an anorak saying things like 'what ho' and 'I'll be jiggered.' God knows what he thought I would be like. Fortunately we hit it off. Roger was relaxed and funny. He took his hobby seriously but was not obsessive about it. More than anything he treated his role as 'a fun way to recreate the past'.

For the first section of the Gettysburg tour Roger and I left the car and walked along the ridge to the north of the town. It was a freezing day, the sky a glacial blue flecked with clouds of pink and silver. Everything was encrusted in frost – the trees, the battle monuments and the windows of Gettysburg's dark, austere-looking college. Very few other tourists were about.

'When Arthur arrived it was swelteringly hot,' explained Roger, glancing at the sky, 'but it looks like it's going to snow for you.'

As we walked Roger reminded me about the build up to Gettysburg: the fact that by the summer of 1863 the Confederate army, under Robert E. Lee, had won a string of glorious victories. This run of good fortune had culminated at Chancellorsville, only weeks before, in which the underdog Rebels had secured one of their most inspired successes. Despite the loss of Stonewall Jackson to friendly fire at that battle, the Confederates were in a buoyant mood on the road to Gettysburg. Ironically they were converging on the little town from the north whereas the Northerners were heading up from a southerly direction.

Roger lifted a pair of vintage binoculars up to his eyes and panned the tussocky skyline. A tour bus, the first of the day, drove by, its passengers rubbing at the condensation on the windows.

'What about the Union?' I asked. 'Were they strong too?'

'The Union knew that they had to win a victory,' replied Roger, lowering his binoculars. 'You have to remember the army of the Potomac was a great army, Tom, a brave army. It just had a succession of dud leaders.'

Roger listed some of the Union generals. There was General McLellen, who was popular and superbly efficient but very cautious in battle. 'He didn't want his army to get dirty,' explained Roger. Then there had been 'overconfident, under-competent' General Pope and that 'muddled mutton chops' General Burnside, the man who had the word sideburns named after him. At Gettysburg the army was in the hands of an anxious new boy, General Meade, still an unknown quantity as a leader.

'So Union morale was low after all their defeats?' I suggested.

'Not entirely,' corrected Roger, blowing on his hands. 'The Union troops knew that General Grant was about to take Vicksburg in Mississippi and this bolstered them. Also this was the first time they were fighting the Southerners on Northern turf, fighting on their own land. This would have put fire in their hearts too.'

We jumped back in the car, both shivering. Roger flicked a switch and the heater whirred to life. Thick spots of snow had started to fall; the sort of snow that sticks on your clothes and doesn't melt for ten seconds. I noticed Roger's nose had turned a shade of bruised purple but his commentary kept rolling.

Roger told me that on the first day of the battle – 1 July – the Confederates achieved a solid victory, pushing the Northern army out of the town. Also, a key Union officer, General John Reynolds, had been shot dead, just hours after proposing to his fiancée. However, the Union still held the high ground to the south of Gettysburg and Lee knew it was vital to knock them off it on the second day.

We were now driving south, past a slew of famous landmarks: Seminary Ridge, The Peach Orchard and on towards Little Round Top, a small hill fronted by a moraine of vast boulders known as the Devil's Den. All along this stretch of ground the Confederates had made determined offensives against the Union positions on 2 July. It proved largely disastrous.

General Barksdale, charging at the head of his Mississippi regiment, his white hair billowing like a Norseman, was shot from his saddle. Dogged Texan General John Hood lost the use of his arm and a large portion of his men while advancing up Little Round Top. On the Union side, politician turned soldier Major-General Dan Sickles ignored orders and left a huge gap in the blue line. Late in the afternoon he had his leg blown off by a cannon ball. He left the battlefield on a stretcher, calmly smoking a cigar. His main claim to fame before the war had been to shoot dead his wife's lover and successfully plead his innocence on grounds of insanity.

'Sickles was a right one,' tut-tutted Roger. 'After the war he donated his missing leg to a museum in Washington and went to visit it every year on the anniversary it was shot off.'

On reaching Little Round Top, Roger and I jumped out of the car and walked up the slope that General Hood's troops would have confronted, commencing from the huge, pock-marked boulders at Devil's Den.

Roger explained that the South may well have triumphed at Gettysburg had they not been pushed back by 350 brave men dug in behind a stone wall midway up Little Round Top. These resilient defenders were the 20th Maine, commanded by Joshua Chamberlain, who before the war had been a college professor. By the end of the fierce Southern assault Chamberlain had lost a third of his troops and was almost out of ammunition. In this desperate situation he issued one of the most extraordinary orders of the Civil War. He told his men to fix bayonets and charge downhill. It proved a master-stroke, and the stunned Southerners, mostly Alabamians, either fled or surrendered. The Union had held the high ground.

'Chamberlain was one of the great heroes of the war,' Roger told me as we weaved our way through the pine trees. 'Wounded six times. Loved by his men. For my money his finest hour was at the surrender at Appomattox. Ignoring protocol, he ordered his men to stand at attention out of respect for the defeated South. A beautiful moment. A true Northern gent.'

We sat back in the car, Roger's moustache was flecked with snow and steam was rising from his uniform like mist.

'The war created a lot of heroes, didn't it?' I said.

'Well, yes,' agreed Roger, throwing his sword in the back seat. 'I suppose it did. Before the war many of its key players weren't thought to be much cop.'

He mentioned Stonewall Jackson, a dismal lecturer at Lexington Military College, Ulysses S. Grant, seen as a washed-up drunk, William Tecumseh Sherman, suspected of insanity and even Robert E. Lee who, after losing a battle in West Virginia in 1861, was cruelly nicknamed 'Granny Lee'. All these seeming no-hopers had become some of America's most revered and enduring military heroes.

'But then there's the other side of the coin,' continued Roger, as we drove back across the snowy battlefield, now bathed in a pale celestial light. 'Soldiers whose memories became unfairly tarnished, like General Longstreet.'

'What is it with Longstreet?' I asked. 'From his diary Colonel Arthur loved him.'

'Well, I have a bit of a surprise for you, my boy,' Roger grinned, while wiping his windscreen. 'We're going to meet one of Longstreet's relatives for lunch. Why don't you ask him yourself?'

*   *   *

We found Dan Paterson standing by his ancestor's statue, snow swirling around him. Dan had clearly inherited General James Longstreet's towering physique, just as I had been saddled with Colonel Arthur's far from Herculean stature. The three of us stood huddled up, looking up at the bushy-bearded general on his horse. It was an unusual statue, much less formal than many of the others at Gettysburg, but still striking. Several people had left cigars at its base as a mark of respect: history had it that Longstreet loved cigars.

Dan, a computer expert from Virginia, was a direct descendant of Longstreet on his mother's side. He was an affable, soft-spoken man, who had fought hard to clear his ancestor's name. Even before meeting Dan, I was a Long-street sympathiser. In his diary my ancestor has nothing but praise for the general's energy, bravery and unflappable sense of authority. I was delighted to see a complimentary quote by Colonel Arthur had been carved onto the statue plinth.

Longstreet's critics blame him for the tragedy of Pickett's Charge, which took place on the third and culminating day of the battle of Gettysburg. The charge, a heroic but suicidal assault into the heart of the Union lines led by eager, flashy General Pickett, devastated the Confederate ranks. Over half the Rebel chargers were killed, wounded or captured. One Mississippi company lost every single man. It was an unprece-dented slaughter: in comparison the Charge of the Light Brigade at Balaclava only endured 40 per cent losses. The Confederacy went on to fight for almost two years, but never really recovered their momentum.

'People couldn't face blaming Lee for Pickett's Charge,' Dan told me. 'So Longstreet became a convenient scapegoat. In fact my ancestor had been very reluctant to carry out a frontal charge; he favoured a defensive position. He gave the actual order but was only obeying Lee's instructions.'

There is little doubt now that Lee does bear the blame for Pickett's Charge. To be fair to the 57-year-old General, con-ditions had not been easy for him for the duration of Gettys-burg. J.E.B. Stuart, his usually reliable cavalry leader, had gone joyriding after Union wagons instead of providing much needed logistical information. Lee was also in increasingly fragile health. My ancestor, while noting that Lee's conduct was 'perfectly sublime' after Pickett's Charge, clearly over-hears him confessing to one of his generals: 'all this has been MY fault – it is I that have lost this fight.' Lee even goes as far as offering his resignation after Gettysburg, but Jefferson Davis refuses to accept it.

'You have to remember Lee had a much smaller army than the North,' said Roger, while photographing Longstreet's statue. 'Huge losses were devastating for him. But he also knew without making bold moves, taking risks, he'd never win the upper hand. It was a catch-22.' Roger shook his head. 'Lee had been so successful, so great. I believe at Gettysburg he believed his men to be unbeatable. He was impatient for victory – the last push towards Washington. Longstreet, who hadn't been at the latest Rebel victory at Chancellorsville, was a bit more rational.'

Dan then explained that it was after the war that Longstreet came in for the greatest flak. First, he became a Republican, the party of Lincoln, which made Southern newspapers dub him, 'the most hated man in the South'. Even more damagingly, long after Lee's death, Longstreet publicly proclaimed it was Lee's overconfidence that lost the battle of Gettysburg. It may have been true but many Southerners couldn't stomach it.

'My ancestor was a very progressive man,' said Dan, touching the statue. 'He joined the Republican party out of solid belief, not on a whim. It was a very different party in the 1860s than it is today.' Dan paused, before continuing quietly, almost in a whisper. 'Longstreet wrote letters to Lee until his death. They still had a lot of affection for one another despite their disagreements over Gettysburg. Your ancestor, Colonel Fremantle, picks up on how close the two men are in his diary.'

'Yes, he writes as if they dote on each other,' I agreed.

'Longstreet was from Alabama,' mused Dan. 'He was quiet, not very eloquent, but always a courageous, noble soldier. Months before Gettysburg all his three children died of consumption. He was grief stricken but still put on a brave face. He was a stubborn man but never a traitor. I'm very proud of him.'

The three of us stood in silence, caught between the infinity of the living and the dead, the snow melting on our faces.

*   *   *

Roger drove us to the Farnsworth House Inn in the heart of Gettysburg. It was a fuggy place filled with Civil War memorabilia and local brews, more like an English pub. As Roger strolled in, wiping the snow off his tunic, some of the regulars recognised him.

'Colonel Fremantle, I presume,' said an old man at the bar. 'The British are coming,' piped up another, looking up from his pint.

Roger smiled politely and murmured under his breath: 'It's that bloody movie that does it.'

Actually, the Farnsworth had on display several props used in the film, *Gettysburg*, including Colonel Arthur's black cap. I had seen the film and enjoyed it although I felt my ancestor's portrayal had been limited and stiff, and the ebullience of the man had not been caught in the same way as in the book, *The Killer Angels*.

'I never complain about the movie though,' said Roger, sipping on a rum toddy. 'Very few people had heard of Fremantle before it, now everyone has. That red tunic put him on the map. Of course, it's historically inaccurate but a grey shooting jacket would have been very dull in comparison.'

Roger added that several of the other foreign observers at Gettysburg wore outrageous clothes. Accompanying Fremantle at the battle was Captain Fitzgerald Ross, a portly Austrian with a Scots name, who *Killer Angels* author, Michael Shaara, vividly describes as, 'aglow in the powder-blue uniform of the Austrian Hussars, complete with shining silver chamberpot for the head, waving a blue plume'. While Captain Justus Scheibert, another of the observers, is depicted as a 'beardless Prussian, moody, prim . . . dressed all in white, white coat, floppy white hat, the inevitable glittering monocle'.

'They must have looked a right bunch,' said Roger, peering up at some uniforms amid the Civil War display. 'In one painting of Fremantle at Gettysburg he looks outrageous. The artist sketches him in a top hat with sideburns down to his chin.'

I asked Roger how he first began to portray Colonel Arthur. He explained he had stumbled into the character having seen a Civil War event near his hometown in Florida. He had asked how he could get involved and was told to simply turn up at the next battle in Civil War uniform. Rather than swearing allegiance to North or South, he opted to take on the role of my ancestor.

'I decked myself out in red Mountie jacket and a Cornwall Yacht Club cap embroidered in braid,' remembered Roger, laughing. 'I walked into my first battle and the man portraying General Grant said, "Good morning, Colonel Fremantle." I never looked back. I've got all the proper kit now. It's the best job in the army.'

During the last ten years Roger has researched Colonel Arthur with forensic zeal. He has written a romanticised but very enjoyable novel, *Fremantle*, in which the South win Gettysburg and Colonel Arthur seduces Southern belles with Flashman-like guile. He also spearheaded a campaign to erect a memorial for Colonel Arthur in Brighton, where the old Coldstreamer died in 1901. Roger proudly presided over the ceremony with a bearskin on his head, while a troupe of reenactors in grey and blue fired an immaculate gun salute.

Perhaps Roger's biggest coup has been locating an original copy of *Three Months in the Southern States* printed on wallpaper. Colonel Arthur's diary did well on its publication in London and New York in 1864, but in the Confederacy it was a runaway bestseller. Southerners, who desperately needed a boost at this late stage in the war, couldn't get enough of my ancestor's complimentary words. Due to a severe lack of funds and printing materials in the South, wallpaper had been the best way to keep the popular diary running through the presses.

Over lunch at the Farnsworth Roger finally moved away from Colonel Arthur and talked instead about the strange nature of the Civil War.

He reminded me, while we ate a blood-warming hotpot, of the extraordinary story of Wilmer McLean. At Manassas, the first major battle of the Civil War, a shell had exploded near McLean's home. To escape further damage, the nervous countryman moved his family south to the village of Appomattox. By some strange act of symmetry, three and a half years later the war caught up with him again. It was in his parlour that Generals Lee and Grant met to discuss the Civil War surrender terms in April 1865. Inadvertently Wilmer McLean – who after the war charged tourists to visit his historic home – had been witness to the opening curtain and the closing credits of America's greatest tragedy.

'Sometimes I think the Civil War is one terrible fairy tale,' said Roger. 'Not even Hollywood could make up a plot line like that.'

Dan then began telling us the story about the last living Confederate widow, Alberta Martin, a 91-year-old lady living in Alabama. Incredibly, she had married an octogenarian Civil War veteran, William Martin, while in her early twenties. Even now, Dan said, Mrs Martin was receiving some sort of monthly Civil War pension.

I'm sure stories would have circulated all afternoon, the Farnsworth was that sort of place, but Roger insisted we must be on our way. After swigging down my coffee and bidding Dan farewell I braced myself for the final stage of the tour. It was time for Pickett's Charge.

*   *   *

Roger and I tramped towards the battlefields directly south of Gettysburg. Despite some antebellum buildings much of the town seemed to be surrendering to KFC, Hardees and a host of other fast-food fortresses. Occasional stores selling Civil War paintings, books and weapons helped sustain the historic identity.

Soon we had reached the grassy sweep of the Gettysburg National Military Park. A wide road punctuated with statues and memorials stretched out across a landscape of mucky, half-dissolved snow. Very few people were getting out of their cars. Roger and I agreed to do Pickett's Charge in reverse, starting at The High Water Mark, where the most dogged Confederates had managed to briefly break through the Union lines before being repulsed for good.

'Bugger marching through this sleet,' harrumphed Roger suddenly. 'Let me explain the charge from here.' He pointed towards the apocalyptic skyline, which on 3 July 1863 would have been sunny, bright, clear and exceptionally dangerous.

'The Confederates started off by letting rip with over an hour of artillery fire – one hundred and forty cannons' worth,' Roger told me. 'It was the largest concentration of cannon fire in American history to date.'

Roger explained that at some time around 3 p.m. Longstreet nodded the order to charge. The brooding General had been too gutted to even say Lee's command, aware of the slaughter it would reap. And so the mile-long line of Confederates marched forward, prompting one Union officer to

call it 'the most beautiful thing I ever saw'. It interested me to
learn that curly-haired General Pickett, for all his thirst for
immortality, only commanded one third of the men in the
action that was soon to bear his name.

'It must have been a heart-stopping spectacle,' said Roger,
trudging over to inspect a monument in honour of a Georgian
regiment. 'Magnificent and tragic all at once.'

Roger told me about some of the heroics during that
fateful half-hour charge. He mentioned the Confederate general, Lewis Armistead, who rushed forward with his hat on
the end of his sword. He was finally mown down by soldiers
commanded by his best friend Winfield Scott Hancock, a
Union general. Armistead's dying wish was to see Hancock.
Another Confederate, the ailing Dick Garnett, had once been
accused of cowardice by Stonewall Jackson and wanted to
prove himself. He rode on a horse, almost the only horse on
the charge, knowing that he stood out a mile.

'Garnett was an honourable man,' surmised Roger. 'He
knew he would die, wanted to die; and he did.'

'What about Fremantle?'

'Fremantle was in a state of high excitement,' continued
Roger, rubbing his arms to generate warmth. 'Remember,
Tom, your ancestor had never seen a real battle at this stage in
his career. He was clearly shocked by the piles of dead. He
was also an asthmatic, so the dust and heat must have been
hard on him.'

Roger pointed out that throughout the three days at
Gettysburg, Colonel Arthur always wanted to be in on the
action. He climbed trees, dodged shells, asked questions. He
noticed all sorts of things — Rebel bands playing waltzes and
polkas with mortars blasting overhead, the fact that General
Lee never carried arms, and the scores of barefoot, ragged
Confederate soldiers jauntily marching along with tooth-
brushes in their buttonholes.

For all this he managed to miss the start of Pickett's Charge and only arrived in time to see the overwhelmed Confederates retreating, some using rifles as crutches. He still tells General Longstreet he would not have missed it for the world, to which Longstreet dryly replies, he would have 'liked to have missed it very much'. Even the next day, 4 July, when news filters back that Vicksburg has fallen, Colonel Arthur's faith in the Confederacy remains undimmed.

'What if Jackson had been at Gettysburg?' I asked Roger, as we walked back up the hill. 'He might have persuaded Lee to try a flanking manoeuvre.'

'Oh, what if, what if?' he replied. 'The Civil War is one big what if? What if Lee's order hadn't been mislaid before Antietam? What if the Brits had come on board? Yes, Jackson might have saved the day at Gettysburg, but he might not.' Roger paused, wiping the sleet off his moustache. 'You know why Jackson's called Stonewall, don't you?'

'Of course,' I said breezily. 'At Manassas one of the Confederate generals described Jackson as standing firm as a stone wall.'

'It was General Barnard Bee,' Roger told me, smiling. 'The thing nobody knows is whether Bee was complimenting Jackson, or insulting him for not getting stuck in. We'll never know because Bee was killed minutes later. Personally, I think Jackson was a formidable soldier but the Civil War is all about your own interpretation. That's what I like about it.'

Roger placed his hand on his sword halter. 'William Faulkner once wrote a famous sentence, Tom,' he stated grandly, 'about how at times every Southern boy imagines it is still two o'clock on that July afternoon in 1863, and Pickett's Charge is still to be made.'

'Give them back that half hour of madness and they can change history,' I suggested.

'Maybe,' said Roger. 'Or maybe they would do it all again just the same.'

With that Colonel Arthur walked towards The High Water Mark, his tunic standing out like blood against the bleak, milky skyline.

* * *

Roger left early the following morning. I was grateful to him. His animated presence had shed light not only on Gettysburg battlefield but on Colonel Arthur himself. Now I had only one thing left to do before Browny and I moved on.

I wanted to see where Abraham Lincoln made his Gettysburg Address, perhaps the most famous speech in America's history. Only 269 words, it was certainly one of the most succinct. The monument honouring the event was located in the National Cemetery to the south of the town, a tranquil spot full of shadowy yew trees and well-preserved tombs. I sat down on the grass and pondered the brass plaque on which the address had been engraved. It was really only a monument to a speech, I concluded, but I was much more interested in the man who made it.

Lincoln's road to Gettysburg was never an easy one. His 'white trash' beginnings in the Kentucky backwoods made his early years a constant struggle. All through his life he suffered from bouts of intense misery, especially over the loss of two of his young sons to disease. The responsibility on his shoulders while in the White House – horrific Union casualties, schisms within his party, furious peaceniks – is almost unthinkable. Yet through his career, whether working as a small-town lawyer in Illinois or as sixteenth President, the spark of greatness never left him. The author Harriet Beecher Stowe described Lincoln as a tough bit of rope, which might swing from side to side, but would never break.

Lincoln's ascendancy was meteoric but often turbulent. As a fledgling politician his stance on the abolition of slavery had been lukewarm, especially as the family of his wife, Mary, kept slaves. Only in the 1850s, with the threat of slavery permeating newly settled parts of the West, was he spurred into action. This finally led to his push for a complete Emancipation Proclamation in 1862, during his first presidential term. Even at the time of the Gettysburg Address Lincoln's political future was uncertain. If it had not been for General Sherman's successful conquest of Atlanta the following year, he may well not have retained his toehold on power.

Lincoln did not make his famous speech during the battle of Gettysburg. He delivered it on 19 November, four months after Lee's aborted attack on the town. On arrival at the battlefield Lincoln noticed many of the dead were still visible in their shallow graves. He had come to speak at a dedication ceremony for the new cemetery in Gettysburg: to say something pertinent about the fifty thousand men in blue and grey who had been killed and wounded over those three days in July.

I tried to imagine the scene – the thousands of locals swarming to catch a glimpse of their war-weary President, the stalls selling lemonade, biscuits and all sorts of battle memorabilia. The chief speaker was not in fact Lincoln, but Edward Everett, a seventy-year-old clergyman and former Governor of Massachusetts. Everett rose and spoke with lush verbosity for almost two hours. In contrast Lincoln's speech lasted about two minutes, and at the time created little buzz. One onlooker dubbed it: 'A flat failure.'

But the speech proved a slow burner. By the time of Lincoln's assassination on 14 April 1865 at Ford's Theatre in Washington, its beauty and brevity had been embraced by America. It's not hard to see why. Even the shortest of excerpts is enough to prick the heart.

We cannot dedicate, we cannot consecrate, we cannot hallow this ground. The brave men, living and dead, who struggled here, have consecrated it far above our power to add or detract. The world will little note nor long remember what we say here; but it can never forget what they did here.

. . . we here highly resolve that these dead shall not have died in vain – that this nation, under God, shall have a new birth of freedom – and that government of the people, by the people, for the people, shall not perish from the earth.'

CHAPTER 18

A Hard-won Place

The temperature nosedived after Browny and I headed north from Gettysburg. Our first night was spent in a deserted barn, the icy wind rifling through cracks in its walls. My pasta supper frosted up in no time and soon I was forced to cocoon myself in goose down to retain any sort of body heat. The following morning my hands were so numb it was hard to get a grip on Browny's girth straps. I jogged on the spot, shaking my fingers like a pre-fight boxer to liven up my blood.

The situation did not improve. On arrival in the town of Hanover the next evening, Browny and I were uncharacteristically turned away by a string of local churches and fire stations. Eventually I had no choice but to bivouac in a farm warehouse, stretching myself out amid bags of fertiliser and barley seed. For the first time on the trip Browny endured a night standing on concrete (thinly sprinkled with sawdust) as opposed to grass or straw. She looked so miserable I vowed never to humiliate her like this again. Now we were nearing New York it was becoming relentlessly urban.

We walked through familiar-sounding towns such as York and Lancaster, which all sprawled into one other. We were never far from gas stations, or mini malls or bright signs suspended on poles that advertised TAXIDERMY – WE STUFF ANYTHING! or ST MICHAEL'S CHURCH – GOD LISTENS TO KNEE MAIL! The only places not so evident were bars and liquor stores, this part of Pennsylvania being mostly a dry spot.

Like the rings on a tree stump, the further my journey progressed towards its core the more intense and congested it became. In Texas the little towns had been up to fifty miles apart, but now we were entering the penultimate lap before New York there was almost no room for manoeuvre amid the concrete. God only knows what Manhattan, our bull's eye, would be like. Fine by me, but for Browny it would probably be more like Dante's ninth circle of hell.

But I was being too fatalistic. After clearing Lancaster's dowdy fringes I plumped for a less direct route and branched off down a series of country lanes. Over the last days Browny and I had appeared all over the local media – television, newspapers and radio. I tried to stay upbeat and friendly but the constant questions of passers by were becoming wearisome. 'Hey, we saw you on TV. You're from Australia aren't you?' 'What's your donkey's name?' 'Are you protesting about something, sir?'

I was sick of the vroom of traffic and the dispiriting rash of suburbia surrounding us. But once Browny and I veered back into the boondocks, a fresh landscape, as gently contoured as

Somerset or Dorset, unfolded. It was just what we needed. We were heading into Amish country.

*   *   *

Browny tuned in to the presence of the Amish long before me. It was the evening of 24 March, Palm Sunday, and we were approaching the tiny town of Bird in Hand. Browny began to nicker and whinny, sniffing at the cold air. Then I heard it too, the unmistakable clatter of wagon wheels on bitumen, bringing back with a jolt memories of Justin and Maria rolling along in Texas, the bleak beauty of the desert, the sting of blisters and the smell of hickory.

My reverie did not last long as Browny was becoming increasingly restless. In the distance was an immaculate black stallion, its coat glistening like creosote, pulling a buggy towards us. The horse was barrelling along through the twilight, its smoky breath as blue as gas.

Browny let out a bray and began to prance. I held her tight, running my hand down her lead rope until my fingers touched her shivering snout. She steadied herself but continued to whimper as the wagon hurtled passed us on the opposite side of the road. Through the carriage window I could make out a bearded man in a black hat. He looked stern, but once he turned and saw the mule, he smiled and waved, propping up his young son on his knee for him to get a better look at us.

That night we spent at Bird in Hand's deserted campsite. Sunday evening was the time the Amish met up for their weekly powwows in each other's barns. Up until midnight dozens of buggies tore past: at times their pace was so fierce it reminded me of the chariot race in *Ben Hur*. I sat at a picnic table eating sardines and crackers, utterly entranced, while Browny stamped and hollered in the background. I was looking forward to the following day, when we would enter the heart of Amish territory — a town by the name of Intercourse.

The Amish certainly like to christen their towns with a mishmash of distinctive appellations. Not only is there Bird in Hand and Intercourse, but the village of Blue Ball and, soon after Intercourse, the optimistically titled hamlet of Paradise.

These names have a particularly suggestive quality because the Amish champion a pure and God-fearing lifestyle. They wear simple clothes and shun modern gadgetry — even bicycles are seen as too progressive and, when not travelling in horse-drawn buggies, the Amish use leg-powered, unmotorised scooters as a substitute.

There are over twenty thousand Amish in this area of Pennsylvania (Lancaster County) mostly descended from the original Dutch settlers who arrived over two hundred and fifty years ago. They are Anabaptists and devout conscientious objectors who refused to fight during the Civil War and both World Wars. They do not drink and do not allow themselves to be photographed.

The countryside surrounding Intercourse was impeccable. Barns with roofs shaped like bread bins dominated the land-scape, often standing alongside large, silver silos. We passed a large herd of black cattle. Several of the beasts were balanced precariously on a steep silage mound, as if they had Velcro on their hooves. Near by a straw-hatted man rode on the back of a harrow pulled by a team of mules — each beast about twice the size of Browny. The man looked like a hillbilly surfer, tentatively slicing through the russet-coloured waves. It was a lovely scene, straight out of a Thomas Hardy novel.

Sadly, though, the town of Intercourse was no Christ-minster. Although refreshingly free from the usual Burger Kings and Wal-Marts, it was far from idyllic. I tied Browny up in a paddock behind the visitor's centre and shuffled around with the other tourists, inspecting the souvenir grottoes, the cafeterias and quilt enterprises. It was a popular spot but other than the horse-drawn buggies it all felt rather bogus and twee, with many of the businesses set up by non-Amish hucksters on the make.

It was not until I had the good fortune to bump into the splendidly named Marlin Smucker that I got a more thorough overview. At first Marlin's longish, tawny hair gave an impression of youthfulness, but on closer inspection his face was weather-beaten, revealing deep crow's feet when he smiled. Marlin, who ran a local motel, agreed to bring over some fresh mule rations – alfalfa hay, oats – in his truck. On his return we chatted, leaning over Browny's paddock fence while she feasted.

Marlin was a Mennonite, who, like the Amish, have a large population in Lancaster County. Mennonites share many of the same doctrines – adult baptism, non-violence, a love of the land – but are generally more liberal than the often ultra-traditional Amish. Marlin told me a fascinating story about his grandparents and how they had rebelled against the Amish elders.

As he untied Browny's hay Marlin explained that his grandfather, a very strong character, had disagreed strongly with the Amish belief that education should end at the age of fifteen or sixteen in order that work should begin. He believed every child had the right to go college and because of his stubborn principles he split from the Amish.

This created a near impossible situation for Marlin's grandfather who was shunned by everyone in the Amish community except his grandmother. She continued to bear her 'sinful' husband's children but every time they had a new child she would have to ask for forgiveness from the elders. By the time the third child was born Marlin's grandmother was fed up. I love my husband and want to sleep with him without apologising, was her attitude. So both Marlin's grandparents became Mennonites, enabling their children the right to further education. From that day on they were shunned absolutely by the Amish. The family and friends they had known all their lives completely cut them off.

'That's terrible,' I commented, after Marlin had finished the story. 'You must be furious with the Amish.'

'I certainly disagree about education stopping so young,' agreed Marlin, reaching out to stroke Browny. 'And the shunning system can be harsh. But Amish teenagers have much more choice now.'

Marlin explained that nowadays when they turn sixteen, Amish youths are usually allowed a spell of freedom from their confined worlds. Unleashing these Amish teenagers into fresh environments gave them a chance to experiment with alcohol, sex, even drugs, before deciding whether to join the church or leave the community for good. This period is known as *rumspringa* – their word for 'running around'.

'Do most of them leave?'

'That's the strange thing,' replied Marlin. 'Only 20 per cent leave. The rest return to the church and get soaked up again in the community. You've got to remember Amish life is positive in many ways. They are very hard working and their farms are beautiful. When a neighbour needs a barn putting up or any other help everyone mucks in. They look out for each other.'

A young boy on a scooter rattled past us, thrusting out his leg furiously to power himself along.

'It seems harsh they can't ride bicycles,' I observed, watching the boy swerve to avoid some horse dung.

'It's more to do with keeping everyone within the community,' explained Marlin patiently. 'Bicycles would make it very easy to secretly nip off to town but a foot scooter ensures everyone stays closer to home. In a sense it's only by this kind of strictness that the Amish keep going.' He shrugged his shoulders. 'It must work because their numbers have doubled in this area over the last twenty years, whereas the Mennonites in Pennsylvania are declining. The Amish are clearly doing something right.'

'Having big families?'

'No, no, that's too cynical,' insisted Marlin, shaking his head vigorously.

'There's much to respect about the Amish,' he continued. 'The fact they get excited about real things – their families, their faith, the rain on their crops, their livestock, their wagons. The big stuff, the important stuff. They don't care less who won at the Oscars, the trivia we've all become obsessed with. After their *rumspringa* many young Amish real-ise the traditional life offers something richer.'

'Like Kelly McGillis at the end of *Witness*,' I stated, reveal-ing my only nugget of Amish trivia. 'She stays home rather than heading off with Harrison Ford.'

'Oh, that film has a lot to answer for,' said Marlin, laugh-ing. 'I actually enjoyed it but only as entertainment, not as an accurate depiction of Amish life. Lots of it was shot around Intercourse of course – the barn raising, the fight scene.' He gestured behind us to some imaginary grid references. Marlin reminded me that the Amish couldn't be photographed so none of them was allowed to appear in *Witness*. They were also forbidden to loan out their buggies to the film people – although some still did. He admitted he had a friend who loaned his buggy out for $150 a day and got away with it. The elders never found out.

'If they had would he have been shunned?' I asked.

'No, I doubt it, but it would have been vital for him to apologise.' Marlin stopped and touched his nose conspir-atorially. 'Between you and me, although the elders were very anti the movie lots of Amish teenagers hired out rooms in my motel purely to see it. Especially that scene with Kelly McGillis!'

'I don't blame them.'

'But *Witness* was all make believe,' added Marlin, holding out some more hay to Browny. 'Nobody really knows the Amish except the Amish themselves. The best you could do, Tom, is spend a night with a family. They are noble, secretive people but your mule might prove a good barrier breaker.'

*　　*　　*

The following evening I was searching for a mailbox bearing the name Ephraim Stoltzfus. Browny and I had walked over twenty miles east from Intercourse and by now darkness was swallowing up the last blush of sun. Horse-drawn buggies rattled by, all of them with orange reflective triangles stuck on the back. One or two of the buggies even had flashing indicator lights, their violent *tick tick tick* like that of a grandfather clock.

An Amish farmer I had spoken to on the road assured me the Stoltzfus family would be happy to put me up. What he hadn't told me was that almost all Amish families in the farms beyond Intercourse were called Stoltzfus. I squinted at mailbox after mailbox – Isaac Stoltzfus. Jesse Stoltzfus. John Stoltzfus. But Ephraim Stoltzfus was nowhere to be found. Just as I was beginning to despair a wagon pulled over. Browny yanked her head up, her nostrils flinching, alive to the scent of a new horse.

'We're the next farm on the right,' shouted out an attractive girl with a surprisingly husky voice. She wore a white bonnet on her head. 'We're expecting you.' She then toppled back into the buggy. Seconds later the wagon lurched away abruptly, as if pulled by an invisible cord.

At the top of the next hill I finally saw the name Ephraim Stoltzfus on a grey mailbox. I must have passed at least twenty

Stoltzfus mailboxes that day. Back in Intercourse Marlin had told me that although inbreeding had been a problem in the past, the Amish were now careful to avoid it. They made sure only strangers or distant cousins were paired off or else matches were arranged with other flourishing Amish communities in Ohio, Indiana or even Ontario in Canada.

Ephraim walked up his drive to meet me. He was leading a team of six Belgian shire horses, colossal animals that left hoof prints the size of cooking pots in the dirt. Ephraim was dwarfed by them but showed himself to be in complete control. He was a pale, wiry man sporting a neat pointed beard but no moustache. He wore a black hat and his face boasted the rubbery articulacy of a clown. When he shook my hand, I noticed his forearms were like hawsers.

Ephraim introduced himself and then beckoned over his wife, Sadie, and their seven children, Daniel, Noah, Martha, Esther, Miriam, Ephraim Junior and Jesse, who were aged from eight years old to twenty-one. My first priority was Browny. I unloaded her and led her into a cavernous barn dimly lit by lanterns. She was put in a stall next to the shire horses. The youngest two sons, Jesse and Ephraim Junior, in their straw hats and bright braces, distributed oats and water. They were completely unafraid of crouching underneath the huge horses, who all stood still as statues, while Browny rolled about, whinnying with glee.

Opposite the horses were ranks of dairy cows. From the parlour floor a fog of ammonia and sweet grassy cow breath rose up. Ephraim grabbed my saddlebags and ushered me towards the house for supper.

Although I knew the Amish used no electricity, the extent of the darkness indoors still took me by surprise. Ephraim's children all bounded about the house as if blessed with magic vision. I, however, couldn't see a thing. After almost knocking over a shelf of homemade jams I decided to put on my head torch to save further collisions. The only room that was lit up with propane lanterns was the kitchen where all the family had gathered for dinner.

There was a spread of pork slices, green beans, corn bread and a pitcher of milk on a vast, dimpled table. We all sat down, a wood stove spitting in the background.

'We always have two minutes of silent prayer before eating,' Sadie informed me, while lighting a couple of candles. I could see the children's eyes dart my way, laughter in their eyes. After the silence, Ephraim read some prayers in Pennsylvanian Dutch, the Amish native tongue. We all then recited 'The Lord's My Shepherd' together before tucking in.

The conversation revolved around my nationality. The Amish describe everyone non-Amish as English, whether they are English, American, French or Balinese. I tried to explain that I wasn't American English, but real English, from across the Atlantic. I was astonished that only one of the family, fourteen-year-old Miriam, showed any knowledge of England. She remembered something they had learnt about Henry VIII in school recently but even that was patchy. I drew a triangular map and tried to explain about life across the pond, but I was fighting a losing battle.

The subject with which the family were clearly happiest was the Bible.

'We take the Lord's words seriously,' said Sadie, who like all her daughters was sporting a white bonnet and a black shawl. 'The divisions between the Amish and Mennonites are all to do with how we interpret the Bible. For instance Mennonites tend to drive cars, whereas we don't. But there are divisions within the Amish too.'

'Some of the stricter Amish refuse to even put reflective triangles on their wagons at night,' added Ephraim, 'because it would be ungodly. They are fighting a court case about this now. Others are so devout they have no mirrors in their homes.'

'Did you know there's a talking donkey in the Bible?' Ephraim Junior interrupted, radically changing the subject. I told him I didn't. He eagerly flicked through his children's Bible as far as Numbers 22, and sure enough there was a cartoon-like illustration of a man named Baleem riding on a donkey with a speech bubble over its nose.

'Baleem dies,' said young Ephraim cheerily. 'But don't worry, you have a mule, not a donkey. You should be all right.'

'Yes, why the mule?' asked Sadie, who had begun laying the table for tomorrow's breakfast.

'It's to give my trip a Civil War flavour.'

I explained about Colonel Arthur. Sadie listened intently while positioning the cutlery. At times her eyes blinked wildly as if she had some grit in them. When I finished she told me she could not understand someone wanting to visit America simply to watch a horrible war. I argued that Colonel Arthur travelled more for adventure than merely to be a spectator to the carnage, but sensed my justification sounded rather lame.

'Amish people hate war,' stressed Ephraim, propping his boots against the wood stove. 'In the Civil War some of our people were imprisoned for not enlisting. Our greatest folk stories are about Amish who have been killed standing up for their right not to fight.' He sighed heavily. 'Some people can never just leave us alone and respect our faith.'

'Yes, I can imagine,' I replied. 'My trip has been a bit war obsessed. It's nice to be in a community where war has no place for a change.'

We retired to bed at 8.30 p.m. Most of the family would be up and about by 4.30 a.m., Ephraim informed me as he led the way upstairs. I had a room to myself. The bed was stacked with blankets but had no sheets. A single window, overlooking the milking parlour, let in a cool breeze. I suddenly felt deeply privileged to be part of all this, to be taken in by these gentle farmers.

I looked around my room. The only decoration was a table on top of which sat a frameless mirror, the size of a playing card. During the night the little strip of glass winked at me in the darkness like a secret.

*   *   *

I woke before daybreak and fed Browny. Daniel, the eldest son, was already harnessing up the shire horses ready for a day's ploughing, while Ephraim and the other boys milked the cows. Back at the house Martha and Esther worked on a quilt and Miriam painted some egg shells ready for Easter. Sadie lent over the stove, oil hissing in her frying pan.

After more prayers we breakfasted in the dawn light, mostly in silence. Eggs, bacon, baked beans, corn bread and tinned peaches, all washed down with milk. Towards the end of the meal Sadie asked me if I would like to take Browny to the local school. Perhaps give a talk? I agreed without hesitation and an hour later, packed up the mule and set off with Miriam, Ephraim Junior and Jesse to their classroom in the hamlet of Shady Grove.

That morning there was no stirring of breeze, no murmur of traffic. The only sound was the steady clip clop, clip clop of Browny's hooves. The nascent sun bathed the stubble fields in gold and burnt away the last wisps of morning mist. Children ran past, their satchels butting against their knees, waving at distant farmers behind their mule-drawn ploughs. Miriam picked some yellow flowers and stuck them in Browny's mane. 'Magic!' she told me proudly.

At the school I tied Browny to a hitching rail alongside a black mare, which I imagined belonged to one of the children's parents. Miriam ushered me into the school, a single classroom in a wooden building not unlike an alpine chalet. It was lined with biblical scenes and bright artwork. The names of all the pupils lined one wall. Over half were called Stoltzfus or Stoltzfoos and the rest a mishmash of equally tongue-twisting options.

The teacher was a young girl in her early twenties. Her black dress and severe white bonnet failed to disguise a shy beauty. She tapped a desk and the children were silenced. The class began by singing hymns in Dutch and then one English hymn I did not recognise. The singing was cautious and rather off key. One of the problems was that the class ranged from six-year-olds to sixteen-year-olds, all hitting wildly disparate chords. It seemed extraordinary that children with a decade's difference in age were all taught the same subjects and all by the same teacher.

After the singing I briefly took the stage. I talked of the mule trip highlights, skipping much of the Civil War. The class listened intently but when I asked if there were any questions I was met with an embarrassed silence. Not even the ever-reliable buffalo episode created much of a stir. The teacher picked up one of the children's class books and showed me a page about England. It contained half a dozen dubious facts accompanied by pictures. The only three I remember were:

1 England is famous for Staffordshire pottery. This is very popular.
2 England has many apple trees.
3 England's best-known king is Henry VIII. He had six wives. (This was accompanied by a picture of a fat, smiling man on a throne, brandishing an axe in one hand and a jousting lance in the other.)

I started explaining that there was more to England than Bramley apples and libidinous monarchs but realised I was making little impression. Rather than feeling disappointed I suddenly felt rather grateful. I had been bombarded by so many questions over the last weeks that the silence fell like balm. These girls and boys would most likely end up leading practical, community-tied lives within this magical horizon. If they chose to break away during their *rumspringa*, then they would have to fend for themselves anyway. Whatever their destiny they had little need to learn which of Henry's wives got the chop.

All the class flocked to the door to say goodbye: no cheers or clapping, just the odd wave and smile. I snapped on Browny's lead rope and headed off, savouring the last minutes of walking in this cathedral-like hush, on paths innocent of petrol and scuffed with hoof prints, on paths that in my mind all led to one place, and one place only. A hard-won place. A place called home.

CHAPTER 19

Sobs and Slobbers

Browny and I were soon back on highways bulldozed for maximum speed. No more mules tilling the earth. No more scooters rattling quietly by. New York was less than a month's walk now, and New Jersey only a matter of days away. Even at a remote youth hostel in the woods of Evansburg State Park, where we spent our first night away from the Amish, I sensed the burr of traffic all around; the pulse of escalating humanity.

Southern hospitality should have petered out long ago. Texans told me it would dry up as early as Louisiana, Mississippians told me once I'd reached Atlanta that was it — I would be met with glacial pomposity from there on up. Atlantans told me Richmond would be the last bastion of decency. And once I'd reached Gettysburg I was beyond the pale, the people would cut me dead. Well, here I was, two days shy of the New Jersey border and eating my Easter dinner with a table full of exuberant Yankees. I was coming to the conclusion America was a generous place, black or white, fat or thin, rich or poor, old or young, perhaps, heaven forbid, blue or grey.

While padding our way through a suburb called Lansdale a richly tanned lady in a burgundy tracksuit had beckoned me over from her garden. Her name was Sue Gadelfino and she invited me in for a party. It was getting late in the day and spitting with rain so I was glad to be rescued. Browny was led off into a fenced paddock full of windfall apples, while I was ushered into a room clogged with wine-flushed guests. Lost in my mule gyspy lifestyle I had completely failed to take in it was Easter Monday.

I squeezed myself into the throng. Sue piled my plate full of roast chicken with all the trimmings, while her porcelain-cheeked sixteen-year-old daughter, Loni, poured me some claret from a box. Sue was a cleaner. Her friends and neighbours were all proud blue-collar types: truck drivers, labourers and shop assistants. They treated me, this sodden Englishman, like a long-lost friend. They slapped me on the back, made off-colour jokes about mules, and told me I should settle down and find myself a good 'Noo Jwersey' girl. I'd had so many nights like this in America. Nights where people with no idea who I was, what I was up to, had still taken me in on a whim.

We made some toasts. First to the Queen Mother, whose recent death had sent shockwaves of grief through America. 'Here's to the old lady of England,' shouted a builder called Cliff. 'God bless her, she liked a drink.' We then charged our glasses to the future, to mop pushers all over the world, to brown mules and to peace. I looked around at the surrounding strangers. Oh yes, I thought to myself, it was nights like this I would miss the most.

The following day Browny and I made it to Lynne Allen's house near Buckingham, my last stop-off in Pennsylvania. I had met Lynne at the artists' colony in Sweet Briar. There she had come across as a delightfully free-spirited bohemian, who had been designing books made out of teabags. In fact, she turned out to be a whirlwind of efficiency, as did her Russian husband, Sergei.

Their remote farmhouse was an Alice in Wonderland affair; creaky wooden staircases, low ceilings and Oriental masks. There were surprise nooks galore where you might stumble on anything from a stash of Russian newspapers to a sleeping cat.

Behind the house was a large, topsy-turvy studio. Sergei, a printer, worked on the top floor while Lynne designed her inventive curios downstairs. Browny paraded around in the garden chewing on the clover-rich grass and forsythia bushes. Bin liners suspended from poles flapped in the breeze. The local farmer had erected them to scare off flocks of Canada geese, which sometimes plagued the area. Only the rustle and snap of the wind interrupted the spectral quiet.

It was a perfect place to contemplate, to rally my thoughts, to make up my mind. The big problem was how to cross the Hudson river into Manhattan. The most mule-friendly bridge was at Bear Mountain, near West Point Military Academy, roughly one hundred miles north of New York City. It was a huge detour and would still make access to Manhattan, and ultimately Central Park, very tricky. Like Colonel Arthur, who sensibly took the train straight to the heart of the city, I wanted a more direct approach.

Lynne, Sergei and I frantically rang around ferry companies. When they all turned me down, we tried fishing boats, container vessels, dredgers, yachts and tugs. Understandably none of them was keen to make this special voyage. 'I'd never sail with livestock,' one tug captain told me. 'Try building a raft like that Kon-Tiki man.' Thor Heyerdahl and his crew dealt admirably with the Pacific Ocean but not a cynical beast who also happened to be a confirmed land-lubber. The thought of wetting her hooves always sent Browny into a paroxysm of sulky brays.

Sod it, I thought. My mule may not be good on water but she can deal with any bridge you lay before her. I unfurled a map of New York. I'd never seen an urban sprawl with so little breathing space. With the exception of the elongated green rectangle of Central Park, just about every grid reference was a shade of breezeblock grey. The only thing to do was to go straight for the urban jugular – the George Washington Bridge, even if it did lead me just south of the Bronx, one of the biggest scrums of humanity on earth.

But my mind was made up. The only other option was inconceivable. Walk over the bridge without Browny. My beast had been with me since the Tex-Mex border. Apart from one solitary week in Virginia she had loyally traipsed after me, lugged my kit, kept me company, even listened to me croon-ing old Harry Belafonte songs. She had done the lion's share, not me. We'd see this thing through side by side, or go down in a blaze of glory. If arrested, I would no doubt be sent off to a modern-day Alcatraz while Browny would be sentenced to lugging parties of sumo-bellied daytrippers up and down the Grand Canyon. Still, we'd have given it our best shot.

Just before leaving Lynne and Sergei's place for New Jersey, I made contact with the New York City Port Authority. After being whanged about from one department to the next I finally struck gold. Thankfully, a big cheese called Ralph Molenia loved the idea of our trip and insisted on my mule being escorted over the George Washington Bridge on Sun-day, 14 April, an hour before dawn. This was magnificent news. And we still had a week to get there on time. It just goes to show all you need is one person, one willing voice in the wilderness of officialdom, and the red tape is miraculously zapped.

'Let me tell you something,' said Ralph, in a no-nonsense Jimmy Cagney voice. 'We've escorted missiles over that bridge. We've escorted heads of state, oversized vehicles, toxic waste, all sorts of stuff. But never, *ever*, a mule.'

*   *   *

The following morning I set off late from Lynne and Sergei's farmhouse after a flurry of last-minute organisational calls. Browny and I walked over the New Jersey border in the late afternoon and by the time we reached the little town of Ringoes it was night.

On the way to Ringoes, Browny had started to worry me. She had begun chomping wildly, as if trying to polish off an unusually large and sticky sweet. Her tongue lolled and frothed while strings of slobber swung from the sides of her mouth. She had also started to pee furiously and at very regular intervals. This slowed down our progress radically and by the time I knocked on the door of Ringoes' resident vicar it had gone 8 p.m.

Appearing at a stranger's door well after dark with a urinating brown mule by your side is not the height of good etiquette, even in New Jersey – and especially not in the presence of a man of the cloth. However, I struck it lucky with Pastor Toby Nelson, a kind, cherub-faced man, who let me stake out Browny in his backyard and presented me with the key to the church hall. It was an ideal place to doss down. Right now, though, Browny was foremost on my mind.

I ferreted out my book, *Know Your Horse* by Lieutenant-Colonel W.S. Codrington. I had been told that medically speaking horses and mules were roughly the same. As there was no such book as *Know Your Mule*, this was the next best thing. Other than exhaustion – a crushingly obvious symptom to diagnose even for me – Browny had been a paradigm of good health. This was the first time I had needed to properly examine the sage Colonel Codrington's advice. For some reason – perhaps a long-forgotten episode of *All Creatures Great and Small* – I had a hunch Browny's ailment might be colic. I flicked through the index and looked up the main symptoms. There were four.

1 There is evident unease.
   Yes, there is.
2 When down, the horse may roll and make violent movements.
   Yes, although with Browny violent rolling is also a sign of rude vitality.
3 The horse may attempt to pass water continually.
   Yes, she may, she's pissing mini-Niagaras, actually.
4 Large amounts of wind and small amounts of dropping will be passed.
   Indeed they will.

All of these symptoms were now relevant to Browny. The only thing it didn't mention was frothing at the mouth, but that might well be a side effect. I suddenly panicked. Here we were less than a week from New York and potentially I had a terminally sick beast on my hands. I couldn't bear the injustice after all we'd been through together.

When I explained Browny's predicament to Toby he was instantly on the case. He punched away at his mobile phone and within fifteen minutes a white sports car pulled up. A very glamorous woman with beautifully coiffed, dark hair stepped out. Toby introduced her as Ellen, and told me she was a whiz with animals.

Toby was as good as his word. Having spent so long in my mule's company I could instantly tell if someone spooked her or put her at ease. Ellen was clearly something of a mule whisperer. After spending a minute walking around Browny reassuring her, she stroked her neck and then began tapping her rib cage as if for dry rot. As she continued with her medical examination Ellen relayed soundbites of information. I was glad to learn Browny's eyes were clear, her heart rate was normal and she had full movement in her guts.

'Well, there's good news and bad news,' stated Ellen finally, her breath like fog in the cold night. 'The good news is that Browny doesn't have colic. All she has is a mild dose of the Slobbers. She's been grazing on too much clover.'

The Slobbers! It sounded like the sort of thing Falstaff might be struck down with after too much homebrew sherry. However, it was most likely a spot-on prognosis. Browny had been troughing on both clover and forsythia in Lynne's garden. The Slobbers, although I'm sure it has some fancy Latin name, summed up Browny's dribbling and frantic chewing motions perfectly. It didn't sound too serious and instantly placated my fears.

'Now for the bad news,' added Ellen, stroking Browny's mane.

'You mean the Slobbers wasn't the bad news.'

'No, no, the Slobbers will be gone by morning,' Ellen assured me. 'The really bad news is that Browny is in season.'

'In season!' I protested. 'She's a seventeen-year-old mule! She can't be!'

'Oh, yes, she can.' Ellen laughed at my surprise. 'I once had a thirty-year-old mare who was in season. She jumped into a neighbouring field and got herself pregnant.'

'No way.'

'Browny may not be able to reproduce but she can still mate. The old girl's been on the road a long time.' Ellen jumped back into her sporty car and fired up the engine.

'Remember to keep her away from clover and to keep her on a tight leash. A horny mule can be a hard thing to control.'

You had to hand it to Browny; the beast had impeccable timing. Just as we were about to take on some of the busiest suburbs in the Western world she decided to fire up her usually docile hormones. I suspected fierce and inaccurate squirts of mule urine would not be a popular addition to New Jersey's pavements. All these complications had arisen just as I thought I was in the clear. I should have remembered what Homer wrote about the time for supreme vigilance being at the very end of a journey. Odysseus may have had to deal with sea monsters, whirlpools, and sorceresses turning his men into pigs. What he never had to do was usher an amorous, piss-happy mule through the Bronx. Those Greek heroes, they had it soft.

*   *   *

After Ellen had roared off in her convertible, Toby invited me in for some hot chocolate. Devotional music played quietly in the background as we sat down in his little kitchen. A painted wooden crucifix rested against the salt cellar.

Toby told me that he had been preaching in a church in California before taking the job in Ringoes only a year ago. He said he loved the little community although his world had been turned upside down after the attack on the Twin Towers. As he lived near by he had volunteered to act as a pastor at Ground Zero in the aftermath of September 11.

'It was an extraordinary time,' he told me, cupping his hands around the steaming chocolate. 'There was so much anger and sadness. One of the most haunting things was seeing all the cars left parked at the suburban train stations, the cars of those commuters who never made it home.

'I simply walked around in my dog collar amid the rubble,' Toby said, fingering the rim on his mug. 'Steelworkers, fire fighters, construction folks often came to see me. Great hairy men in hard hats, some hugging me, some in floods of tears. The families of the victims were the hardest. They would shout at me: "How could God do this?" But five minutes later they asked to be blessed.

'Lots of people at Ground Zero had no religion. Probably hadn't been to a church for years. But somehow they wanted more, something beyond humanity. A hunch of something greater. Let me tell you, Tom, I've seen cathedrals, I've held Mother Theresa's hand, but that, that pile of ruins.' Toby nodded his head slowly. 'It was the holiest place I've ever been.'

*   *   *

During the next day's walk thankfully Browny kept her raging hormones in check. Apple and cherry trees were bursting into blossom while white-tailed deer regularly sprang into view. Stumbling along one creek bed I saw what looked like an otter diving under a bridge, although it may have been the more common muskrat. I camped that night in a park in a village called East Millstone and when I woke the canvas was caulked in frost.

We slogged down the pretty Delaware Canal, which, other than the odd surprised jogger, we had to ourselves. Parts of the track were waterlogged and Browny reluctantly sloshed forward, her hooves churning up the slippery ground. In some murkier parts of the canal, bubbles inflated and popped slowly like porridge, while in others the current gushed, pale and frenzied, like milk on the boil. At the town of Bound Brook we left the canal bank and crossed a bridge into the start of suburbia proper, Browny leaving dirty hoof prints on the bitumen.

That night we were put up by Sid and Helen Frank, artist friends of Lynne and Sergei, who lived in the district of

Springfield. When I appeared with Browny the whole Frank clan came out to welcome us. It was like being taken in by a chaotic but very charming family out of a Woody Allen film script. 'Knock yerself out, sweetheart, you're in Noo Jwersey,' Helen encouraged me, miraculously rolling both her 'r's and 'w's. 'Hey, you're gonna need one hell of a pooper scwooper if that mule bombs on the sidewalk.'

The Franks knew New Jersey intimately, and were the perfect family to help me navigate my randy beast across the Hudson. By some colossal stroke of serendipity there was a stable only one mile from the George Washington Bridge. Sid contacted the manager and secured lodging for Browny for our last night on the road. However, I still had two more days of intense suburbs to deal with before that. I'd just have to make it up as I went along.

The night after leaving the Franks was one of the most memorable of the trip. Just south of Paterson – a rough and ready neighbourhood where the beat poet Allen Ginsberg once lived – was a large, hummock-strewn park. At the entrance I flagged down a police car and asked permission to camp there. The obliging cop escorted me up to a forest ridge, where dozens of lean-tos had been set up. Small circles of grey stones where previous adventurers had made fires were dotted all around. But I had the place to myself that night.

After cooking some pasta, I led Browny over to a nearby puddle. She supped on the dark water with her familiar elegance. I was really going to miss little things like this. The simple grace with which my mule slaked her thirst: the utter peace of the moment.

I decided to lead Browny up a little higher to see if we were near the ridge summit. I walked with my head torch providing a jittery beam of light. A bat flew past in a wild trajectory narrowly missing a rope ladder, just one of the many tortuous-looking devices on offer at the nearby assault course. Soon the spongy carpet of pine needles petered out and my boots crunched down on a stone path. We reached a glade and the night sky appeared in full, clear as glass, with a peppering of faint stars. I picked up my pace. I could see a railing ahead signifying the summit. My heart began to race and I felt the urge to run, Browny clopping obediently alongside.

After a quick dash I stopped dead. A rush of blood surged to my head. I stepped gingerly forward, tied Browny to a railing, and slumped down, transfixed. It was one of the most breathtaking sights of my life, a true showstopper. A blaze of lights, some dazzling, some subtle, some yellow, some blue, green or red, some pulsing, some still, some, like the distant aeroplanes, in constant motion. All was quiet except for the thrum of the streets, the odd boop of a car horn or the bark of a lonesome dog.

New York. The Big Apple. Old Gotham. Jesus Christ, it was beautiful. In the heart of it was Manhattan, the winking glass of its many skyscrapers and the duel lances of sky blue light shining out where the Twin Towers once stood. It took me by complete surprise. I had not even seen a signpost to New York yet and here it was before me like some promised land: a canvas of enchanted light. I suppose somewhere as definite as this didn't need a signpost– it was just there, as immutable and rich in the imagination as a fabled mountain or a great sea.

'Bugger me, Brown Girl,' I whispered. 'We've made it.' This burst of relief coupled with New York's astonishing beauty was all a bit much. I have to say my Colonel Arthur stiff upper lip twitched, quavered and ultimately collapsed in a fit of craven shudders. The tears fell freely. Great gasping, joyous cascades of them, the like of which I had not shed since childhood. Thankfully, there was only my stoic old mule to witness this display of salty incontinence. Ever one to keep things in perspective she continued to gaze at me with a look of unshakeable bemusement.

Mule's eye view — two days from New York

Just look at him marching along, doffing his cowboy hat and waving at the passing cars. He doesn't realise I'm the reason these people are waving back, that I'm the star of this show. You'd think he was running for President the way he's sashaying through the traffic bollards. The poor deluded fool. What would he be without me!

Oh, no, please, no, he's just started singing 'I Was Born Under a Wandrin' Star' again. That's the fourteenth time today. What have my lovely, refined ears done to deserve such horror. One minute I was grazing away in my retirement paddock, getting happily plump on Tex-Mex ryegrass. The next thing I'm trussed up with saddlebags and paraded half way across the New World by this short arse conquistador who sings like he's just swallowed a bucket full of shingle. The whole thing is quite preposterous.

Oh, mother of all mules, he's changed his mind and is now serenading me with that 'Take Me Home Country Roads' chestnut. His voice is even worse than Hangdog Roy, a busker who played guitar for us at the campground this morning. That's the other thing about the boss; he has to talk to everyone.

Roy was this haggard old troubador who sang heartbreakingly bleak bluegrass tunes. In the space of ten minutes he had crooned about alcoholism, adultery, marital cruelty and the death of his sheepdog. Roy's voice was so harsh it sounded like he had experienced all of his lyrics first hand, possibly within the last twenty-four hours. But let me tell you something, Hangdog Roy sounded like Sinatra compared to my boss. In fact I would rather hear Roy sing a ballad about losing his favourite mule in a tragic harvesting accident than ever hear the boss yodel 'Country Roads' again.

This journey really has been extraordinary. I've sprouted a winter coat shaggy enough to insulate an ice age mammoth. I've walked over the Mississippi river accompanied by a police car with a whirring blue nipple on its roof, I've rolled on the battlefield at Gettysburg, shared a paddock with prize stallions, with goats, with antelopes and even with a lusty old buffalo down in South Carolina.

Oh, yes, one or two glory days have interrupted the hard slog, like that time I slipped away from the boss in Texas. What a triumph — they don't call me the Hooved Houdini for nothing. It was such a buzz, galloping over the highway with him sprinting after me. His tough-guy adventurer facade was instantly shattered; his face looked as frazzled as his hero, Don Quixote, charging towards those windmills. I let him catch me, of course, but it was fun while it lasted.

To be fair, though, the boss is more attentive now. He's finally beginning to see how valuable I am to him. Recently he visited Richmond and stopped off at a statue commemorating all the horses and mules that were killed between 1861 and 1865. He's finally done some homework and accepts the crucial role my long-eared brethren played in the Civil War.

Most creatures have potent phrases to describe themselves. You know what I mean — a troop of kangaroos, a leap of leopards, a crash of rhinos. Then there's the slightly grander ones like a parliament of owls, a business of ferrets and my personal favourite, a smack of jellyfish. And us mules? Want to know how nature remembers us dry-wombed freaks? A barren of mules! Could anything sound more dispiriting.

Many years ago some literary wag commented that a mule is 'without pride of ancestry or hope of posterity'. What a terrible slur! It's ridiculous to write off our contribution to the world like that.

The Roman Emperor Nero supposedly loved his mules so much he ordered them to be shod with silver shoes. Even that tedious merchant Marco Polo praises the mules of Central Asia in his journals. Meanwhile, across the Atlantic George Washington was supposedly the first American to bring mules in to his fledgling country. He was given a large jackass by the King of Spain that sired several splendid mules. Even today, I'm told, there are mules in the grounds of Mount Vernon, Washington's home in Maryland.

But my favourite episode revolves around the Arctic explorer Robert Falcon Scott. Most people remember Scott's tragic fate, and that of Captain 'may be some time' Oates, but they forget the seven heroic mules that strode off on a relief expedition to find the doomed explorers. In the winter of 1912 each of these noble beasts lugged a massive sledge all the way to Scott's camp. Other than the paltry corn rations, the mules lived off a strange diet of sugar, tea leaves and even tobacco. Over the month-long journey, two of the mules died of exhaustion. The other five survived, but were shot a year later when no longer of use to the Arctic team who tended them. Such is the gratitude of humans.

Oh, dear, I can see the boss is getting tetchy. He wants me to wrap up my side of the story, but there's one more thing I'd like to add. This is directed exclusively to the driver who threw a bottle at me near Grove Hill in Alabama shortly before Christmas:

1 *You are a foolish Yahoo.*
2 *I have a hoof with your name on it.*
3 *You missed.*

CHAPTER 20

All American

The climax of a journey is often reached long before breasting the finishing tape. My mule trip was no exception. Spending time with the Amish family and marching with Colonel Arthur through the snow at Gettysburg had both been grand finales in their own way. But even they paled in comparison to that overwhelming night looking down on the lights of Manhattan. It had been an unsurpassable high note that now hung in the air waiting for the conductor to swing his baton with a flourish and put an end to it all.

I was glad. Suddenly I'd had enough. Enough of never knowing where I would spend the night, enough of navigating my beast through urban gridlocks, enough of telling strangers the difference between a donkey and a mule, or which state I liked best, or why I was such a 'crazy, goddamn son of a bitch', enough of seeking out fresh pasture, or a bag of oats, or a farrier and, though I hate to admit it, enough of putting one foot in front of the other, of walking, moving. Enough! I just wanted to reach New York, my mule by my side, and go home. I'm quite sure Browny felt the same way.

Considering New Jersey is America's most densely populated state, and Browny and I were in the thick of it, the last two days on the road were surprisingly easygoing. Amazingly, we found ourselves on the best pavements to date. Even better, as almost everyone in America drives, we had all the walking space to ourselves. Browny strutted along with a streetwise insouciance, the princess of all pedestrians.

A bit of circus atmosphere took over. Cars honked horns, school children waved, passing policemen and fire-fighters stopped to have their picture taken with us. Every time Browny 'bombed', I raked her dung into a bin liner or else covertly booted it into the nearest municipal shrubbery.

We spent our penultimate night camping on the lawn of Paramus police station and the next day strolled through the exotic-sounding suburbs of Teaneck and Bogota to Overpeck Stables, only two miles from the Hudson river. Plodding down the stable's meandering driveway we were swooped on by a New York-based television crew.

The reporter turned out to be a true ice maiden. Her wan face was coated with enough talc to dust a doughnut. She thrust a microphone in my face and asked terse, negatively slanted questions. 'What was your worst moment?' 'Did you get sick?' 'Did this mule go all the way or did other ones die first?' Dusty Donna, for want of a better name, oozed a soul-sapping greyness about her. She obviously wanted to be out covering a major political scoop or at the very least hobnobbing with celebrity A-listers. Talking to me was clearly the media equivalent of mucking out a horsebox.

Dusty Donna was so different to all the perky local reporters I had dealt with on the trip so far. She was also the first journalist who took absolutely no notice of Browny. It hit home that soon my charmed mule-man status would be over. I would have to face the real world again. Dusty Donna's waspish probing made me realise the sand in my fantasy hourglass was running out; it was as if part of me was slipping away with it.

After the interview I needed a boost. Overpeck Stables, emitting an earthy pong of hay and sawdust from its front gate, proved just the right environment. The peach-cheeked, bosomy manager, Debbie, generated warmth and vim in the way Donna drained it. She gave us a grand welcome and immediately took a shine to Browny, fiercely rejecting any offers of payment. My little mule looked a tad incongruous among all the immaculate stallions belonging to horsey New Yorkers. She reminded me of a Thelwell pony accidentally painted on a canvas full of George Stubbs thoroughbreds.

Browny was marshalled into a straw-fluffed Sheraton of a pen. A gaggle of attractive stable girls clucked around her. She was in caring, capable hands for her last night on the road. I was glad; she deserved it.

*   *   *

And so the final day loomed. At 4 a.m. the following morning I loaded my loyal old friend for the last time. Even in the drizzly darkness putting on her saddlebags seemed as natural as tying a shoelace. I smiled as I remembered my first ham-fisted attempts at packing Browny near the Tex-Mex border. But there was no hoof pawing or nickers of disapproval today; over 2,700 miles had been clocked up on the mulometer since then. We'd got to know each other pretty well. I fed her a sweet corn husk and off we launched into the New Jersey puddles.

After a quick tramp through the deserted precinct of Fort Lee we reached the George Washington Bridge just as dawn was breaking. A cluster of Port Authority workers stood watching the two lasers of blue light that had been shining up since last autumn from Ground Zero. As Browny and I approached, the distant blue lights suddenly vanished. 'That's the last time we'll see them,' one of the men told me, emotion in his voice. 'They've been turned off for good. It's time to build a permanent memorial now, time to move on.'

Several workers took pictures of each other with Browny before I hauled her off to confront the river. Some soldiers were standing sentinel, shouldering guns. They laughed and wished us good luck, gesturing the way onto the bridge's wide sidewalk. The escorting car, with its pulsing but silent roof light, ran along side us. The driver yodelled encouragement in between drags on his cigarette. But Browny didn't need any prompting; the old beast didn't bat an eyelid. Here we were hundreds of feet off the ground and entering one of the biggest cities on earth. Oh, yes, the mule whisperer at last.

The view did not disappoint. Manhattan's skyscrapers loomed like pale castles in the murky half-light. Far below stretched the Hudson, a wide band of glimmering mercury, shooting out towards its invisible horizons. It was all rather dream-like and before I knew it we were on the other side, decanted onto the Upper Manhattan coastline.

The Port Authority vehicle escorted us back down a twisty hill to the riverbank. We passed a tiny, red, Hansel and Gretel-style lighthouse, which looked almost as out of place in this land of skyscrapers as my mule. Soon we reached Harlem. We sauntered on by the infamous Cotton Club, which had been belting out groundbreaking jazz and blues since Fats Waller was around in the 1920s. On we marched through the elegant halls of Columbia University, a hotbed of student unrest during the Vietnam War, and into the shadows cast by the beautiful facade of St John the Divine Cathedral.

By the time we neared Central Park a motley entourage of pilgrims had tagged on. Rather like Chaucer's band of Canterbury yarn-spinners, we were an ever-expanding unit. Margo appeared, Lynne, Sid, Helen and all their family; then there was Liz Todd, Heather and Xeno Stravapolous, all generous souls who had somehow helped me to reach this point.

'Hey, my friend,' shouted an Italian-sounding hot dog vendor, whose booth was propped up near the cathedral. 'I'll give you a hundred dollars for your donkey.'

'Sorry,' I said, doffing my hat. 'Not for a million. Not today.'

Once in Central Park we found a spot in the sunshine. I tied Browny to a chestnut tree, unloaded her, and watched her roll. It had been a moment I had already visualised so many times. Within seconds Browny was up on her feet and tearing at the coarse city grass. I laughed at the sheer abrupt-ness of it all. My friends took it in turns to pet the mule goodbye. Nobody else outside of our little party paid her much attention now. To any fresh onlookers Browny, without the saddlebags, without the 20-mile-a-day agenda, was just another beast. For me too, my muleman days were almost numbered. Not quite yet though.

It was still early but already roller bladers were whipping round the park and baseball games were getting started. A clown on stilts teetered past chased by a posse of excited children. Two lovers lay entwined on the damp grass, still as marble, oblivious to the ambient hubbub. One by one our group drifted away. I hadn't got the right words so I hugged each of them and we all said things like good luck, take care, all the best.

Finally it was just Margo and me. We were watching the mule from one of the park benches. The sun was warm now. I tentatively put my arm around Margo. She put her arm around me and we sat there in silence with the big city waking up around us.

'Snow from the moon, Brown Girl,' I thought to myself. 'Snow from the moon.'

*   *   *

Colonel Arthur didn't have such a breezy time reaching New York. After witnessing Gettysburg he retreated into Maryland with General Longstreet's men before striking off north once more. He didn't get far. Just outside Hagerstown he was arrested on suspicion of being a Rebel spy. This is hardly surprising considering he was wearing grey breeches and smelt like a badger.

My ancestor was approached by a 'truculent-looking individual with an enormous moustache' who, the nervous Colonel noted, fixed 'his eyes long and steadfastly upon my trousers' and remarked in surly tones 'Them breeches is a damned bad colour.' Despite proclaiming his innocence and apologising for his ripe wardrobe Colonel Arthur was promptly carted off in a prison buggy. He was fortunate to be dumped at the Union HQ of the good-natured General Kelley, who, instantly realising he was a British officer, set him free. I'm proud of Colonel Arthur. He must surely be the only Englishman in history with the dubious honour of being arrested as both a Yankee and a Rebel spy.

Most of my ancestor's Confederate friends feared he might come to a sticky end once he ventured north. General Longstreet, however, retained the utmost faith in Colonel Arthur and insisted: 'A man who has travelled all through Texas as successfully as the Colonel, is safe to get through the Yankee lines all right.'

Longstreet was spot on. After reaching Johnstone by horse-drawn buggy, Arthur caught a succession of steam trains into the heart of New York. The exhausted young soldier collapsed on a bed at the Fifth Avenue Hotel, one of the plushest lodgings in town.

Colonel Arthur could not relax just yet though. His first morning in Manhattan, 13 July, he woke up to witness the worst riot in American history. It was sparked by a compulsory draft, forcing New Yorkers to sign up and fight the South. The anti-war rioting and looting lasted four days until quashed by the police along with heavy back up from the army. Most of the rioters were dirt-poor European immigrants (many of them Irish) who were not only resentful of the rich but also hostile towards any potential competition from black workers.

Colonel Arthur was in the heart of the uproar. He witnessed a black man being pursued by a baying lynch mob, a draft office on Broadway being torched and, most shockingly, a violent gang storming and burning down the city's Coloured Orphan Asylum. Fortuitously, all the two hundred or so children escaped in time. At the end of the violence New York was in turmoil. Over a hundred people had been killed, most of them rioters. However, Lincoln stood firm on the draft. It was successfully reintroduced a month later after a fresh injection of troops to keep control.

By 15 July it was time for Colonel Arthur to sail home. Three months and thirteen days after docking at the Tex-Mex border he secured a cabin on the *China*, a steamer plying from New York to London. On board he engaged in a hearty debate with some 'intelligent Northern gentlemen' and, despite having just witnessed the horror of Gettysburg, argued categorically that the South would still win the war.

How could my ancestor get it so wrong? He could be blinkered and partisan at times but for the most part he was

an observant, at times sensitive man. He had certainly cata-
logued the South's many strengths, the indomitable pluck of
its soldiers, the brilliance of Lee, its resilient women. Then
there was the constant resourcefulness of the Southern
people, such as building an entire munitions industry from
scratch, or putting disabled veterans to work as horse grooms
or factory hands in order to stretch every ounce of man-
power.

But Colonel Arthur spotted some serious cracks in the
Confederacy too; the shoddy discipline and the shattered
infrastructure, the restrictive Union blockade and the military feuds. He had also witnessed the collapse of Vicksburg
and the tragic folly of Pickett's Charge. So why did my
ancestor continue to smoke his pipedreams and predict a
Southern triumph?

The historian Walter Lord puts it beautifully:

> By the time he [Fremantle] left he was hopelessly under the
> spell of frontier days, rattling trains, river boats, campfires
> and close escapes. He had succumbed to the threadbare
> graciousness of Charleston, the thunder of Gettysburg, the
> soft breeze of a starlit night at Shelbyville. Fremantle, in
> short, was in love with the South, and his heart now ruled his
> mind.

Travelling in my ancestor's footsteps almost one hundred and
forty years later, I could now finally see what he meant.

*   *   *

My time in New York was less turbulent than Colonel
Arthur's. There was no rioting or looting, although on my
first evening it was sad to witness rival groups of Palestinian
and Jewish sympathisers hurling abuse at each other from
opposite ends of Union Square.

This aside, the city boasted an inspiring buoyancy. It had its Sunday best on, as they say in Mississippi. Ripe-smelling blossom, white and pink, was bursting into bloom, the skies were an unbelievable blue and the al fresco cafes were alive with gossip and laughter.

Of course, there were still scars, still sad legacies. One officer from the Port Authority had been close to tears recalling that over sixty of his men had been killed on September 11. From Brooklyn to the Bronx there were indications of the impact everywhere, most noticeably in the many Stars and Stripes still flying across the city. PROUD TO BE A NEW YORKER – MORE THAN EVER heralded the posters. And it is a city that, despite its immensity, really does seem to have a strong sense of community, a collective pulse that bonds its wildly disparate population.

But could the same be said of America as a whole? Yes, I think so, but in truth I cannot be sure. After seven months I felt I had barely scratched beneath the surface of Uncle Sam's huge and complex underbelly.

Many things had disappointed me on my walk, though. I seemed to be surrounded by a culture of convenience, where huge, identical malls create far too many urban eyesores, where the car is king and the pedestrian is an alien, a land of drive-ins and drive-bys, a throw-away culture with a surfeit of trash not only on highway verges but on televisions and dinner tables too. At times America came across as a place that takes far too much for granted. Not so much a superpower as a blatantly superior one.

But there was much to admire on my travels too. What impressed me most, other than the boundless optimism of the American people, was their generosity. Never before have I travelled in a country so effusively kind to me: from Texas to New York I was offered shelter, water, money, food, whiskey and, of course, no end of goodies for my mule. We were endlessly spurred on: 'God Speed', 'Happy Trails', 'Yeee-haaa', and whenever the going got tough I knew help would always be at hand. This big-heartedness, without doubt, will be my most abiding memory of the walk and of America.

However, despite their tolerance towards me as a stranger, I noticed Americans tended to be suspicious of one another. 'Watch out for the crazies' they warned as Browny and I marched off into the middle distance. 'Don't trust anyone.' 'Be careful, there's a lot of meanness about.' Some of this was good-natured concern but much of it was also blatant paranoia. Of course, I had to watch my back at times but I sensed many Americans almost relished the existence of a universal bogeyman. It made guns under pillows and a distrust of the outside world all the more justifiable. For many it also created a terrible sense of loneliness and isolation.

All I can say is that if I, a firearm-free Englishman with a poor sense of geography who rarely boos at a goose, let alone a bogeyman, can make it 2,700 miles through thirteen states with the loss of only three toenails, surely it can't be so bad out there.

No one can deny that America possesses an admirable sense of camaraderie. When John Steinbeck returned from his travels with Charley in the winter of 1960, he ranted about many aspects of his country – its racial prejudice and environmental complacency – but deep down nothing could dent his patriotism.

'Americans are much more American', wrote Steinbeck, 'than they are Northerners, Southerners, Westerners, or Easterners. And descendants of English, Jewish, German, Polish are essentially American. This is not patriotic whoop-de-do; it is carefully observed fact. California Chinese, Boston Irish, Wisconsin German, yes, and Alabama Negroes, have more in common than they have apart.'

These words, to my mind, still ring true today. In fact, now that America's racial jumble is ever more complex, they are especially relevant. Steinbeck's message, however, is far from original, and echoes back to almost a century before when America's most savage and costly conflict reached its denouement.

On 9 April 1865, two years after Colonel Arthur had sailed home from New York, Generals Robert E. Lee and Ulysses S. Grant converged on the village of Appomattox in south Virginia. The Civil War, which had lasted four years and left over 620,000 men dead, was drawing to a close. Grant, wearing his mud-spattered trousers and Lee, immaculate in a full-dress uniform, quietly negotiated the surrender in Wilmer McLean's famous parlour.

Both men, indeed both armies, displayed exceptional dignity. Having accepted the generous terms of his adversary, Lee, ever the gentleman, rose up to shake hands with the Union staff, including the Seneca Indian, Ely Parker, General Grant's military secretary. Noticing Parker's swarthy features Lee commented: 'I am glad to see one real American here.'

After a pause, the Indian replied clearly: 'We are all Americans.'

* * *

Like Colonel Arthur I was lucky to spend my last days in America in splendid surroundings. Rather than the Fifth Avenue Hotel I was a guest at the Manhattan home of my ever-sociable cousins Hugh and Susan, who live five minutes' walk from Central Park. Their apartment is full of Mexican objets d'art and ruled over by an exotic, astonishingly hairy Burmese cat called Asparagus. I slept like a prince on a voluminous sofa bed. The first morning I woke up with sunbeams lancing through the blinds and yeasty pongs from a nearby bakery wafting up. It was bliss.

My main practical concern – other than securing a flight home – was transporting Browny back to Twin Oaks ranch. Overpeck Stables were generously looking after her in the interim. I finally tracked down a company that agreed to stick her in the back of a Mexico-bound trailer with a couple of pedigree racehorses. She would be picked up in a week.

Cousin Hugh drove me up to West Point Military Academy where we inspected the US army's three remaining mules, one of which was called Traveller. They were used very rarely now, the resident vet told us, only as mascots on special occasions. However, I was happy to learn that the academy was hoping to set up a Military Mule Museum within the year, exhibiting all things mulish. This would surely be the first of its kind.

Even more pleasing, as I write this, a report has come in from Morocco claiming a mule has given birth to a live foal for the first time ever. If this proves true it is triumphant news for skinners the world over. Could this mean the potential patter of little hooves at Twin Oaks one day? A Browny dynasty might be on the cards after all.

During my last few days I spent as much time as possible with Margo. Of course it was a doomed relationship. She was a beautiful and successful New York writer and I was a bum with a mule. In fact, now I was just a bum. It was great to meet up with her in the evenings though. We walked, hand in hand, around the fountains and statues of The Metropolitan and kissed in the parks of Greenwich Village. She joked that she would never forgive me if ever I called her Browny by mistake.

In what seemed like a flash it was time to fly home. I visited Browny for the last time. There was nothing more to be said. I had been gradually saying goodbye to my mule for the last month. I fed her some carrots, rubbed her forehead, thanked her and left. Next week she would be back in the Tex-Mex sunshine.

Before my flight Margo and I lunched near Brooklyn Bridge and then walked over to Ground Zero. The whole experience was rather grim. All the tourists were beckoned onto a suspended pier above the ruins. Other than some bulldozers and a huge crane, which towered over the site like a mutant phoenix, there was very little to see. It dawned on me we had come to look at nothing: a void of rubble, dust and human loss. Rather than a respectful hush there was a lot of chattering and clicking of cameras. It was over six months since the Twin Towers fell and I sensed most us here were not mourners, but simply voyeurs. It didn't feel right somehow.

In contrast to the depressing ruins, the tributes displayed on the railings of a nearby church were very moving. There were flowers and poems, photographs and dozens of flags, several of which had been battered and faded by the weather. The simplest were often the most powerful. 'Daddy, a Kiss for you in Heaven' read one, with a snapshot of a smiling, moustachioed fire fighter in a yellow helmet. GRIEF IS THE PRICE WE PAY FOR LOVE had been printed neatly on a kite-sized St George pennant. A wreath of red roses hung from the church gate. On a card in the middle of it someone had scribbled: 'Peace on Earth, Good Will to all Men'.

The tranquillity of this sanctuary soon evaporated when Margo and I reached the next street up from the church. Here New York life bustled on at the same furious pace. Having wandered around the tributes for over an hour I was running late. Margo weaved me through the crowds and we caught the subway back to Hugh's apartment. We stood on Park Avenue, holding one another in a bear-like clinch. The French have a great expression, *l'esprit d'escalier*, meaning the thing you wished you'd said when descending the staircase, the missed riposte, the forgotten *bon mot*, the goodbye left hanging. As usual I couldn't rustle up anything remotely poignant or eloquent so I simply kissed Margo. She reciprocated then flashed me one of her heart-thumping smiles and off she glided under an avenue of cherry trees.

Back in the apartment I shoved all my stuff into a rucksack, spooned out a tin of chicken livers for the mewing Asparagus, dashed downstairs and hailed a cab. By the time I alighted at Newark airport, it was dark. I looked back at Manhattan. It was a dull night, thick with nocturnal cloud. All that could be seen above the skyscrapers was the moon. It gave off no more light than a smudged ghost, but it still looked somehow brilliant.

Epilogue

And you can't help but worry for them, love them,
want for them – those who go on down the close,
foetid galleries of time and space without you.

Tim Winton, *Cloudstreet*

General Lee is sitting next to me primping his beard. We are surveying a hotly contested skirmish on the hill below. Ranks of blue and grey troops have been hammering lead at each other for the last fifteen minutes. Amazingly, not one man has fallen. Plumes of smoke drift up from the crackling muskets, while a couple of cannons boom away beneath a rusty leaved oak tree. Eventually a Union soldier lurches wildly, and rolls headlong down the ridge and furrow. He comes to a halt, shudders briefly and then lies still, spread-eagled amid the dandelions.

'It's about time somebody copped it,' said a dry-voiced man to my right. He was puffing on a pipe, its smoke mingling pleasantly with the cannon fire. 'Yankees always drop dead like it's Oscar night, worse than bloody footballers.'

A swervy line of Confederates all yelling like banshees charge up the hill. They crest a ridge but a barrage of Union fire takes its toll. One butternut-clad soldier clutches his chest, grimaces and topples into the pasture; another young hero throws his arms in the air and collapses belly up on top of his friend. Both corpses stare wide-eyed at the dark clouds scudding above them. Nurses in white bonnets scuttle around tending the wounded with bandages and whiskey. A Union drummer beats out a steady rhythm while next to him a standard bearer in a slouch hat waves the regimental colours.

Before long the Rebels are pushed back and the skirmish peters out. It has been an impressive fray; but it's not 1863. For starters all the corpses have risen up, brushed themselves down and merrily bounded off to rejoin their regiments. Then there's General Lee. He certainly looks the part, tall, handsome, and of calm demeanour, but he sounds even less like a high-class Virginian than I do. He is also wearing a Millets lumberjack shirt.

General Lee is actually Neville Wantling, an ex-coal miner from Lancashire, who has been portraying his Confederate hero for the best part of twenty years. At today's battle he is only spectating, acting as my guide, so mufti is in order. However, when in full regimental dress with a jewelled sword in his hand, Neville is a deadringer for the white-whiskered general and has become something of a celebrity in America where he has attended dozens of reenactments.

When I first heard that England had an active American Civil War reenactment society (known as SOSKAN, the Southern Skirmish Association) I scoffed at the idea. Come off it. The Norman Conquest, sure, I'd believe that. The Wars of the Roses, the English Civil War or either of the World Wars all smacked of credibility: but the American Civil War? Pull the other one! Now, having seen roughly two hundred Englishmen clad in blue and butternut slog it out on a hill in Avon, I realized my cynicism was unfounded. Even more astonishing, Neville told me there were Yankees and Rebels still clashing at mini-Gettysburgs and Antietams as far afield as Germany, Australia and even Brazil.

Churchill called the American Civil War the 'noblest and least avoidable of all the great mass conflicts', at least prior to the First World War. Clearly, even today, it was not only Americans who were obsessed. I wanted to find out why.

The morning following the battle Neville and I returned to the reenactors' camp. Lines of white tents, blurred by mist, panned out across the grubby field. Groups of soldiers hunkered around fires to warm their hands and boil their billycans. One Union officer was twanging on a banjo.

I struck up a conversation with a Massachusetts regiment, who had been up all night guarding the explosives *caisson*. They were a varied bunch: a chef from Dorset, a postman from Kent, a London welder and a couple of ex-squaddies. Their conversation shifted from Stonewall Jackson's nicknames to the recent *Hunley* submarine excavation. Before long it was clear they all knew much more about the war than I. The reason for their hobby was varied.

'I couldn't get in the army because of my eyes,' said Bill, the postman, adjusting his John Lennon specs. 'At least here I can fight in some capacity. What the soldiers went through in that war we can only guess at. I've led a soft life in comparison. Doing this gets me back to basics, maybe helps relieve some of the guilt.'

'Yes,' agreed Max, the jovial, big-bellied chef, cutting up a hunk of salt pork. 'Things were simpler back then. If someone was told to charge up a hill at the enemy he did it. No questions asked. People had clear definitions of right and wrong. Today we are all pulled in so many directions.'

'Come on,' interrupted Mike, a welder with a Rasputin-style beard. 'Admit it, we do this for fun. I love the history side but it's mostly an escape, a break from the humdrum. No girlfriend ever gets jealous of a man who puts on smelly clothes and goes off to imitate long-dead Americans.' He tugged at his luxuriant side-whiskers. 'I used to play at Vikings before the Civil War hooked me.'

'What next, Mike?' piped up another soldier. 'You'd make a great Lara Croft.'

Later in the morning I got talking to Sue, one of the few female troops. Sue was a stocky, straight-talking Confederate who ran a Civil War shop in Newton Abbot. She was furious that I had recognized her gender.

'You're supposed to think I'm a man,' she protested. 'I should have put my fake sideburns on but it's a bore if they fall off in battle, or worse still, catch fire!'

'Do you die in battle like the men?'

'Of course I do,' insisted Sue, swigging on some chicory coffee. 'Plenty of women fought in the Civil War. Some of them died, so it would be a cop-out if I didn't.'

'Why the Civil War?'

'It's because it's so relevant today,' she replied. 'I fight as a Confederate because I see myself as a country girl. My father was pushed off his land by a greedy landlord when I was a child. I see the American South as a simple rural place compared to the slick industrial North. These days there's still many of the same issues. Town versus country. State versus government. Not only in America but over here too.'

Sue put down her coffee and tucked into a rasher of bacon with her fingers. 'I live off bacon and baked beans just to afford this damn hobby,' she stated, laughing. A squad of Confederate soldiers marched by as we spoke, a bearded officer barking orders at them.

'That there,' Sue gestured at the troops with her thumb, 'is more addictive than any drug, it truly is. I take it seriously but some reenactors go too far, some even pull out fillings from their teeth because they didn't exist in 1863. That's a bit much.' Sue reached over for her rifle. 'Strange eh,' she said, polishing the barrels. 'That a 140-year-old war at the other side of the world can take over your life.'

Unlike Sue, Neville had been strangely quiet about his love for the Civil War. Like his great hero, Robert E. Lee, he was a calm, taciturn man. I decided to ask him one last time before we parted ways at the car park. It soon became clear it was Lee rather than the war itself that first seduced him.

'Lee was as near as a man came to being a god,' Neville said simply, while shaking my hand. 'At least he was in the eyes of his troops.' He lowered his head sadly. 'I can't think of anyone like that now.'

It was a fair enough answer even though I didn't agree with it. At the beginning of my walk, as I waded through the cacti at Palmito Ranch, Kevin Garcia had likened some of the Civil War generals to Greek gods. Back then, swept up by the grandeur of the Tex-Mex desert, I had been prepared to stretch my imagination and believe him. Now, 2,700 miles later and standing in the English autumn drizzle, it was clearer than ever Lee was no god. Nor was Lincoln, Grant, Stonewall or Colonel Arthur. They were only men, good men, brave men, proud men and at times cruel men: all of them as fallible as one another.

The key players of the Civil War certainly boasted some divine traits: the vanity of Achilles, the heroic stubbornness of Hector and the self-destructive glory of Ajax. Now, 140 years later, coalminers, chefs, postmen and cross-dressing farmers' daughters were still battling for immortality in the English countryside. Ridiculous, of course: in fact undeniably rum behaviour. But in this tame, modern world perhaps it's good to know some men still play at being gods, if only for the odd weekend.

*   *   *

It's the Sunday after New Year and I'm standing by Colonel Arthur's grave in Brighton. He would have liked it here. The cemetery is home to many military types, mostly old sailors, with anchors and mermaids chiselled in their memory. Stone angels with their wings spread akimbo perch all around, as in the churchyards of the Deep South. A solitary yew shelters Arthur's tomb, its plump red berries plopping down on him whenever the sea wind picks up. A fountain trickles near by and there is birdsong in the air. FORGOTTEN HERO REMEMBERED reads his inscription. 1835–1901.

Colonel Arthur's wife, Mary, died three years before him. In his twilight years the elderly Coldstreamer became a keen yachtsman, the sea air helping to alleviate his phlegmy lungs. It was perhaps apt that he dropped dead at the Royal Yacht Squadron in Cowes after suffering a massive asthma attack. He was sixty-five. I like to think of him rasping his last words, a glass of brandy in his fist, surrounded by kindred sea dogs, his head swirling with derring-do of days gone by. He certainly had quite a trove of memories to draw from.

After his American busman's holiday in the summer of 1863 my ancestor had excelled himself. He served with distinction in Sudan in the wake of General Gordon's death, was promoted to a full general and later became Governor of Malta. Shortly before retiring to Brighton he was knighted by Queen Victoria. However, as the historian Walter Lord notes, for all his impeccable sense of duty Colonel Arthur's Civil War adventure was undoubtedly his finest hour. Everything after Gettysburg, however worthy, somehow pales in comparison.

I paid my last respects to the man who had consumed my life for the past year and walked back through town. The jaunty turrets of Brighton's Pavilion prodded the dismal afternoon sky.

Before long I was crunching along the beach. Dirty waves crashed up ahead, their frothy spume lapping against the pebbles. I took off my rucksack and sat down, inhaling the briny stink of the ocean. Near the pier a young couple flew a kite shaped like an octopus that shimmered in the quiet breeze. Apart from them I was alone.

It was time to finish off the trip. I pulled out a bunch of stuff from my rucksack: Colonel Arthur's diary, some sepia Civil War prints, a copy of Wilfred Thesiger's *A Vanished World* and one of Browny's shoes. I tipped out some final snapshots and pinned them down with beach stones: Margo at Sweet Briar, James limping across the Mississippi, Justin on his wagon, Trenton in his caravan, and a host of others. I looked down at the clumsy montage, soaking it all up one last time, merging the past and the present. The future. Then, bit by bit, I put it away, until only the faces of strangers remained.

Bibliography

Lt-Colonel Arthur Fremantle, *The Fremantle Diary: Three Months in the Southern States*, edited by Walter Lord (Little Brown and Company, Boston, 1954)

Geoffrey C. Ward with Ric Burns and Ken Burns, *The Civil War: An Illustrated History of the War between the States* (Pimlico, London, 1991)

James M. McPherson, *Battle Cry of Freedom* (Oxford University Press, 1988)

Tony Horwitz, *Confederates in the Attic* (Vintage, New York, 1998)

Bruce Aiken, *Ballots, Bullets and Barking Dogs* (Bruce Aiken, Brownsville, 1996)

Paul Johnson, *A History of the American People* (Phoenix Press, London, 2000)

Emmett M. Essin, *Shavetails and Bell Sharps: The History of the US Army Mule* (University of Nebraska Press, 1997)

The Vintage Book of Walking, edited by Duncan Minshull (Vintage, London, 2000)

Bruce Chatwin, *The Songlines* (Jonathan Cape Ltd, London, 1987)

Gary Younge, *No Place Like Home* (Picador, London, 1999)

Bill Bryson, *A Walk in the Woods* (Black Swan, London, 2000)

Robert Louis Stevenson, *Travels with a Donkey in the Cévennes* (The Marlboro Press, Illinois, 1996), first published 1879

Dervla Murphy, *Eight Feet in the Andes: Travels with a Mule from Cajamarca to Cuzco* (John Murray, London, 1983)

John Steinbeck, *Travels with Charley* – with an Introduction by Jay Parini (Penguin Classics, London, 2000), first published by The Viking Press in America, 1962

Elizabeth A. Topping, *What's a Poor Girl To Do? Prostitution in Mid-Nineteenth Century America* (Thomas Publications, Gettysburg, 2001)

Webb Garrison, *A Treasury of Civil War Tales* (Rutledge Hill Press, Nashville, 1988)

John B. Billings, *Hard Tack and Coffee* (George M. Smith and Co., Boston, 1887)

Jan Morris, *Lincoln: A Foreigner's Quest* (Penguin, London, 2000)

Sam R. Watkins, *Co Aytch: a Confederate Memoir of the Civil War* (Touchstone, 1997)

Index

Other titles available from Constable & Robinson Ltd

Children of Kali   Kevin Rushby   **£7.99 [   ]**
The thugs, in the 1830s, were the enemy within the British Empire, and the colonial
reaction to them still haunts India. This is a journey into the dark and mysterious world
of Indian crime, past and present, where the line between good and evil can be as
murky as the Ganges.

The Middle-Aged Mountaineer   Jim Curran   **£7.99 [   ]**
In the summer of 2000 Jim Curran set off to cycle from north to south of Britain.
Carrying his climbing equipment with him. His route took in old climbs and climbing
friends, plus new climbs and new friends met in lay-bys and pubs along the way.
Unfortunately that summer was one of the wettest on records but, for the reader, it only
adds to the fun.

The Great Hedge of India   Roy Moxham   **£7.99 [   ]**
This is the quest for a lost wonder of the world: a mighty hedge, that spanned the Indian
subcontinent in the middle of the 19th century, set in place to allow the collection of the
Salt Tax by British customs officers. Roy Moxham sets off to find out what happened to
this forgotten hedge and whether any remnant exists today.

Robinson books are available from all good bookshops or can be ordered direct from
the Publisher. Just tick the title you want and fill in the form below.

TBS Direct
Colchester Road, Frating Green, Colchester, Essex CO7 7DW
Tel: +44 (0) 1206 255777
Fax: +44 (0) 1206 255914
Email: sales@tbs-ltd.co.uk

UK/BFPO customers please allow £1.00 for p&p for the first book, plus 50p for the
second, plus 30p for each additional book up to a maximum charge of £3.00.

Overseas customers (inc. Ireland), please allow £2.00 for the first book, plus £1.00 for
the second, plus 50p for each additional book.

Please send me the titles ticked above.

NAME (block letters) ....

ADDRESS ....

....

POSTCODE ....

I enclose a cheque/PO (payable to TBS Direct) for ....

I wish to pay by Switch/Credit card

Number ....

Card Expiry Date ....

Switch Issue Number ....